HAUNTED PLACES IN AMERICA

A Guide to Spooked and Spooky Public Places in the United States

CHARLES A. COULOMBE

THE LYONS PRESS
Guilford, Connecticut
An Imprint of The Globe Pequot Press

The Lyons Press is an imprint of The Globe Pequot Press.

10 9 8 7 6 5 4 3 2 1

Printed in the United States of America

Designed by Claire Zoghb

ISBN 1-59228-415-9

Library of Congress Cataloging-in-Publication data is available on file.

Dedication

To
Ryan Brookhart
With whom I have shared some bizarre adventures
And many good times,
This book is dedicated.

THE CHURCH FORBIDS THE DEAD TO BE EVOKED, BUT THERE IS NOTHING TO FORBID THE DEAD MAKING THE GESTURE THEMSELVES, SINCE IT IS CLEAR THAT ONLY BY DIVINE PERMISSION COULD THEY DO SO. A CATHOLIC WITH THE MEDIUM'S GIFT HAS ONLY TO SIT STILL TO BECOME AWARE OF THE PASSING SPIRITS. THE PARAPHERNALIA OF A SÉANCE IS QUITE UNNECESSARY.

—*Sir Shane Leslie,* The Ghost Book

IT WOULD RATHER SEEM THAT SOME STRICT LAW OF THE UNKNOWN STATE FORBIDS SUCH APPARITIONS, UNLESS ESPECIALLY PERMITTED. DOUBTLESS WELL FOR US IT IS SO.

HOW IT WOULD ALTER THE WHOLE COURSE OF HUMAN EXISTENCE, IF SUCH APPARITIONS CONSTANTLY TOOK PLACE. WHETHER THEY LOST OR WHETHER THEY STILL RETAINED THEIR TERROR, IT WOULD HARDLY BE COMPATIBLE WITH WORLDLY BUSINESS THAT THEY SHOULD BE PERMITTED. IN ALL SUCH STORIES A SUPERINTENDING PROVIDENCE SEEMS MOST CLEARLY MANIFEST.

—*Dr J. M. Neale,* Communications with the Unseen World

Contents

Acknowledgments

Any book dealing with such a wide variety of people, places, and things necessarily requires a lot of support. To mention a very few, I'd like to thank my agent, Jake Elwell, and the gang at Lyons: Tom Meagher, Diana Nuhn, and freelancer Chris Jagger. Jane Doherty and the staff at the Proprietary House in Perth Amboy, New Jersey require special mention, as does my old friend, Bernard Guste, owner of Antoine's Restaurant in New Orleans. I'd also like * to especially thank Jeannette Coyne, Matt Lewis, and Chris and Irene Hoag, as well as my cousins, Ashley and John Barrett.

Introduction

U sually, haunting is a private affair. The people whose home is so afflicted generally do not want publicity, and often live in silence with their eerie secret for years. Often, only family and close friends are aware that something unearthly shares the home of their loved ones; invitations to outsiders are few. But many public places around the United States also have their quota of haunts, and so must share them with their public.

One such is the Aztec Hotel, in Monrovia, California. Built in 1926, and located on old Route 66, the hotel served not only as a gateway to Los Angeles, but as a getaway for famous (and not so famous) members of the silent film colony. Not surprisingly, it boasted a speakeasy in its basement until Prohibition ended in 1933. No less unsurprisingly, its history, like that of most hotels, offers a selection of unpleasant deaths: overdoses, abortions gone awry, and suicides. One of these calamities claimed the life of a young girl staying in Room 120. Many claim that she continues to dwell in the room where she died; others point to the basement area as a prime source of eerie happenings.

In October of 2003, I was privileged to join a group of about sixteen people from the San Gabriel Valley Paranormal Researchers in a "ghost hunt" at the Aztec. Half of those present were self-proclaimed "psychics"; the other half parapsychologists, armed with all sorts of odd instruments for gauging air pressure, temperature, and the like. One lady psychic began telling us about a female spirit who was ensconced in the lounge; next to the chair from which she was speaking was another, inhabited, so it appeared, by an uncommunicative male entity. Robin, the top SGVPR official present, asked me if I cared to try the "divining rods." These were two brass L-shaped items, with the shorter part of the L encased in a sort of handle that allowed the larger part to revolve all the way around.

"Grasp the handles, and then ask, 'What is yes?'" he instructed. I did so, and the two rods stuck straight out in front of me. "Now ask, 'What is no?' " Again I followed his instructions, and the two rods crossed in front of me. "It differs from person to person," Robin explained.

Turning my rods to the empty chair wherein the male entity was supposed to be sitting, I inquired, "Were you here in the '20s?" The rods crossed—"No." "The '30s?" Yes. "'40s?" Yes. "'50s?" After some hesitation, the rods straightened out. "The '60s?" Definitively, the rods crossed. "Did you die in the late '50s, then?" Yes. I asked the psychic if she could get anything out of him. "I'm getting the name 'George.' He is similarly dressed to you, in a dark suit like yours. He finds you sympathetic," she added. "Uh-huh," I replied.

The rest of the evening was spent prowling the old hotel, especially Room 120, where, using the rod system and the interpretation of several female psychics, I gleaned that the ghost there had died of post-abortion hemorrhaging. Other spirits wandering about were suicides and the like.

At last we decamped downstairs, and in the main room, where the bar was supposed to be, I tried the rods again. "Is there anyone there?" Yes. "Male?" Yes. "Did you drink down here when it was a speakeasy?" Yes. "Gin?" Yes. "Rye?" Yes. "Rich delicious chocolate milk?" The rods crossed very quickly. Snagging the first psychic, I asked her what she could get out of this one. "Why, it's your friend George! He must have followed you down!" With that encouraging word, she went off to other beings.

Shortly afterwards, I left. My twenty-two-year-old nephew, Guy, who had accompanied me, asked, "Well, Uncle, was it real? What do you think?" I told him I didn't know what to think. Were the psychics deluding themselves? Were winds or magnetism moving the rods, or was there something actually present? I didn't know, and I still don't know.

But it was certainly an interesting experience. A month later, I would encounter a haunting at the apartment of two young cousins of mine in Greenwich Village that was much less ambiguous, encompassing as it did a sudden drop in temperature, the flashing on and off of Christmas lights and the movement of a curious silver-dollar-sized point of light around their living room. I have heard a ghostly choir singing in an empty Catholic chapel in Athlone, Ireland, and had the back of my chair kicked by a phantom foot at the Lexington Restaurant in St. Paul, Minnesota. What is one to make of these experiences?

Spiritualists have a developed mythology centering around contact with supposed spirits of the dead, comprising séances, spirit guides, "Summerland" (a sort of ghostly waiting room prior to reincarnation), and the like. Medieval Catholics taught that ghosts were either spirits returning from Purgatory to ask for prayers and Masses, right wrongs, or deliver messages; demons masquerading as the departed; or damned souls. Some modern parapsychologists hold that many hauntings are simply reenactments of emotionally charged events somehow impressed on a given room or place, and that poltergeists are essentially the unleashed energies of disturbed adolescents. Many rationalists reject all such happenings as fraud, trickery, or self-delusion.

In the early '80s, there was a famous poltergeist case in suburban Los Angeles; a team of scientists from UCLA even confessed themselves baffled. The late and renowned *Los Angeles Times* columnist Jack Smith, a thoroughgoing materialist, poured scorn on the proceedings as pure nonsense. The owner of the house wrote Smith, inviting him to visit and see for himself. To his credit, Smith published the letter, and in his column replied that he would not go. If he went, he wrote, and the occurrence turned out to be real, he would have to entirely revise his world-view, "and," he confessed, "I am simply too old to do that." Smith aside, materialism has little answer for things that go bump in the night, save to categorically deny their existence. It would seem, on the basis of the sheer number of such things reported daily throughout the world, that this is a blind end in the search for truth in this area. Undoubtedly, many such experiences leave one wondering whether or not anything really happened after all. But some are so extraordinary as to leave no doubt. Certainly, whatever explanation one accepts for them, once one encounters these things, he or she will never look at the universe the same way again.

The places we will explore in this book are all open to the public; many have even capitalized on their haunted reputation. Probably most of their clients never encounter anything strange. But if you are one of the "lucky" ones, you will come away from such a place with far more than a mere holiday memory. So ready your insights, as we begin our exploration of America's Haunted Places.

Charles A. Coulombe
Arcadia, California
Hallowe'en 2003

The Blonde Sings On . . .
and On . . . in Alabama

Alabama is a Deep South state with all the charm one associates with that region. Outside the bustling industrial center of Birmingham and the capital at Montgomery, there are quiet rivers, beautiful plantation homes, and huge fields of cotton and other crops. In the north, the Appalachians peter out, and in the south, historic Mobile and a number of old fishing communities add their own charm.

But this idyllic picture conceals a bloody past. Alabama was a home to the Cherokee and Creek nations, two of the "Five Civilized Tribes." Their inter-tribal warfare left its mark, a mark that was only deepened when the French, Spanish, British, and at last Americans fought both directly and through their Indian allies. When these last were mostly driven from the region in the early nineteenth century, their place was taken by plantation agriculture and with it the institution of slavery. This came to an end with the Civil War. But the blood shed in the conflict, and the evils of Reconstruction that followed, left a legacy of bitterness that was not dissipated by the Civil Rights struggles of the late twentieth century.

All of these players and events made a mark on the state's weird lore: many a stately home boasts its spirit inhabitant, and the folk beliefs of black and white alike are filled with stories of witchcraft and hoodoo. But there is also a fine tradition of learning in Alabama. Not least of its beneficiaries is the renowned Athens State University at Huntsville.

Today, Athens State University is Alabama's upper-division University, and offers junior- and senior-level courses to complete baccalaureate degrees in thirty-three different majors. Paradoxically, ASU is both the oldest and youngest institution of higher learning in Alabama's state educational system. It was founded in 1822 by local citizens. They purchased five acres of land, erected a building, and began Athens Female Academy. Ownership of the school was transferred in 1842 to the Tennessee Conference of the Methodist Church. With the birth of the North Alabama Conference of the Methodist Church in 1870, the College came under the jurisdiction of that body. On May 10, 1974, the Board of Trustees asked the North Alabama Conference to seek for the institution an affiliation with the State of Alabama. The Conference, at its annual meeting in June 1974, gave the Board of Trustees this permission, and authorized the transfer of the institution to the State of Alabama.

It would be strange indeed if such a venerable place lacked a ghost. In ASU's case, the primary haunting occurs at McCandless Hall. Containing a small theater and faculty offices for the School of Arts and Sciences, the red brick and white columned building would seem an unlikely setting for the supernatural.

Nevertheless, so many a current and former student maintains, it is haunted by the ghost of Abigail Lylia Burns. Described in popular legend as a very beautiful young blonde, she is said to have been studying opera singing at Athens State College. Armed with a soprano voice, she planned to become a professional opera singer after school. Supposedly, when McCandless Hall and its theater were dedicated in 1914, she sang as part of the opening ceremonies. Receiving a standing ovation, she swore to return when she became a professional. On her way home, however, the horses pulling her carriage were frightened by a storm, and the conveyance was wrecked. Abigail did not survive the accident, and a beech tree was planted in her honor near the building whose opening she had graced with her song.

Generations of students claim that Abigail returned in any case. Many believe that they have seen her in various spots in McCandless Hall (especially in the auditorium) wearing the white formal dress she wore the night she died. Hundreds of people annually attend the memorial concert at the Huntsville Opera Theater in Alabama to see if she will put in an appearance. Still others claim to have seen her gazing out from a third-floor window when the building was locked up, bathed in an eerie blue light and still clutching the bouquet of flowers she was thrown after her successful performance. Some students smell those flowers on the third floor, other strange shapes are seen, and footsteps without feet heard.

What makes all of this a bit odd is that, despite all the phenomena, research has proved there was no Abigail Burns at ASU between 1908 and 1922. Whatever walks at McCandless, it's not her.

A better-attested historical personage is Women's Education pioneer Madam Childs. In life she doubled her academic work with the role of proctor. Apparently very strict, she is claimed to stalk the women's dormitories, frightening girls who stay out past curfew. Founder's Hall is also said to be haunted—or at least, its attic is. While the unearthly tenant there has neither name nor face, he does make the attic freeze at times, even during the hottest days.

Despite all of this supernatural activity, the campus continues to shelter a highly regarded university, and to welcome visitor and prospective student alike. Just be careful in McCandless Hall— you might be in for an impromptu concert from beyond!

Athens State University
300 North Beaty Street
Athens, AL 35611-1999
(800) 522-0272

Some Guests Never Leave
Alaska's Golden North Hotel

A laska is our largest state and, at the same time, our most mysterious. Thinly settled over most of its wide acreage, it remains a refuge for wildlife, some of which (such as the grizzly bear and gray wolf) are either rare or extinct in the Lower 48, as well as for species restricted to the far north alone.

Alaska's history and folklore are likewise unique. In addition to the Athabascan Indians (distant cousins to the Apache and Navajo of the Southwest), Alaska is home to the Eskimos or Inuit and to the Aleuts as well—people who retain links to related tribes in Siberia. The Inuit can be found in Greenland and Canada as well. Where most of the United States were colonized by the French, Spanish, or British, Alaska was reached in the mid-eighteenth century by the Russians. These last arrived in the last gasp of the advance—spearheaded by Cossacks—which led them across Asia from the Ural Mountains to the Pacific.

The Russians introduced their religion and folklore to the state; but in 1867, they sold their American colony to the government in Washington, evacuating most of their pure-blood settlers. Left behind were many half-breeds and the largest number of Eastern Orthodox believers in North America. The strange tales of the natives and the Russians mixed and merged, but for three decades after the arrival of U.S. authorities, the territory slumbered.

In 1897, however, gold was discovered in Alaska, beginning a gold rush similar to that which had hit California fifty years earlier. Immigrants poured in from all over the world to get rich quick, and towns sprang up overnight to service them and take their money. One of these was Skagway.

That city was host to the Golden North Hotel. Opened in 1898, it is Alaska's oldest operating hotel. It was moved in 1907 by horse and capstan to its present location. But the change in place did not affect the hotel's permanent guests.

The year the place opened, a young would-be gold miner left his fiancée, Mary, at the hotel, planning to come back for her after he struck it rich. He intended to leave her in comfort until he returned. Unfortunately, Mary fell sick with pneumonia in his absence. Although some claim that her lover died in the mines, and others maintain that he returned with money too late to save her, one thing is certain: Mary died in Room 23, choking to death from her disease.

Ever since, guests in Room 23 have often awakened in the middle of the night, choking and gasping for breath. Some claim to have seen a figure of a woman, sometimes reaching out as if to choke them. In 1998, to honor the centennial both of the hotel and Mary's demise, the Golden North opened up a microbrewery producing a pale ale dedicated to Mary.

She is not, however, the only strange presence in the old hotel. Guests in Room 14 have often seen a "gray light form" or an "orb of light" moving around. Usually one or more of the observers will feel lightheaded or dizzy. Occurring in the early hours of the morning, the effect fades after a couple of hours. There is no story or explanation behind this phenomenon. But do ask for either room if you stay here!

Golden North Hotel
Third Avenue SE at Broadway Street
Skagway, AK 99840
(907) 983-2294

Arizona's Monte Vista Hotel Appeals To Celebrities—Alive and Otherwise

Arizona is a beautiful state, with every kind of terrain from deserts to forested mountains. The Grand Canyon attracts thousands of visitors, as do the state's many other historic sites. Ranging from Spanish missions such as Tumacacori and San Xavier del Bac, to old west towns like Tombstone (home of the famous gunfight at the OK Corral), these places reflect the romantic stories and wild legends of the various groups who have called Arizona home.

When the first Spanish explorers came to the state in the sixteenth century, they found tribes like the Papago and the Pima already ensconced. But in addition to their own tribal myths, some of these tribesmen were already familiar with the Catholic religion of their new visitors. They claimed that a mysterious woman in blue had come among them, teaching them new doctrines. Some of the explorers, returning to their homeland, met a nun named Maria de Agreda. Without having left her convent, she was able to describe (to the shock of her listeners) the appearance and customs of the Arizona Indians they believed themselves to have been the first Europeans to visit. This was apparently an example of the strange phenomenon of bilocation.

It was also a fitting commencement to the area's bizarre history. For the Spanish missionaries and soldiers who established forts and missions in the area soon began to leave otherworldly vestiges of their stay behind: ghost stories centering around old missions and forts are a big part of Arizona's weird lore.

When the Americans annexed Arizona in 1848, they soon began to add their own. The Superstition Mountains well earn their name, with odd tales such as that of the "Lost Dutchman Mine." Even the most recently settled part of the state, in the northern mountains, garnered its own share of legends.

Flagstaff, founded in 1882, is an important part of this sort of activity. Its cold bracing air has attracted many visionaries. They began flooding in with the railroad in the 1890s; among them was Bostonian Percival Lowell, who established his observatory there in the early twentieth century and enthralled his contemporaries with his speculations about intelligent life on the planet Mars. In the 1920s, the nascent Route 66 brought many more seekers to the area, and nearby Sedona is now a New Age fortress of sorts, complete with UFO believers, Vortex seekers, and all sorts of intriguing folk.

But one of the most important sites in Arizona for the seeker of ghosts is the old Hotel Monte Vista, located in the center of Flagstaff itself. Brooding over the city at the corners of Aspen and San Francisco Streets, the Hotel Monte Vista stands as a symbol for Flagstaff. This is fitting, for the hotel is one of only a few in this country built through public subscription.

In 1924, an astronomer at Lowell Observatory named V. M. Slipher spearheaded a local fundraising campaign that resulted in an ordinance establishing a municipal bond to build the Hotel

Monte Vista. Flagstaff's role as a tourist center was growing, and the town's leaders were concerned that not enough lodging was available. Mr. Slipher pushed his idea through the electorate and designed and oversaw much of the actual construction. Part of the Old Post Office, built in 1917, was incorporated into the hotel and is still connected to it.

The hotel quickly became a popular spot for tourists and glamorous folk from around the world; locals also came to love the place, and the phrase, "Meet me at the Monte V," became an oft-repeated Flagstaff slogan.

The year of the Monte Vista's completion, Mary Costigan became the first American woman granted a radio-broadcasting license; her three-hour radio show aired daily from her second-floor studio at the Hotel Monte Vista, Room 105. In 1931, a major Flagstaff bootlegging operation was put to an end by local officials. The main speakeasy involved was the Hotel Monte Vista's lounge. From 1935–1940, locals Fred Nackard and Rex Gobel ran slot machines out of the hotel lounge and lobby, the only slot machines ever to operate in Flagstaff.

When Western movies became popular during the '40s and '50s, more than one hundred were filmed in the Sedona and Oak Creek Canyon, both close to Flagstaff. Since there were no other hotels in the region at that time, Hollywood stars made the Hotel Monte Vista their home away from home. Rooms are named after some of the famous guests who have stayed here. A few celebrities holding this honor are Bing Crosby, Jane Russell, Gary Cooper, and Spencer Tracy. You can even spend the night in the room where a scene from *Casablanca* was filmed.

These illustrious guests gave shoe-shiner Gregory Martinez and porter bellhop Isaac Henderson a national reputation. Both were offered parts in Hollywood movies, but neither ever accepted, choosing to remain on staff. Barber Samuel Cancinas, who worked out of the hotel for twelve years, was once flown to Phoenix upon special request to cut Harry Truman's hair.

The film colony also gave the hotel's otherworldly staff its reputation. In the late 1950s, John Wayne reported seeing a friendly ghost in his hotel room. Word of his experience quickly spread, and now more than fifty such stories are told about the hotel. The "phantom bellboy" knocks at the Zane Grey Room announcing in a muffled voice, "Room service." When guests open the door, however, no one is standing there—nor is anyone running off down the corridor.

"In 1970," Ellen Roberts, the desk clerk, says, "three men robbed a nearby bank and, to celebrate, they decided to stop by our lounge and have a drink—even though one of the men had been shot during their escape. While having his drink, the wounded man died, and some feel he's the spirit that's haunting this area of the building." Former owner Johnny Johnson believed that it was indeed the voice of the would-be robber that greeted him with an eerie "Hello," or "Good morning," each day.

Some repairs were needed following a fight in Room 220. Finishing his work, a maintenance man turned off the light and locked the door. He returned a mere five minutes later to find the light back on, the television going full blast, and the bed linens stripped. In the early 1980s, a strange, long-term boarder rented this room (he was known to hang raw meat from the chandelier) and when he passed away, his body wasn't recovered for two or three days. Was his ghost responsible for the upheaval that took place in the empty, locked room?

"When a father and son checked out of the Gary Cooper Room, the father made the comment that during the night, he suddenly sat straight up in bed feeling like someone was staring at him," Ellen Roberts recalls. "His son started to kid him but he was very sincere and kept stressing that he knew someone had been watching him. The red-light district was south of the railroad tracks, not too far from the Hotel Monte Vista, and two prostitutes were murdered in that room. Another version of the story is that they died after they were thrown out the window."

These occurrences are only a few of the peculiar goings-on at the hotel: late at night, the lobby telephone rings; a ghostly woman appears outside the Zane Grey Room; and a man coughs continuously through the night. A woman who was murdered in her second-floor room has never been seen, but dogs brought anywhere near the room go crazy and tear things up. Room 305 is one of the most active rooms in the hotel. There is a rocking chair in that room that insists on staying in the same place by the window. No matter where the staff puts it, the next morning it will be in its familiar place. These are just a few of the fellow guests waiting to meet you at the Monte V.

Hotel Monte Vista
100 North San Francisco Street
Flagstaff, AZ
(800) 545-3068

An Arkansas Health Resort's
Inmates Keep Coming Back

Famous (or infamous) as the home state of former President Bill Clinton, Arkansas boasts an interesting history—in some ways typical of the Deep South, and in other ways worlds apart. The first European settlers were the French, who settled Arkansas Post in the eighteenth century, but for the most part left the rest of the area to its native inhabitants. In 1803, the region passed into American hands with the Louisiana Purchase. The low-country half of the state, connected as it was with the Mississippi River, was soon flooded by settlers from the rest of the South, accompanied by their slaves. Soon a flourishing plantation culture grew up, with all its accompanying strains and folklore. As a result, Arkansas seceded from the Union with the rest of her neighbors, suffering in her turn the pains of the Civil War and Reconstruction.

But in the Ozark Mountains, settlers from the Appalachians set up a very different culture from that of the flatlanders. These mostly Scotch-Irish folk imported the strange tales and odd customs that had served them so well in the mountains of Tennessee, Kentucky, Virginia, and North Carolina. In the Ozarks as well are a number of healing springs—not least of which may be found in the town of Eureka Springs.

Dr. Alvah Jackson is claimed to be the first to discover the healing waters of Eureka Springs, back in 1856. That was the year he used them to cure his son of an eye ailment. Thus began "Dr. Jackson's Cave Hospital," where the good doctor cared for wounded Civil War soldiers. When that conflict ended, he began selling "Dr. Jackson's Eye Water" to a grateful public. In 1879, the doctor's friend and hunting companion Judge J. B. Saunders was cured of a crippling disease by a visit to Basin Spring, and thereafter began actively promoting the springs to friends and family throughout the state.

As a result, the city of Eureka Springs was founded and named on July 4, 1879. As word of Eureka's miraculous waters began to spread, thousands of visitors poured in to the original encampment of tents and cabins. By the end of that year, the estimated population of Eureka Springs reached 10,000 people. In 1881, the town was declared a "City of the First Class," the fourth largest city in Arkansas.

Five years later, the Crescent Hotel was opened to provide grand accommodation in a manner befitting the prosperous town. On May 26, the companies who had sponsored the place—Eureka Springs Improvement Company and The Frisco Railroad—staged a gala opening, for what they modestly called "America's most luxurious resort hotel."

Afterwards, though, the hotel's history was checkered: it served successively as a hotel, women's conservatory, junior college, health resort, and is now once again a hotel. This past has left its heritage of hauntings.

During construction of the building, a workman fell from the roof. He died when he landed where Room 218 is; not surprisingly, it is considered the most haunted room in the hotel. Doors slam shut, strange sounds are heard, and people have been shaken awake at night.

But it is not the only haunted room in the hotel. Guests staying in Room 424 have had several odd experiences, and in Rooms 313 and 202, ghosts were even photographed. Some guests have reported seeing a middle-aged man with a beard, in formal clothes, at the bar. When those who view him speak to him, he vanishes without replying! From these and many other rooms, guests emerge in the morning with hair-raising tales of nighttime visitants. The hotel even encourages visitors to tell them of their experiences for posting on the hotel's website. If you are looking for otherworldly roommates, the Crescent Hotel may be just the place for you!

Crescent Hotel & Spa
75 Prospect Avenue
Eureka Springs, AR 72632
(800) 342-9766

A Woman Wronged Won't Check Out of California's Aztec Hotel

California has always been a refuge and an El Dorado for those seeking to remake themselves. Its Indian tribes were generally driven over the deserts surrounding the state to seek asylum from more powerful nations among its oak trees—sources of acorns and refuge for rabbits, the two staples of the native diet. These first Californians were visionaries of a sort as well: the Jimson Weed Cult, centering around the hallucinogenic properties of that plant, was the dominant religious force in southern California before the arrival of the Europeans.

Fearing that Russians from Alaska would seize the area, King Charles III of Spain ordered Fr. Junipero Serra, superior of the Franciscan Missions in Baja California, to spearhead settlement to the north. The eventual result, by the time of Mexican independence in 1821, was a chain of twenty-one missions extending from San Diego to Sonoma. Four *presidios* (forts) guarded San Diego, Santa Barbara, Monterey—which served as the new province's capital—and San Francisco. Two towns (San Jose and Los Angeles) and a network of *ranchos* completed the face of Spanish and then Mexican California, with the King's Highway—*El Camino Real*—acting as the link between them all.

Three years after California fell to the Americans in 1846, the discovery of gold created a wave of immigration to the state larger than any other in history. The earlier inhabitants, Indians and Spanish alike, were swamped in a mass migration from all over the country and the world, which has not yet stopped, although dreams of gold have given way to other inducements. In 1919, the nascent film industry moved to Hollywood from New York, and the final element in California's history and culture was added.

In southern California especially, the arrival of the movies transformed the rural face of the area. Within two decades a dizzying array of churches, mansions, hotels, restaurants, and any number of other buildings were erected, in every imaginable architectural style. A veneer of Hollywood decadence was thrown over the Southland, which likewise persists to the present day.

All of these groups had strange lore of their own: Spanish folktales of *brujería* and hauntings were added to by late nineteenth-century immigrants from the Midwest. But the movie stars really completed the picture. Actors are by and large a superstitious bunch, and the strange climate and high-pressure environment of the movies exacerbated this tendency. One result has been an enormous number of haunted sites, representing all of the state's formative groups. Phantom friars have been seen at missions Carmel and San Antonio; the pioneer Whaley Mansion in San Diego has so many and such active ghosts that the state assembly voted it California's official state haunted house. Among many other examples, such stars as Montgomery Clift and Marilyn Monroe have reputedly returned to their old stomping grounds at Hollywood's Roosevelt Hotel.

Among many such places to choose from, a particularly chilling site is the Aztec Hotel in Monrovia, which we first met in the introduction. Monrovia itself is the fourth oldest general law city in Los Angeles County. It was established in 1887 as an incorporated city; originally a collection of orange ranches, its first inhabitants wanted to escape the evils both of Los Angeles and vice-ridden Arcadia next door. The new city council's first order of business was to ban the sale of alcohol. From that staid beginning, Monrovia has grown into a lovely residential community of some 37,000 residents. Its craftsman homes are the goal of an annual pilgrimage, and its downtown section is often used by filmmakers for its "small-town" atmosphere.

One of the key reasons for Monrovia's transformation was the creation of Route 66 in 1922, which encompassed Foothill Boulevard, one of the city's major thoroughfares. Four years after the route came through, noted architect Robert Stacy-Judd—whose prior career had been limited to Egyptian-themed movie theaters in England—built the Aztec Hotel on the boulevard.

Done in Mayan theme, the ornate lobby and bar's brass railings and stained glass lured many members of the film community out to the San Gabriel foothills where Monrovia lies. In its early days, the hotel even boasted a speakeasy in the basement. As the decades wore on, however, the clientele became seedier, dropping from minor-league Mafiosi on the lam and girls in trouble looking for abortionists, to mere heroin addicts looking to score. The end of the twentieth century was not a pretty time for the old hotel.

Luckily, in recent years new owner Kathy Reese has breathed life into the old place, redecorating and restoring the building, and attracting a much more elevated clientele. But all the work in the world can't change a building's past—or its permanent residents.

In Room 120, a girl jilted by her lover accidentally hit her head on the radiator and died. She is often felt, sometimes heard, and occasionally seen by those who stay there today. Odd whisperings and closing and opening doors are heard in the basement where the speakeasy once entertained refugees from Prohibition. But odd occurrences are not confined to those two hot—or cold—spots.

Front desk receptionists, maintenance workers, and bar tenders alike have reported strange occurrences in almost every part of the hotel, and the San Gabriel Valley Paranormal Researchers consider it to be one of the most haunted structures in the area. This writer himself went on one of their ghost hunts, and can testify to the eerie atmosphere of the building, as well as its top-notch service. If you're trying to relive a bit of old Route 66, why not spend time with a few folk who never left it?

Aztec Hotel
311 West Foothill Boulevard
Monrovia, CA 91016
(626) 358-3231

Colorado's Stanley Hotel Inspired Stephen King, but Has Ghosts of Its Own

Colorado is an intriguing place, in many, many ways. The Rocky Mountains occupy the center of the state, giving the capital, Denver, its nickname of "Mile High City." In total contrast to the more or less arid plains surrounding them, the Rockies offer an incredible array of scenery, as well as—now, as in the past—refuge to all sorts of game. Bison, deer, and many other edible beasts thronged the "parks" in the region. "Park" in this case does not mean a protected tract of land, but is rather a geological term meaning a glacially cut level valley between mountain ranges.

Attracted both by the cool climate of the mountains and the profusion of game, Ute and Arapaho tribesmen made their homes in the Rockies during the summer. Winter snows would drive them back to the relative warmth of the plains. Although France, Spain, Great Britain, and, later, the United States would claim the land, actual settlement only began in the 1840s, with the arrival of

Hispanic pioneers from New Mexico in the south-central part of the state. Despite soon coming under the American flag, they have retained their culture and their legends until today.

But American sovereignty meant American settlers: the plains filled up with farmers, the mountains with trappers, guides, ranchers, and later miners. Although Denver grew into a large city, many Colorado Rockies towns remain small—resorts catering to visitors seeking both nineteenth-century quaintness and stunning mountain views. One such is Estes Park, home to the Stanley Hotel, perhaps (thanks to Stephen King) America's most famous haunted hotel.

Set in a typical park-valley, and named after its first settler, Joel Estes, the town enters history in 1859. In that year, Estes, having found the site on a hunting expedition, thought that cattle would do as well as elk and deer in the rich grass of the park; of course, he loved the mountain scenery as well. He moved his family into two log cabins.

Trapping, hunting, prospecting, and finally tourism attracted other visitors. In 1864, the little settlement was given its name by William Byers, the editor of the *Rocky Mountain News*. But in 1877, a man arrived who would change the face of the town (and add a bit of supernatural flair to it). This was Wyndham Thomas Wyndham-Quin, Fourth Earl of Dunraven. The Irish lord had just explored the Yellowstone, writing a book about his experiences the year before coming to Estes Park. A keen sportsman, he saw many possibilities for Estes Park.

He also had a great interest in ghosts, having been raised in haunted Adare Manor. In 1869, he had witnessed the famous nineteenth-century medium, David Dunglas Home, levitating outside a window. But His Lordship's life (and death) had stranger turns to take yet.

At Estes Park, he saw the resort potential of the area, bought a private hunting reserve, and (with investment from his neighbors) built a hotel intended for European visitors. While it gained a great reputation, not enough tourists arrived and the hotel folded. Lord Dunraven's neighbors drove him out of town as a fraud. On his return to Ireland he took up the management of Adare Manor, yacht racing, and Irish politics, dying in 1926 at the age of 85. But as we shall see, it is not Adare Manor where His Lordship's ghost walks!

Estes Park continued to modestly prosper, reporting a total of two hundred people in the 1900 census, most involved in ranching or tourism. The telephone had come in, and lodges for visitors sprang up among the hills. Five years later, the downtown was platted.

Incorporated in 1917, the town has grown up considerably, without losing its charm. Some of this growth is due to the increased numbers of tourists attracted by the nearby Rocky Mountain National Park, opened in 1915; the park has also played an important part in reclamation projects. But the man who put Estes Park on the map was the builder of the Stanley Hotel, F. O. Stanley.

Stanley was a wealthy man, having (with his twin brother, F. E.) invented, manufactured, and marketed the Stanley Steamer automobile. A native of Massachusetts, Stanley was forced to leave his native state when he became infected with tuberculosis. Attracted to Colorado by its dry elevation, he arrived in Estes Park aboard his Stanley Steamer on June 3, 1903. He fell in love with the town, and set to work improving his new home. Not only did he build the road to Lyons, Colorado, in 1907, he also redesigned the Stanley Steamer truck to create the first motor bus, the Stanley Mountain Wagon. This conveyance brought tourists from Lyons, Loveland, Longmont, and other Front Range railheads to Estes Park.

But where to house them? F. O. had an answer for that, too. He would build a hotel. Buying Lord Dunraven's disused property, he built the Georgian Revival Stanley Hotel, opening in 1909.

Where the Irish Earl's attempt had failed, the Yankee car manufacturer succeeded.

The palatial building and its beautiful grounds have attracted innumerable celebrities. Early on, the "Unsinkable" Molly Brown (so-called from her surviving the sinking of the *Titanic*) arrived. Pope John Paul II visited the area in 1993, followed a year later by the Emperor and Empress of Japan. Others include Jim Carrey, Peter Gabriel, Elliott Gould, Steven Weber, Judy Collins, Bob Dylan, Jeff Daniels, Ed McCaffery, Brooks Robinson, Johnny Rutherford, Reynelda Muse, Bill Walton, Amy Grant, Scott Carpenter, and Jerry Seinfeld.

But the guest who has done the most to popularize the hotel is horror writer Stephen King. In the late summer of 1973, King was at a crossroads. *Carrie* had made him famous, and his chilling vampire novel, *Salem's Lot*, was awaiting publication. For a change of scene, he moved his family to Boulder, from Maine, hoping for inspiration. But nothing clicked.

King found the Stanley while driving one day, and was impressed that the road to Estes Park was often closed in winter. Arriving at the Stanley, he began to see a story—a tale about a family trapped in a grand hotel in the Rockies over the winter. This story became *The Shining*, and the Stanley turned into the evil Overlook Hotel. Two movies have been made of the novel, the second (which was made for TV) actually shot at the Stanley.

But imaginary spooks also find their real-life counterparts at the Stanley. Since his death in 1940, F. O. Stanley himself is often seen in the lobby and the Billiard Room (his favorite room during his lifetime). Apparently, Stanley once appeared during a tour group's visit to the Billiard Room behind a member of the tour. Bartenders have seen him strolling through the bar, though he disappears whenever they try to cut him off at the kitchen.

His wife Flora is also on hand, playing in the ballroom although it is many years since she died. Employees and guests hear music coming from the room, and looking inside see the piano keys moving. But the music and the keys stop whenever anyone actually sets foot in the room.

Lord Dunraven, as mentioned, does not prowl the corridors of Adare Manor (now, ironically, also a hotel), but he may be encountered in Room 407 at the Stanley. There, he stands in the corner of the room near the bathroom door. Witnesses have reported that a light in that corner turns on and off. On one occasion, while the light was off, the guests that night told the ghost that they knew he was there, they would only be staying two nights, and would he please turn the light back on—His Lordship obliged. Later, though, when the lights were turned off and they were trying to sleep, the elevator kept operating noisily. As it turned out, however, the elevator was not operating at that time.

But many other rooms also have their unearthly tenants. Guests in Rooms 217 and 401 often complain of strange sights and sounds. When Room 407 is not booked, people often see someone looking out the window. Children apparently haunt Room 418, frightening the cleaning crews with the noises they make, and leaving impressions in the empty bed. Guests who stay in the room often complain of children playing in the hallways at night—even when no children are registered at the hotel!

But there is another child ghost who does not stay put in 418. He has been known to appear to staff in many parts of the hotel. Fittingly, Stephen King himself is said to have seen this junior apparition.

So haunted is the hotel, that rather than attempt to hide these stories, the management have capitalized on it. Twice daily on Wednesday and Saturday, and once on Sunday, ghost story tours are offered that feature the hotel's "history and stories about F. O. Stanley; the retelling of documented accounts of the paranormal; some explanations for the hauntings of the hotel; information about the hotel's relationship to Stephen King and *The Shining*;

and the occasional visit from one of the many spooks, specters, and ghosts of the Stanley Hotel."

If you are looking for roommates from beyond, check into the Stanley!

The Stanley Hotel
333 Wonderview
P.O. Box 1767
Estes Park, CO 80517
_(970) 586-3371 or_
_(800) 976-1377_

A Love Triangle Never Ends
at a Connecticut Restaurant

onnecticut was settled in the seventeenth century by Puritans from Massachusetts who sought an even stricter interpretation of Puritanism than that prevailing in Boston. Like their more "liberal" brethren in that province, however, the Connecticut Yankees lived in deadly fear of the Devil and his witch-minions; these were considered just a hair more dangerous than Anglicans or the even more despised Catholics.

Although witch-fears passed from legal processes to folklore, Old Nick seemingly kept his eye on the Nutmeg State. Many are the strange sites Connecticut boasts, most notably Dudleytown, a literal ghost town near Cornwall. The many immigrants of all nationalities who poured into the state in the nineteenth century added their own weird lore. "Haunted Connecticut" is more than a tourist office phrase.

One of the most typical towns in the state is Simsbury. Settled in the 1640s, the area was named Simsbury in 1670. Six years later,

King Philip's War broke out. Throughout New England, towns were raided by Indians intent on stopping the flood of English settlers. King Philip himself watched from a nearby ridge to see the infant settlement burn completely to the ground—the only town in Connecticut to do so.

The town recovered quickly, however. Its growth was spurred in 1705 by the opening of a copper mine. During the American Revolution, a thousand Simsbury men joined the rebel forces; one hundred of them fought at Bunker Hill. The now-played-out copper mine was transformed by Connecticut authorities into the fearsome prison of New-Gate, where many a loyalist paid for his refusal to change allegiance with death from exposure or starvation. After independence, Simsbury gave the new nation its first temperance society, the "Aquatics."

Thirteen years after King Philip watched the town burn, a tract of land just below the spot where he sat was granted by the Crown to a Colonel Pettibone. Eventually, the holding passed to his descendant, Colonel Jonathan Pettibone, Jr., in 1777. The inheritor built a tavern on the site eleven years later. The Pettibone Tavern was one of the first inns in the area to provide food and lodging for travelers; unfortunately, it burned to the ground in 1800, being rebuilt by the colonel the following year. George Washington stayed there while on a Connecticut visit.

As is usual with long-standing taverns, the Pettibone acquired during its long history a reputation for being haunted. The incident that is claimed to have sparked the haunting concerned an ocean-going member of the family, one Captain Pettibone. Supposedly, the captain's wife, Abigail, amused herself with other men while her husband was at sea. On one occasion, the captain returned early from a trip to England, and found his wayward wife in bed with another man in what became Room 6 of the tavern. Captain Pettibone's trusty cutlass ended the lives of the adulterous pair, and the Pettibone family went to great lengths to remove all traces of Abigail's existence—going so far as to cut her picture out of the family portrait, and concealing it within the wall. Recent research has failed to turn up any documentary proof of the event, however.

The Pettibones sold the tavern to Charles Croft in 1885, after which time it passed through a succession of owners. Under their management, the inn acquired a reputation for being haunted. Guests and staff encountered apparitions and other strange goings-on both in the restaurant and the guest rooms of the upper two stories. But after the Chart House chain acquired the place in 1973, and turned it into a steak and seafood restaurant, the fun really began. The new owners put through extensive renovations—precisely the sort of activity that is said to stir up supernatural manifestations in old houses.

Among other changes, the Chart House closed off the top floor, and turned the second floor into a bar (notorious Room 6—already renowned for its haunting—was turned into a ladies' room, complete with mirror). They continued to run the restaurant on the ground floor. While digging in the walls during renovation, workers found the cutout of a woman's face that had obviously been taken from a family portrait. Convinced that this was Abigail, the management ordered the fragment restored to the painting, which now hangs in the foyer.

Since the renovations, ghosts appear to run wild in the place. A cocktail waitress encountered a phantom Civil War soldier in the kitchen, who laughed as he spoke to her. The waitress ran screaming from the room, and never returned to work there. The candles in the dining rooms have relit themselves after everyone has left for the evening, and one woman broke up with her fiancé after feeling someone push her down the staircase—she was convinced that he had done it, despite the physical distance between them. One former headwaiter, accompanied by two waiters, heard a woman singing in the tavern, even after all the guests had left and the building had been searched thoroughly (during which the music stopped until the trio went outside). Women in the lady's room (formerly the infamous Room 6) have seen reflections other than their own in the mirror, and a large picture in one of the dining rooms—bolted to the wall—was broken off at night and laid on the floor, without alerting the movement-activated alarm system. The attic, too, is a very spooky place, complete with odd sounds and the occasional severe drop in temperature. One of the dining rooms, the Red Room, always smells of wood smoke, although it hasn't had a fireplace in years—it does have the temperature drop, though, and a sconce did fly off the wall at the manager when he tried to lift the carpet. The basement, too, has its share of chills.

All in all, it is a thoroughly haunted house; but the food is definitely made by the living for the living, and is an important reason to brave the ghosts—if they don't actually attract you, that is!

The Chart House/Pettibone Tavern
4 Hartford Road
Simsbury, CT 06084
(860) 658-1118

The Governor Shares His Mansion
with the Unearthly in Delaware

Delaware is our second smallest state. In the popular imagination, it is known chiefly for being the home of the du Pont clan, and for being the first state to ratify the constitution. But there is much more to Delaware. Although Wilmington, the du Pont stronghold, and surrounding New Castle County are fairly developed, as one ventures further south through Kent and Sussex Counties the state takes on a rural and even remote air—for such a small place, Delaware takes its regional differences seriously. Many old English customs and beliefs are kept up by the small farmers, larger landholders, and blacks in Kent and Sussex. The mysterious Moors, a people of mixed black, white, and Indian descent, in particular treasure tales of magic, ghosts, and witches, as well as various romantic stories of their own origins.

The reasons for this odd situation lie in Delaware's past. Although the coast was visited in the sixteenth century by Spanish and Portuguese explorers—in 1609 by Henry Hudson, the following year by Samuel Argall (who named the bay he sailed into in honor of Lord De La Warr, governor of Virginia), three years later by Cornelius May, and at last by Cornelius Hendricksen in 1614— permanent settlement did not occur until 1631. In that year, thirty Dutchmen settled at Zwaanendael, near modern Lewes. Two years later, they were all dead—killed by Indians.

In 1638, the Swedes settled at present Wilmington. This was the beginning of New Sweden, founded by Peter Minuit, ironically a Dutchman who founded New Amsterdam (now New York). But having fallen out with the Dutch West India Company, Minuit entered the service of Queen Christina of Sweden. In her honor, Minuit named the new settlement Fort Christina. Young, beautiful, and headstrong, the queen later renounced her throne in order to convert to Catholicism, and went into exile in Rome. Greta Garbo later played her in *Queen Christina*, and, judging by her performance, felt that she was a kindred spirit.

In New Sweden, however, the colonists had problems of their own. In 1651, a group of Dutch from the New Netherlands colony established a post, Fort Casimir, at the site of modern New Castle. Three years later, the Swedes seized it, thus provoking an attack the following year by Peter Stuyvesant, the Dutch governor. He seized New Sweden, which at that date comprised most of Delaware and adjoining portions of Pennsylvania and New Jersey, and annexed it to New Netherlands. Nevertheless, the Swedes and Finns sent over by the Queen, and their descendants, continued to have a lingering cultural affect on the area. The Finnish log cabin became a mainstay of frontier life, and is now considered as American as apple pie.

The conquest of New Netherlands by James, duke of York (brother of the English king, Charles II), meant the raising of the English flag over Delaware. In 1681, the king granted part of the conquest to William Penn—the colony of Pennsylvania. The following year, the Duke gave Delaware to Penn to guarantee him an outlet to the sea. By this donation, the counties of New Castle, St. Jones, and Deale became part of Pennsylvania; in 1682 these "Three Lower Counties" were constituted as territories with full privileges under Penn's "Frame of Government." St. Jones and Deale were respectively renamed Kent and Sussex Counties.

But these decisions did not please the Delawareans overmuch. Of primarily Anglican, Presbyterian, and Lutheran affiliations (with some few Catholics from Maryland), they looked with suspicion on Penn's Quaker commonwealth. The resulting litigation was settled in 1701. Although Delaware accepted the Penn charter of 1701, provisions were added giving the "Three Lower Counties Upon the Delaware" (as the colony was called officially) the right to a separate assembly. They would share the governor Penn and his heirs appointed for Pennsylvania, but he would be considered a royal governor in Delaware. The assembly did not actually meet until 1704, when New Castle became its seat and Delaware's first capital. Nevertheless, the Penns remained proprietors; disputes between them and successive Lords Baltimore over the boundary between Maryland and Delaware continued through the colonial period, and were not finally settled until the 1950s.

The countdown to the Revolution found the wealthier sort in New Castle County in favor of independence, Kent County divided, and Sussex County loyal to the throne. At the time of the Declaration of Independence, Delaware's leadership not only broke away from the crown, but also broke all ties to Pennsylvania. The Loyalists were rigorously suppressed, and the Delaware First Regiment—the "Blue Hen's Chickens"—and other state troops fought in all the major battles from Long Island to the siege of Yorktown. The only one fought in Delaware was Cooch's Bridge, near Newark, on September 3, 1777. The incursion of the British had the effect of frightening the state government, which fled New Castle for the safety of Dover, where it has remained ever since.

After the Revolution, gristmills on the Brandywine and Christina rivers turned Wilmington into a center for cloth, paper, and flour manufacture. In 1786, the state's own John Dickinson presided over the Annapolis Convention. This gathering called for the federal Constitutional Convention that met in Philadelphia the following year. Delaware was the first of the thirteen original states to ratify—unanimously—the new federal Constitution.

The French Revolution of 1789 sent many French royalists into exile in the United States. In 1802, one of these, named Eleuthère Irénée du Pont, established a gunpowder mill on the Brandywine River. This marks the beginning of that remarkable family's connection with Delaware. At various times, they have been accused of running the state like a feudal fiefdom. Whether or not that is true, they certainly have had an influence, not only through industrial and financial might, but also through culture. The splendid museums of Winterthur and Nemours, near Wilmington, started out as du Pont mansions.

But the industries they brought to the Wilmington area heightened divisions in the state. Before the Civil War, Delaware was a slave state. In the early nineteenth century, however, the number of Delaware slaves declined and the number of free blacks grew. Although more and more Delawareans favored emancipating slaves and sending them to Liberia, few were outright abolitionists; segregation was strong.

When the war broke out, Delaware remained loyal to the Union. Nevertheless, "Copperhead" sentiment was strong, and grew stronger as the war continued. Not only did Delaware refuse to accept Lincoln's first emancipation proposal in 1861, the state also did not ratify the Thirteenth, Fourteenth, and Fifteenth Amendments to the U.S. Constitution until 1901.

William Penn laid out Dover in 1683; in 1717 the city of Dover was incorporated by the Delaware General Assembly. As we saw, it became the capital of the state in 1777. After 1797 (when the title was changed from President, as laid down in the 1776 state constitution), the Governor presided over the town's political and social life. But it has only been since 1965 that the state's chief executives have resided in the old mansion called Woodburn. Nevertheless, the building's history goes back to the eighteenth century. In 1684, the land on which Woodburn is located was part of 412 acres given to one David Morgan. Although we cannot be sure, it seems that Morgan's family named the property Woodburn.

On November 2, 1784, Sheriff John Clayton sold the current tract to Charles Hillyard III. Hillyard came of a family that had held land grants in Delaware as early as the 1680s. It was then that Charles Hillyard's great-grandfather, John, had come to Kent County, receiving a land grant of about two thousand acres. Charles, after buying the Woodburn property, built the house around 1798. As befitted his background, he erected a Middle Period Georgian palace. Featuring three full floors, attic, and cellar, Woodburn boasts brickwork laid in Flemish bond. Most notable of the rooms open to the public are the Entrance Hall, the Drawing Room, and the Dining Room, all enhanced by fine Middle Georgian woodwork in such things as paneling, molding, and rails.

The enormous mansion was immediately filled: Hillyard and his wife Mary had ten children between the years 1782 and 1798. At fifty-four he died in his home on January 25, 1814, predeceased by his wife. Their daughter Mary and her husband, Martin W. Bates, bought the place on Charles's death, and lived on in the home for the next eleven years. A self-made man, Bates later became a U.S. senator.

On August 4, 1825, Daniel Cowgill, Sr. bought Woodburn from Martin Bates for $3,000. Cowgill was a newlywed, having married Mary Naudain just before moving into the house. Cowgill and his family became increasingly abolitionist: during the 1840s and 1850s the house served as a station on the Underground Railroad. It is said that a tunnel ran from a secret room in the basement underneath the rear grounds of the property out to the St. Jones River. From there, escaped slaves snuck into boats, traveling from the St. Jones River, north along the Delaware River to the neighboring free states. In Delaware, itself a slave state, this was a perilous occupation.

On September 15, 1877, Edward H. Wilson married Coralee Cowgill, granddaughter of Daniel and daughter of his son Clayton, in the house's Great Hall. Later, Woodburn was transferred to them and to Harriet Louise (Cowgill) Haman by Daniel, Sr. and Clayton. A number of notable owners followed in quick succession. In 1912, U.S. Senator Daniel O. Hastings bought it. The senator used the place primarily as a summer home, and added a brick porch on the three sides of the house, pillars on the south side, a French doorway in the drawing room, a reflecting pool in the garden, and removed the fireplace from the Great Hall. He sold Woodburn on September 12, 1918, to Mr. and Mrs. Frank Hall.

They in their turn also made a number of changes to Woodburn; but the high cost of maintaining the house forced the Halls to move to Bellevue Stratford in Philadelphia after World War II. After his wife died in 1952, Mr. Hall held an auction for the contents of the home, and then sold the house and one and a half acres of land. The remaining land was sold to the Elizabeth Murphy School.

The last private owners, the Murray family, sold the house to the state in 1965 for use as the Governor's Mansion. Delaware's chief executives have lived there ever since, and the house has become the venue for many official functions.

The first governor to live there, Charles L. Terry, Jr. (1965–1969), gave leave to his wife to outfit Woodburn as a proper official residence, and opened it to the public for tours. They also began the tradition of open house at Christmas. Governor Sherman W. Tribbitt (1973–1977) and his family were the first to use the house as their primary residence. Mrs. Tribbitt also began such customs at the house as exchange student tours, the Delaware

Mother of the Year Tea, and press breakfasts. They also initiated the custom of planting a tree on the grounds. While governor from 1977 to 1985, Pierre S. du Pont, IV, his wife, and their four children started hosting a Halloween celebration. Woodburn and its grounds were turned into a haunted house for the amusement of local children. But in actuality, it had already been one for quite some time.

Around 1815, the Bates family was host to Lorenzo Dow, the famous Methodist missionary. At breakfast one morning, Mrs. Bates asked the preacher to say grace. He asked if they shouldn't wait for the other houseguest. Surprised, his hostess told him that there were no other guests. Dow then described in some detail the older gentleman in powdered wig, knee britches, and ruffled shirt whom he had encountered on the staircase. Mrs. Bates was rather upset—Dow had described Charles Hillyard, her father and the builder of Woodburn, who had died the previous year.

Regardless of whether Mr. Hillyard returned again during his daughter's tenancy, he has come back since. In the 1870s, another houseguest had a fainting spell after seeing him sitting by the fireplace. Hillyard was renowned for his love of wine, a love that seems to continue beyond the grave. Governor Charles Terry Jr. blamed the ghost for draining off some of his vintage wines in the cellar of the mansion. One of his servants saw the ghost drink from a decanter in the dining room. Earlier residents would set out wine decanters, which drained overnight, in hopes of preserving their own better bottles. Frank Hall also saw him many times on the stairway during his own long tenure. Inspired by Hall's example, Governor Tribbitt's wife, Jeanne, would regularly check the stairway for Hillyard's apparition, and also left wine out for him on numerous occasions. But apparently he has no truck with those looking for him: none of those attempts brought any results.

Another revenant is a small girl in a red-checked gingham dress and bonnet. Carrying a candle and walking on the grounds around the reflecting pool added to the property by Senator Hastings, she must be of twentieth-century vintage. First seen playing by the pool during the 1940s, she has never been identified. When Governor Michael Castle held his inauguration party in January of 1985, his guests complained that an invisible presence pulled at their clothing; one woman saw an apparition of a little girl in a corner of the reception room. Was it the girl from the reflecting pool?

Out on the south lawn near Kings Highway, close to the south porch, is a large tree with a huge hole in its trunk. Screams are heard emanating from it, often at Halloween, and at times the figure of a man hanging from two branches of the tree is seen. Moaning and rattling of chains sometimes emanates from the basement as well, and popular legend suggests two opposite origins for these phenomena, which said legend also claims to be linked.

Both stories go back to the days of the Underground Railroad, when the Cargills held sway. According to the first tale, a slave fleeing pursuit was caught hiding in the tree trunk's hole. The screams are supposed to be his; the chain rattling in the basements is said to be either his or that of another slave who was sold out.

The alternative tradition is that the ghost that haunts the tree was actually a slave kidnapper, who had climbed the tree in hopes of finding runaways sponsored by Cargill. Instead, he slipped—his head caught between two branches. Thus he is supposed to be the hanging apparition according to this school, who also attribute the basement noises to him.

As mentioned, the living, official tenants of Woodburn have tried to solve the mansion's mysteries. Undaunted by her lack of success with Charles Hillyard, Jeanne Tribbitt sought to confirm the presence of the other ghosts who share the house and grounds with Hillyard, to no avail. Governor du Pont allowed college students to investigate the premises, but they came up with little evidence. Since a ghost crashed his inauguration party, it is no wonder that Governor Castle reported a few ghostly encounters himself. He permitted a teacher and three of her students, equipped with tape recorders and Ouija boards, to spend the night at Woodburn. In the morning they were all quite frightened, insisting that a portrait of a woman in one of the rooms had kept smiling at them.

Tours of Woodburn are open to the public Monday through Fridays, 8:30 AM to 4:00 PM, by appointment only. Will you be able to learn more than the current staff? Who knows? But should you encounter Woodburn's builder, see if he will share his wine.

The Governor's Mansion (Woodburn)
151 Kings Highway
Dover, DE 19901
(302) 739-5656
www.state.de.us/capitolpd/governor.htm

Florida's Biltmore Hotel is Still Refuge for Capone's Man

Florida is not only the sole tropical state in the continental United States, it was also the first to receive European settlement, by the Spanish in the sixteenth century. Even today, their remaining settlements at St. Augustine and Pensacola are filled with tales of ghosts and weird happenings. Another strand of the strange came to Key West with the Conchs, Bahamian descendants of Americans who fled after the Revolution because of their loyalty to the Crown. After Florida was annexed to the United States in 1819, Scotch-Irish "Crackers" moved into the northern part of the state, bringing with them their stories of "ha'nts," while American blacks brought in their unique lore as well. Cubans brought their Santeria and Brujeria to Tampa and Miami.

The southern part of the state owes its settlement to nineteenth-century tycoon Henry Flagler, who settled in St. Augustine, developed Palm Beach, and built a railroad down the East Coast. In 1895, an inhabitant of the small fishing village of Miami, Julia

Tuttle, mailed Flagler an orange blossom during a frost that had even chilled St. Augustine. Flagler extended his railroad down to this refuge, and two years later opened up the luxurious five-story Royal Palm Hotel. Alongside more humble tourists, the likes of John D. Rockefeller, Andrew Carnegie, and the Vanderbilt family (who built a mansion on Fisher Island) flocked to the spot. Mansions soon blossomed along Brickell Avenue—Millionaire's Row. Pan Am began flights between Miami and Latin America in the 1920s, and Miami had arrived.

Among the first settlers brought by Flagler's railroad was the Merrick family, who arrived in 1899 and bought 160 acres to be turned into a guava and avocado plantation. Called "Guavonia," it passed to George Merrick eleven years after his father's death. After a decade in the business, the younger Merrick began to dream of building a city on the property. It would be a pre-planned town that would encompass both residential and commercial properties, all built in Mediterranean style. Not only would it be a self-contained realm, it would also serve as a center of international trade. Thus was born what in time became Coral Gables. By 1924, Merrick realized that Coral Gables would need a hotel worthy of such a center. The next year, the city was founded, and construction began on the Biltmore hotel. Using the same firm who produced New York's Empire State Building, the combined Moorish, Italian, and Gothic hotel opened on January 15, 1926.

From the beginning, the Biltmore attracted the cream of Miami-area visitors, with a tower modeled after Spain's fabled Giralda tower, two eighteen-hole golf courses, twenty-six gondolas in the canals, weekly foxhunts, a water show, and polo grounds. The hotel also boasted a thirteenth floor—a rarity among hotels. There was only one suite on that top level, with only one elevator. It soon became sought after by the many wealthy folk who came to stay.

Johnny Weismuller and Esther Williams used the pool, and the stunning lobby was filled with such luminaries as Ginger Rogers,

Judy Garland, Bing Crosby, the Duke and Duchess of Windsor, and innumerable Roosevelts and Vanderbilts. But as with many grand hotels, there was a seamy underside to the Biltmore's glamour. Often the wealthiest patrons, during the hotel's first decade, were unable to book the suite on the thirteenth floor. The mob had discovered Coral Gables, and often enough a Capone lieutenant, one Thomas "Fats" Walsh, ran an illegal casino for high rollers in the suite. All went well until one night when Walsh was shot to death in front of his opulent guests, dying on the floor of the bathroom.

Nevertheless, life at the Biltmore went on, and many a celebrated guest was happy that the suite was now available more often. But if life was beautiful in the privileged precincts of the Biltmore, the world outside was careening toward war. After Pearl Harbor, in common with many such hostelries across the country, the Biltmore was taken over by the War Department for the duration, being given to the Veterans' Administration to serve as a hospital. Unfortunately for the old place, the duration stretched on past 1945 to 1968, when the abused building was finally released from government service. It sat abandoned until 1973, when the city of Coral Gables took it over. Rather than tear it down, the city poured time and money into the hotel, and it reopened on New Year's Eve, 1987. Restored as a lavish four-diamond, four-star hotel, and eighteen-hole, par-71 golf course, the Biltmore once again attracted Miami and international society, and was designated a National Historic Landmark in 1996. Its beauty lured singers Ricky Martin and Christina Aguilera to film music videos in the lobby, which is once again one of the hallmarks of the hotel.

But the Biltmore's checkered history has also left a roster of permanent guests, who occasionally mingle with the living. During the period that the Biltmore lay empty, passersby saw strange lights and heard band music and laughter coming from the shuttered hotel. Reopened to the public, both sets of guests began to interact. In the tower room, whence a woman dressed in white mounted a fatal jump to save her child, overnighters occasionally are confronted by her ghost. In some rooms lights turn on without a switch being touched, and doors open by themselves. Couples in 1920s formal wear have been seen dancing in the ballroom. Ghosts have been captured by cameras in Room 702, and a slender young man in a hospital gown (probably a World War II hold-over) has been seen.

The elevator leading to the suite on the thirteenth floor has a mind of its own—or else is run by the shade of Fats Walsh. It will start by itself, and mount to the floor, regardless of whether or not any living person is in it; bellhops intent on going elsewhere find themselves stopped at the suite itself, while lights in both elevator and suite flicker on and off as they please. On one occasion a guest declared that "Walsh got what he deserved." The elevator stopped screechingly in mid-flight, and would not move again until the hapless visitor apologized. Walsh's blood remains, irremovable, on the bathroom floor of the suite, and it is claimed that he once explained the details of his murder to the members of a séance held there. Not surprisingly, he has actually been seen as well. For a mere $2,850 a night, you can find out for yourself if the suite is haunted.

Although the hotel management officially discourages belief in ghosts at the Biltmore, they do tolerate a ghost tour every Thursday evening at 8:00 PM.

The Biltmore
1200 Anastasia Avenue
Coral Gables, FL
_(305) 445-1926_
Fax: (305) 913-3159

A Revolutionary War Vet Haunts His Restaurant Home in Georgia

Coastal Georgia was settled by the Spanish in the 1500s. The Indian tribes there were not only converted to Catholicism, but their languages were also reduced to writing. Indian chiefs carried on long correspondence with the king of Spain, and their numbers grew.

But the founding of Charleston, South Carolina, by the British in 1672 signaled the beginning of the end of this interlude. With their Creek Indian allies, the newcomers waged unceasing war against the Spanish and the Hispanicized Georgian Indians. By the end of the century they had withdrawn to Florida, leaving a wasteland behind them. In 1732, James Oglethorpe founded the city of Savannah as capital of the new colony of Georgia, named after King George II.

With its close ties to the Crown, the American Revolution came to Georgia not as a struggle for freedom by the people, but as a bloody civil war. Loyalists and rebels asked for and received no mercy from one another, and many a ghostly apparition owes its origins to that dark and terrible time in the state's history. (Not surprisingly, many another spirit walks after an untimely death in the second and better-known Civil War, almost a century later.)

Although the outer reaches of Georgia suffered terribly in this manner, the refined seaside capital of Savannah was not spared its share of the horror either. Here, too, families were divided in their loyalties. While the lower classes bore much of the brunt of the fighting, some of the most illustrious names in the province found themselves on either side of the conflict. So it was with the Habersham clan.

Born a younger son of a noble family in Beverly, Yorkshire, in 1712, the Honorable James Habersham came to Savannah on May 7, 1738 with James Whitefield (later co-founder, with John Wesley—who also visited Georgia—of Methodism). The pair opened a school for orphans and destitute children at Bethesda, nine miles from Savannah. Six years later, Habersham gave up philanthropy and became a merchant. In 1750 he was appointed with Pickering Robinson a commissioner to promote silk cultivation in the colony; in 1754 he became secretary of the province (predecessor of today's Georgia secretary of state) and one of the councilors—the King's Council for Georgia served both as the Governor's Cabinet and as the Upper House of the Assembly. In 1767 he became one of the presidents of that body. So trustworthy was he in that capacity, that when Sir James Wright, the South Carolina-born governor, took a leave of absence in England from 1769 to 1772, he officiated as acting governor. His public life did not interfere with his private endeavors, and he raised at Bethesda the first cotton in the state, sending the first few bales that were exported from the province to England. In 1771 he built a beautiful new town house of red brick on Abercorn Street, accounted one of the finest in the colonies.

But tragedy was lying in wait for James Habersham, despite his wealth and position. Although he had opposed the Stamp Act, he remained fiercely loyal to the king and to his friend, Sir James

Wright. As the clouds of war began to gather, however, he found that his three sons were no support to him. Joseph, John, and James, Jr. all took the rebel side, and many were the arguments the old man and his sons had in the basement of the house on Abercorn Street. The boys joined the "Sons of Liberty" in 1774, and when news came of the battles at Lexington and Concord on June 11, 1775, John led the group who seized the powder in Savannah's royal magazine. That same month, John was appointed to the rebel council of safety, in July leading a party that captured a government ship with munitions, including 15,000 pounds of powder. In these actions he was supported by his brothers, but so overwrought by the situation was his father that he left the colony about May 1775, and found refuge in New Brunswick, New Jersey (still under the rule of Sir William Franklin, who faced a similar family split with his father Benjamin) where in a home on the banks of the Raritan River he died the following August 28.

It was probably just as well, as he was spared witnessing an act that might have pushed him over the edge. On January 18, 1776, Joseph Habersham raised a group of volunteers, and stormed Government House, residence of Governor Wright (and now the site of Telfair Academy). This was an easy task, since the governor had no troops. John and a handpicked group burst into the Audience Chamber, where Sir James was meeting with the council. Upon hearing his words—"Sir James, you are my prisoner"—the councilors fled. Wright was held under house arrest, but escaped after three weeks, by stepping out of the back part of his house at night; before his absence was discovered he was safe on board a British ship that was lying at the mouth of the river.

The three brothers played their part in the Revolution, James, Jr. inheriting the house. He and his brothers did well under the new regime, despite Savannah being besieged twice, falling to the British the second time. At the close of the war Joseph held the rank of lieutenant-colonel in the army, was a member of the state assembly and its speaker in 1785 and 1790, was postmaster general of the United States from February 25, 1795, to November 28, 1801, and was president of the branch of the United States bank at Savannah from 1802 until the expiration of its charter. John, after the Revolution, was by Washington appointed Indian agent, was a member of the continental congress from Georgia in 1785–6, and was collector of customs at Savannah in 1789–99. James, Jr., apart from enjoying his father's residence, served on the board of trustees created in 1785 to establish the University of Georgia, and was speaker of the General Assembly in 1782 and 1784. But his joy was not to last. Apparently, in 1799, Junior is said to have hanged himself in the basement where he and his brothers had argued so long with their father.

Despite this setback, the house continued, surviving the great fire of 1820. But over the years the red brick's color bled out, leaving the building an odd shade of pink. When it was reincarnated as a restaurant in the twentieth century, it was dubbed the "Olde Pink House," which it remains. Here Savannah's elite dine in style on such local specialties as She-crab soup, Caesar salad with fried oysters, grouper, trout, flounder, Blue Crab in Vidalia onion sauce, pork, shrimp, duck, and veal. There is also a tavern downstairs, with live music on Saturdays. But apparently there are other-worldly attractions as well.

Since the restaurant has opened there have been reports of a male figure in the uniform of a continental general in the old places, especially downstairs. It is claimed that he may be seen in the autumn and winter especially, merely lighting candles the rest of the year. Sunday afternoons are said to be a particularly good time for seeing him. Not surprisingly, local tradition maintains that it is James, Jr. watching his old home.

Certainly, his picture, showing him as a general at age thirty-seven, may be seen in the foyer. Many report that the picture's eyes follow them, and some employees insist on keeping their backs to the portrait at all times when duty forces them into the foyer.

But worse may await the visitor elsewhere in the building. Habersham is claimed to be the most witnessed ghost in Savannah, a city that has more than its share. One old patron, supposing the apparition to be a re-enactor or prankster, asked him, "Tell me old boy, how was the war?" Habersham's phantom ignored him and walked past.

In the tavern occupying the basement, there is supposed to be a hidden vault. Next to its bricked-up entrance is an ancient velveteen chair formerly owned by Junior himself. Here he is held to occasionally materialize, watching over his guests. There are rumored to be other spirits inhabiting the place, including a woman. But if you do make your way there, don't ask too many questions of odd-looking folk you may encounter. They just might answer back.

Olde Pink House
23 Abercorn Street
Savannah, GA 31401
(912) 232-4286

Hawaii's Royal Palace
Still Hosts a Prince

Although many of the United States were originally colonies, and retain various relics of royal rule, only Hawaii boasts an actual royal palace. This is because the state had its own kings, from the time that Kamehameha I united the islands in the eighteenth century to the day Queen Liliuokalani was overthrown by American settlers in 1893.

Although the islands have been primarily Christian since the mid-nineteenth century, a great deal of native Polynesian supernatural lore survives. Even certain streets are said to be haunted, although few if any *haoles* (whites) have seen the spectral columns of "marchers" said to parade in plain sight.

The kings of Hawaii tried to reconcile modern European and American traditions with their own customs. One of these efforts at modernization was to turn the native kingship into a contemporary monarchy. This required a palace. The first one, built of wood, succumbed to the ravages of damp and termites. At last, King David

Kalakaua resolved to build one in stone. After demolishing the former residence, the king laid the cornerstone of a new palace on the last day of 1879. Completed and furnished by 1882, Iolani Palace cost the kingdom of Hawaii just under $360,000. It was the official residence of King Kalakaua from 1882 until his death in 1891, and of his sister and successor, Queen Liliuokalani, until her overthrow.

Sumptuously furnished, it hosted the coronation of King Kalakaua and Queen Kapiolani in 1883, as well as the king's fiftieth birthday celebration. But after his death, the new queen's position became increasingly threatened by the American settlers. Although the rooms she nervously walked through boasted gifts from French, British, Russian, and German monarchs, no help was forthcoming. Not only was the queen at last deposed, she was tried and found guilty of treason against the republic that unseated her. For a short time she was under house arrest, until moving into her husband's family home at Washington Place.

From 1893 to 1968, Iolani Palace served successively as the capitol of the Republic, the Territory, and finally the State of Hawaii. When the new state capitol was completed in 1969, the palace was vacated and restored to its former splendor as a museum. The grounds too have been restored, and the Royal Hawaiian band plays at times in the coronation pavilion.

But it would be strange, indeed, if the often tragic history of the palace had not left its mark upon the place. Often, when visitors have left, security guards will see unexplained lights and shadows, hearing footsteps when no one else is present. At times, wet footprints will appear in the halls—said to be left by a Hawaiian prince who was dunked in water as a punishment, and died of pneumonia. They say he still seeks his family.

Nor is the strangeness confined to the palace itself. Folk enjoying the gardens will smell odd scents, and hear unseen guards walking their rounds, invisible keys jingling as they walk. Unable to maintain their queen's authority in life, they still try to do so in death.

Most haunted of all is a disused, round concrete fountain with stairs going underground. It is the site where King Kalakaua had the palace well dug for emergency use. Shortly after their victory over the monarchy, about a century ago, the triumphant republicans erected a decorative fountain that has since decayed through neglect. Near this symbol of Hawaiian defeat, a glowing phantom girl in a white dress may sometimes be seen. At sunset, she emerges from the locked doorway beneath the fountain, ascends eight stairs to the ground level, and floats about the palace exterior. She cries out to passersby, attempting to lure them to their doom—so far, unsuccessfully.

One shade is missing from Iolani Palace, however—Queen Liliuokalani herself. But the wronged sovereign has been spotted elsewhere, both at the new state capitol (where she apparently objects to the placement of her statue in an obscure spot), at the Bishop Museum, and at Washington Place, now the Governor's Mansion, where she spent her last years in exile. But fear not; at her palace you may still encounter some of her loyal entourage.

Iolani Palace
364 South King Street
Honolulu, HI
(808) 538-1471

A Serial Killer's Victim Haunts
a Church-Turned-Theater in Idaho

The state of Idaho was once part of the Oregon Country, a vast wilderness of forests, mountains, and game. The first permanent European settlements were the posts of the Hudson's Bay Company, soon followed by various Catholics and other missionaries. The oldest building in Idaho is the chapel of the Cataldo Mission.

Idaho history is replete with strange tales of the Old West: Indians, trappers, settlers, miners, and the like. The first explorers to pass through was the Corps of Discovery, headed by Captains Meriwether Lewis and William Clark, and dispatched by President Thomas Jefferson in 1804. The mission of the Lewis and Clark Expedition was to explore the newly acquired Louisiana Purchase and blaze a trail through to the Pacific Ocean. The intrepid band reached Idaho's Clearwater Valley in 1805. Following the Clearwater River from the Bitterroot Mountains to its merger with the Snake River, they found the site of the present

day twin cities of Lewiston, Idaho, and Clarkston, Washington—
named, of course, in their honor.

They found the area inhabited by the NiMiiPuu nation,
dubbed by French-Canadian trappers the "Nez Perce" (pierced
nose). A peaceful people, they welcomed the explorers, as they
would—to their cost—many later arrivals. Unremitting pressure
by white settlers led the Nez Perce to fight a tragic war under their
celebrated leader, Chief Joseph. Despite their defeat, today the Nez
Perce tribe is a federally recognized sovereign nation with inher-
ent rights preserved by treaty. Their tribal headquarters are located in Lapwai, Idaho, near Lewiston. NiMiiPuu (pronounced
Nee-mee-poo) or "the People" have much to offer visitors.

In 1863, the little settlement became Idaho's first capital, a
distinction held only a year until the Territorial Legislature
approved moving the capital to Boise, where it remained after
statehood in 1890. Nevertheless, immigrants continued to pour
into the Lewis-Clark valley: miners, merchants, railroads, mill
workers, and farmers. Lewiston became a regional service and
shopping center for north-central Idaho and eastern Washington
and Oregon. Because the river is still navigable this far up, the
city is the site of the farthest inland seaport, the Port of Lewiston, 465 miles from the Pacific Ocean. The valley, because of its
mild winter climate, is referred to as the Banana Belt; golfing is
year-round.

Despite this heritage, the ghost story we are concerned with
does not involve settlers, soldiers, missionaries, trappers, or Indians (though plenty of others in the state do). Not only that, it
involves a church!

In 1907, the Lewiston Methodist Church erected an impressive sandstone castle-like structure, replete with twenty stained
glass windows. In 1972, the Lewiston Civic Theatre bought the
church, at first sharing joint occupancy with the congregation.
The minister even delivered a rousing sermon through the sunroof

of a VW Beetle, part of the set of "The Me Nobody Knows," the theater's first production at the venue. Eventually, the congregation moved to an ultramodern church building, and the structure was renamed the Anne Bollinger Performing Arts Center, after the famed opera singer. In 1980, the building was placed on the National Register of Historic Places, and continues to serve as a venue for the Civic Theatre's productions.

But the old building, given up as it had been to the gentler pastimes of religion and culture, was soon to play a part in one of the grisliest episodes in Idaho's history. Apparently, a serial killer has been operating in the Lewiston-Spokane area. In 1979, twelve-year-old Christina White of Asotin, Washington, was attending the Asotin County Fair. She called her mother from a friend's home to say she was feeling ill, whereupon her mother told her to walk back to the fair when she felt better. She never arrived. Two years later, Kristen David, a twenty-two-year-old University of Idaho student from Lewiston, also disappeared. Eight days after her disappearance, her headless torso and leg were found along the Snake River in Clarkston. The next day, Kristen's head, arms, and part of a leg were found.

In September of 1982, Kristina Nelson, twenty-one, and Jacqueline Miller, eighteen, who had attended a performance at the Civic Theatre that night, disappeared. So, too, did the janitor, thirty-five-year-old Steven Pearsall. Almost two years after their disappearance, the bodies of the women were found on a brushy slope in Kendrick. Although Pearsall has never turned up, he is not believed to be their killer.

But if their bodies vanished, Jacqueline's spirit has not, apparently. It is said that at night she can be seen climbing up the stairs; she also is supposed to play the usual sort of phantom tricks. But she does not walk the theater alone. There is also an apparition of a jilted bride, left at the altar when the theater was the Methodist church: she is seen roaming through the seats crying. A now-deceased director has been observed at times observing the latest production. Every theater is said to be haunted, but if you attend a performance at this one, look closely at your fellow audience members!

Lewiston Civic Theatre
805 6th Avenue
Lewiston, ID 83501
(208) 746-3401

Illinois' Red Lion Pub Fights for Its Title of "Most Haunted"

As might be guessed by its French name, Illinois was first settled by *voyageurs* from Quebec and by farmers from Louisiana. In the early days, the bulk of the population resided in the south of the state, along the Mississippi River. Such old settlements as Cahokia, Kaskaskia, Prairie du Rocher, and Metropopolis (formerly Massac) are testimonies to these intrepid folk. Not surprisingly, some of the old lore brought from medieval France has survived in those favored spots.

The arrival of the Americans after 1783, however, precipitated an enormous change. The Indians were for the most part removed to the Indian Territory west of the Mississippi (modern Kansas and Oklahoma) and settlers from all over Europe and the east filled up the state. Most telling, for the future, was the incorporation of the settlement of Chicago in 1837. Over the following "Century of Progress" (as the Centennial Exposition in 1937 dubbed it), Chicago became not merely the largest city in Illinois, but the second biggest in the nation—a position it would hold until edged out by Los Angeles in the late twentieth century.

As with any big city, Chicago became host to any number of ethnic enclaves and their attendant institutions: churches, fraternal societies, restaurants, and bars. In the 1920s, during Prohibition, the city became renowned for its lawlessness and the size and power of its criminal gangs; it is no wonder that Al Capone is perhaps, even today, the best-known Chicagoan. With such a past, the city is a vast repository of strange and unearthly tales.

One establishment that carries on memories of both sides of Chicago's heritage is the famed Red Lion Pub, on the city's north side. It is located directly across the street from the Biograph Theater where John Dillinger, accompanied by the mysterious "lady in red," was shot by federal agents in 1934. Built in 1882, its past has included use as a gambling hall, apartments, a laundry house, and a novelty shop.

One John Cordwell, former city planner, acquired it in 1984, and opened the place as an English pub. Although John died in February 1999, his widow, Dr. Justine Cordwell (a noted anthropologist specializing in urban studies—a good complement to her late husband's career) continues to run the place. When Cordwell bought the building, he began extensive renovations; as often happens in such cases, it was then that odd phenomena began to occur. It started with the installation of a stained glass window in memory of John's father. Cordwell Senior had died in England without benefit of a proper interment. People started reporting feeling dizzy when passing the window, and claimed to sense a "presence."

Having gained for itself the reputation of being "the most haunted bar in Chicago," (quite a boast, in a city filled with them) seemingly every patron and employee has a story to tell. One waitress was locked in the upstairs ladies' room by an unknown agency. Unable to get out, she began screaming. Members of the staff rushed to her aid, and one of them was easily able to open the door from outside. This has happened repeatedly to others, and is ascribed to a mentally handicapped girl who died in the upstairs area during the 1950s. She also pushes people on the stairs.

This has not been the only strange occurrence upstairs. One regular patron went up there after closing time one night, only to find that the layout was different from normal. A scene played out in front of him, ending with a young woman lying on the floor, covered in blood. His screams for help brought John and the others in the main bar upstairs in a hurry. When they arrived, all was normal and the woman had vanished; the patron was very upset, to say the least.

Nor have these been the only goings-on. A ghost dressed like a cowboy haunts the main bar, calling people by name and quickly disappearing when they look. Every now and then the scent of lavender wafts through the entire establishment, causing patrons to look, unsuccessfully, for its source.

If a little shabby looking, the Red Lion is a warm and welcoming refuge from the rigors of Chicago's winter. The food is good, and the companionship jovial. But don't be surprised if you run into someone—or something—strange.

Red Lion Pub
2446 North Lincoln
Chicago, IL 60614
(773) 348-2695
www.hauntingsresearchgroup.homestead.com/redlion.html

Hannah House in Indiana Offers
Ghostly Sights, Sounds–and Smells!

L ike its neighbor to the west, Indiana's first settlers were
Frenchmen, traveling up various rivers. They founded the
city of Vincennes, which even today hosts tales of such
uniquely French oddities as the *Loup-Garou*, the werewolf. As
with Illinois also, the American takeover in 1783 resulted in re-
moval of most of the Indians, and their replacement with a dizzying array of nationalities. The axis of settlement also shifted
northward, so that Indianapolis, in the center of the state, is both
the capital and largest city.

But the rapid settlement of Indianapolis before the Civil War
resulted in numerous attempts to give the city a veneer of sophistication by building homes and public buildings in the most up-
to-date European styles. One such product is the Hannah House
at the corner of National and Madison Avenues. The twenty-
four-room red brick structure was erected in 1858 for Indiana
State Legislator Alexander Moore Hannah, who adapted the

contemporary Italianate style (with touches of Greek Revival) for his new mansion.

Hannah was born in Wayne County in 1821. Having trained as a harness-maker, he left his business in 1850, bound for California and its Gold Rush. There he earned enough money to become part owner of a barley and vegetable ranch. In 1855, he sold his share of the ranch and returned to Indiana, settling in Indianapolis and working for the Indiana Central Railroad. Hannah's father, Samuel, was president of the railroad; he also owned extensive property in Marion County. Alexander acquired 240 acres south of Indianapolis, beginning construction of the Hannah House. Although the design of the house is attributed to him, he seems to have been affected by the many trade publications and architectural guides popular in the 1850s. He was certainly a man to keep abreast of developments, at a time when technology was advancing further and faster than ever before. Known throughout his lifetime as a progressive farmer, Hannah applied the latest scientific techniques in raising wheat, corn, oats, and hay, and such livestock as cattle, sheep, and hogs. His forward-looking applied to transportation as well: the first toll-road in Marion County, the Indianapolis-Southport Toll Road, crossed Hannah's property. From 1860 to 1895, he collected the tolls from travelers along his section of gravel-surfaced road. His politics were also advanced: in a border state with a large number of southern sympathizers, Hannah was a convinced abolitionist. It was rumored that for the two years before the Civil War actually broke out, Hannah House was a station on the Underground Railroad, smuggling slaves to Canada.

In 1872, Alexander married Elizabeth Jackson. To accommodate his new lifestyle, he built a service building southeast of the kitchen wing, housing the smokehouse, washhouse, milk-cooling room, and servant's quarters. In his later years, Hannah was a member of the Indiana General Assembly, serving at various times as postmaster, sheriff, and clerk of the circuit court. The major east-west street south of his house was named "Hannah Avenue" in his honor. Marrying so late in life, Hannah had no heirs (although his wife was said to have given birth to a stillborn child); his farm was subdivided and sold after his death in 1895.

Roman Oehler, German immigrant, Civil War vet, and prosperous jeweler, purchased the house and twenty-one acres of surrounding property in 1899. During his occupancy, the porch on the front of the house was replaced with a wider one of concrete; several still extant outbuildings were also constructed. Oehler's daughter, Romena Oehler Elder, with her husband and family, were the third owners of the house, occupying it until 1962. In that year, David Elder assumed responsibility for caring for the place, although he didn't live there. From 1968 to 1978, a Mr. and Mrs. O'Brien rented the mansion, opening an antique store in one part of it, and living in another part. Hannah House was placed on the National Register of Historic Places in 1978. From 1980 to 1982, the place was used as the annual "haunted house project" of the Indianapolis Jaycees. They would take kids on a tour of the spooky old mansion, with frightening special effects added for entertainment.

From 1981 to 1999, the house was restored and renovated; still owned and operated by the descendants of Roman Oehler, it is now used for private parties and functions. The historic mansion hosts weddings and receptions, corporate dinners, birthday and anniversary parties, class reunions, an annual Easter egg hunt, and monthly open house tours. Apparently, it hosts other, less conventional activities as well.

David Elder was perhaps the first to suspect that something strange was happening in the mansion. One day, while doing various chores around the old place, he suddenly heard a terrific crash of breaking glass coming from the basement. Rushing downstairs, he found nothing wrong, although he did notice a number of old fruit jars stacked up. The second-floor bedroom where Elizabeth Jackson Hannah gave birth to her stillborn would at different times give forth either an odor of rotting flesh, or of roses. Normally used for storage, its door would swing open, even when locked. When this would occur, other things would happen: strange noises, unseen footsteps, whispering voices, cold drafts blowing in places without outlets, and other doors and windows opening and closing without help from the living.

When the O'Briens moved in, the fun really began in earnest. A painter saw doors swing open and pictures slide from their moorings as he walked by. He fled after a spoon that Mrs. O'Brien had put on a tray flew across the room. Both husband and wife saw a man with mutton-chop whiskers in a black suit who would disappear in front of them, and their son and daughter-in-law, their young granddaughter, carried on a conversation with someone she said "looked like a grandfather." Although the staircase to the second floor was carpeted, footsteps with rustling clothing could be heard. Mr. O'Brien saw the door to the attic open by itself, after the handle deliberately turned. One night, while he watched TV in one of the upstairs bedrooms, Mr. O'Brien heard groaning from the second floor hallway. He yelled at it to stop and leave them alone. Four years after they moved into the house, the ghostly activity stopped.

But after the O'Briens left, the unseen denizens of the mansion began their tricks again. When the Jaycee coordinator and some of his staff were preparing the place to serve as the Halloween haunted house in 1980, they took a break in the summer kitchen. This adjoined the staircase formerly used by the servants to go up to the second floor. Loud scratching sounds started coming from inside the staircase landing wall, for which no cause could be found before they stopped. On another night, the coordinator and a friend listened to the stereo unit playing scary sound effects, when the unit was switched off. This happened repeatedly.

Since then, many other phenomena have occurred. There are cold spots that move; in addition to the man in black (assumed to be old Alexander Hannah himself), the ghost of an unidentified woman has been seen in a second-floor window. A TV crew in October of 1981 visited Hannah House and experienced chandeliers and picture frames moving unaccountably, as well as sounds of unknown origin. Apparitions of supposed slaves have been seen hiding in the basement.

This last event points up a legend of the house. As mentioned, the mansion was supposedly part of the Underground Railroad for escaping slaves that ran through Indiana to Canada. The story goes that Hannah hid the runaways in his mansion's basement, until they could be moved to the next "station." One night, it is said, a lantern accidentally was knocked over, causing a fire in the basement. Many of the slaves hiding there were killed, and duly buried in simple coffins in the basement. But no one has proved this story to be true or otherwise.

Today, the smell of rotting flesh seems to be absent, but disembodied moaning and whining continues. Doors in the house still suddenly open and close by themselves, and old drafts are also sometimes felt when there are no windows or doors open. Whether or not you'll encounter these things yourself, a tour at the Hannah House might well be more than you bargain for!

Hannah House
3801 Madison Avenue
Indianapolis, IN 46225
(317) 787-8486 or
(317) 881-9136
www.hannahmansion.com

An Opera House in Iowa
Offers Nightly Performances,
without Living Actors

owa passed under American sovereignty in 1803, together with the rest of the Louisiana Purchase. The only major European settlement in the state at that time was at the site of modern-day Dubuque. The city owes its name to one Julien Dubuque, a French-Canadian fur trader who settled in the area in the 1780s. He originally came to the area to trade with the local Mesquakie Indians who occupied the land at that time. But when he learned of plentiful lead mines located on their property, Dubuque's attention wandered from trading to mining. In 1788, the Mesquakie granted Dubuque control of their lead mines; he in turn named this region, just south of the present-day city, the Mines of Spain.

Until his death in 1810, Dubuque worked the mines. At his death, the Mesquakie reclaimed the Mines of Spain for themselves. But in 1822 the federal government licensed settlers to mine lead in the area; settlers rushed in, and ten years later, as a result of the Blackhawk War, the tribe was forced to cede the region to the government. In 1833, the area was officially opened for settlement as the city of Dubuque.

As the years went by, Dubuque filled out, acquiring all of the accoutrements of contemporary urban living. The city hall was built in 1857, and the county courthouse in 1891. Despite the city's reputation for a lack of interest in the arts and in sophistication generally (remember Harold Ross's famous declaration about the *New Yorker* that "It is not edited for the old lady in Dubuque"), early residents' thirst for culture led to the erection, in 1889–90, of the Grand Opera House.

Built in the Richardsonian architectural style, the Grand's original facade is constructed of St. Louis brick facing with Bayfield red sandstone trim. Opening night performance on August 14, 1890, was the opera, *Carmen*. Eight hundred people came to see the performance, paying five dollars a head; in today's money, this would be around a hundred dollars. In later performances, such greats as George M. Cohan, Lillian Russell, Ethel Barrymore, and Sara Bernhardt would all tread the Grand's stage. Perhaps the most elaborate production ever put on at the Grand Opera House was *Ben Hur*, replete with chariots and live horses and elephants on the stage.

In the 1920s, the owners of the theater closed it for three months for remodeling. As with so many similar venues across the country, the theater was to become a movie palace. During this time, the second balcony and all of the box seats were removed, the orchestra pit was covered over, the semi-circular stage front was straightened, gas fixtures were replaced with electric lights, and a big screen and a projector were installed. For the next fifty-eight years the Grand Opera House was a movie theater known as the Grand. But multi-screens doomed the cinematic incarnation of the Grand, as they have so many other beautiful old movie theaters. In 1986, the Grand Opera House became home to the Barn Community Theatre Company; it has once again merited a reputation as one of Iowa's foremost theatrical venues.

But, apparently, something was up at the Grand soon after it became a movie theater in 1928. The Dubuque police department began a record of calls from theater cleaning ladies reporting strange voices in the building at night. Since the Barn took over the Grand, they themselves have collected many tales of odd activities in the building, ranging from ghostly voices to bizarre electrical problems. The company also records the theft of small items in the theater and various other pranks. Voices of people who are not present are heard; disembodied singing occurs; invisible piano playing and footsteps are experienced, as well as the old standbys of cold blasts of air and lights turning themselves off.

In 1991, things heated up. Apparitions started to be reported in the theater. One of the employees saw two women sitting in the auditorium seats, who vanished before his eyes. An apparition turned up on a tape being shot of a stage performance as well. Apparently, the show goes on at the Grand Opera House—whether or not there is anyone to see it!

Grand Opera House
135 West 8th Street
Dubuque, IA
(563) 588-4356
www.thegrandoperahouse.com

A Kansas College Athlete
Sticks Around His Alma Mater,
Even After Death

Before the first white settlers came, a large Kaw Indian village stood near the mouth of the Big Blue River on the present site of Manhattan, Kansas. Although most of the Indians of Kansas were peaceful, the Santa Fe Trail wound its way through the future state, and the settlers traversing its length needed security. For that reason, a fort was established in 1853 near present-day Manhattan to protect movement of people and trade over both the Oregon-California and Santa Fe Trails. It was named Fort Riley in honor of Major General Bennett C. Riley, leader of the first military escort along the Santa Fe Trail. Taking advantage of the protection offered by the fort, in the following year two settlements were established, Canton and Poleska. They were soon consolidated under the name of Boston, in tribute to the Free-State sentiments of many of these settlers. When a large new colony of settlers arrived, the name was changed to Manhattan, which became the seat of Riley County.

Blue Mont College, the forerunner of Kansas State University, was founded in 1859. Three years later, Congress granted Kansas 90,000 acres to found an agricultural college; the following year, Kansas State University in Manhattan was established as the nation's original land-grant university. It is an odd fact that university and college campuses rank alongside hotels, restaurants, and theaters as favored public spots for hauntings; certainly KSU has its share of supposed ghosts. But the most talked-about example on campus is the Purple Masque Theater, a room located in the East Stadium Building. Originally, East Stadium was an athletic building, and adjunct to the nearby Memorial Stadium. But in 1965, when KSU's auditorium burned down, the theater department built the Purple Masque in one room of East Stadium as a black box theater, a free space capable of being rearranged for every new production. It is set up as a theater in the round, with audience members on all sides of the small stage.

In addition to its reputation as a venue for fine (but necessarily small) performances, it has gained great fame through its alleged ghostly connections. The story goes that, back in the 1950s, a young football player named Nick was hurt while playing at Memorial Stadium. Supposedly, he died in the cafeteria area of the athletic dorms under the bleachers, where the theater is now housed. The legend continues further that while on their way to watch him play, Nick's parents were killed in a car accident. He is said to still be waiting for his parents to arrive. The problem with this charming tale is that, according to university archives, there was no football player named Nick, nor any record of a football player dying during a game. Nor was there ever a cafeteria in Memorial Stadium.

But regardless of who or what is doing it, footsteps are heard stomping up and down hallways, on staircases and on the theater stage. Chairs are moved and theater props are hidden at night, and paint is mysteriously sprayed over things. Witnesses have seen wooden boxes stacked in the dressing room jump to the floor and then re-stack themselves. A fire extinguisher was seen spinning around in mid-air, spraying white foam as it traveled. No ghostly football player has been seen, but a Confederate soldier has been observed sitting in a phantom chair atop the stage. While there is no historical explanation offered for this last sighting, that old college spirit does seem to be alive at the Purple Masque!

Kansas State University
Manhattan, KS 66506
(785) 532-6011

In Kentucky,
a Mysterious Disappearance and a
Misplaced Grave Fuel Hauntings

What is now Kentucky was, before the arrival of the Euro-peans, prized by all the surrounding Indian tribes as rich hunting ground. Unfortunately, this led to its being fought over by them. The standard translation of the name "Kentucky" is "the dark and bloody ground," supposedly in reference to this tragic state of affairs. However that may be, there were few estab-lished Indian settlements there by the time British explorers began ranging over the land in the eighteenth century.

One of the first of these pathfinders was the celebrated Daniel Boone, who helped establish Kentucky's first forts at Harrodsburg and Boonesborough. As the Revolution heated up, loyalists and rebels alike sought refuge beyond the Alleghenies. The city of Lex-ington was founded in 1775, seventeen years before Kentucky be-came a state. Louisville, named after Louis XVI of France (without whom the rebellious colonists could not have won), was founded by George Rogers Clark in 1778; this was done as part of Clark's effort in attaching Kentucky to Virginia. English-descended Virginians poured into the area. But in 1785 a "league" of sixty Catholic families was formed in Maryland. Many more such Catholic Marylanders were to follow in the years to come, settling in what today is called the "Holy Land" of Kentucky—Nelson, Washington, and Marion Counties. Thus a unique element was added to the Kentucky frontier. Many Scotch-Irish mountaineers simply moved further west from their settlements in what are now West Virginia and Virginia, thus making the eastern part of the state an integral part of Appalachian culture.

All of these areas have their own strange lore: witches, ghosts, and healers. But we will turn our attention to the state capital (and seat of Franklin County), Frankfort.

Settlement of the immediate area began in the 1780s. Rather than being named after either of the two Frankfurts in Germany, in this case the title apparently is derived from Stephen Frank, a settler killed at what came to be known as Frank's Ford. The town was established in 1786 as Frankfort, Virginia, and replaced Lexington as capital of the new state in 1792. Two years later, a post office was opened. Shortly after that occurrence there began the saga of one of the most famous haunted houses in all Kentucky: Liberty Hall.

In 1786, General James Wilkinson received a grant of land from Virginia Governor Patrick Henry for the land that is now downtown Frankfort. Wilkinson proceeded to lay out a town and name the streets for friends, famous persons, places, and himself. His original streets form the boundaries of three of the four sides of Liberty Hall Historic Site. Wilkinson, who in 1787–90 was active in the movement among Kentuckians to bring Kentucky under the Spanish flag, eventually sold the tract that is now Liberty Hall to local settler Andrew Holmes. In 1796 he in turn sold the four acres that form the site to Kentucky's first United States senator, John Brown.

Brown was one of Kentucky's great early statesmen, and is often called its founding father. An initial supporter of Wilkinson's scheme, he eventually supported Kentucky's long-delayed statehood when it was granted (as did Wilkinson, in the end). Despite the controversy surrounding his early role, his personal honesty and integrity were so renowned that his fellow citizens elected him to a number of important political positions.

Born near Lexington, Virginia, in 1757, John Brown and his parents moved to Kentucky because John's father, Reverend John Brown, became minister to two local Presbyterian churches. The older Browns were born in Ireland. John was raised in his father's church, and was sent to Augusta Academy and the College of New Jersey (now Princeton). Initially intending to study medicine there, Brown was forced to leave when the Revolution raged through the area and the college closed. For two years he served in the rebel forces, entering the College of William and Mary in 1778. Two years later, his schooling there ended when the forces of the Crown arrived. He then studied law in Thomas Jefferson's office in Charlottesville. He then set out his shingle in Danville, Kentucky, becoming active in local politics. Brown served in the Virginia State Senate from 1783 to 1788; in 1787, he represented the county of Kentucky in the state of Virginia at the Continental Congress, for one year. In 1788, under the new Constitution, Brown was elected to the United States House of Representatives. Serving as a representative for four years, he presented to Congress a petition to separate the county of Kentucky from the state of Virginia. It was during this seemingly endless interval that Wilkinson's plan to join Kentucky to Spain acquired its popularity; this vanished in June of 1792, when Kentucky became the fifteenth state. Brown became Kentucky's first United States senator. He served in the Senate until 1805, twice holding the position of president pro tempore.

As befitted his position in society, Brown bought the Wilkinson tract from Holmes in 1796, and built Liberty Hall on it. The first few years of his ownership were consumed with the building of the Hall: built in Federal style, it is, even now, one of the finest of its kind in the state. It is claimed that the mansion was designed by Thomas Jefferson. Three years later, Brown wed Margaretta Mason of New York City, when he was forty-one and she was twenty-six. On November 10, 1799, their first child, Mason, was born. In 1800, Brown purchased a ferry crossing the Kentucky River from the end of Wilkinson Street to the beginning of the road to Louisville. Brown also managed hundreds of acres of property in central Kentucky, as well as 20,000 acres near Chillicothe, Ohio. That same year, Brown moved into the Hall, his wife and baby son joining him in the spring of 1801. Their second son, Orlando, was born on September 26, 1801. Two more sons (who both died as infants) followed, as well as a daughter who died at age seven from mercury poisoning resulting from the use of a medication called Calomel.

In 1805, defeated for re-election to the Senate, Brown retired to Liberty Hall. He remained active in public affairs for the remaining thirty years of his life. Unbroken by his defeat, Brown acted as a host for visiting celebrities. When, in the same year that he lost his Senate seat, a beautiful Spanish opera star was invited to Frankfort, to perform in a concert, the Browns invited her to stay with them. A party was held in her honor, but during the festivities, the diva went out to explore the garden. Last seen walking down to the Kentucky River, she vanished. Although an extensive search was made of the area and the river dragged, she was never found. Indians or vagabonds were blamed, but the mystery has never been solved.

Brown became a founding member of the Frankfort Water Company and director of the first bank of Kentucky; in 1812 he was appointed by the legislature to oversee the construction of a public house of worship on the public square of Frankfort.

In 1817, when Mrs. Brown lost another infant, the family sent for her aunt, Mrs. Margaret Varick—who had raised Mrs. Brown when her mother had died—to come out from New York to attend and comfort Mrs. Brown. Mrs. Varick, who loved her niece as her own daughter, readily complied. Unfortunately, the trip by coach and horseback was a terrible strain on the aged and frail lady. Totally exhausted, she died of a heart attack in one of Liberty Hall's upstairs bedrooms soon after her arrival. Buried at first in the small family plot in the outside gardens, when the entire family plot was moved to the bigger cemetery in Frankfort her remains were lost.

Undeterred by this latest tragedy, the Browns entertained the cream of American society; their 1819 guest list alone included President James Monroe, Colonel Zachary Taylor, Colonel Andrew Jackson, General Lafayette, and Aaron Burr. In later years, William Harrison and Theodore Roosevelt also visited the Hall.

In 1829 Brown became the sheriff of Franklin County. John Brown served on the board that oversaw the brick capitol building, as well as the limestone one that replaced it, known today as the Old Capitol. Brown died in Lexington on August 29, 1837.

In 1934, Mary Mason Scott, John Brown's great granddaughter, passed away, leaving Liberty Hall to her brother, John Matthew Scott. As a successful attorney in Louisville he did not want the burden of Liberty Hall. Scott sold the Hall to a nonprofit organization; in 1955, together with the neighboring family home, the Orlando Brown House, which came to them at the same time, the National Society of the Colonial Dames of America in the Commonwealth of Kentucky opened the house as a museum. They continue to run the property as a "living museum of Kentucky history" to this day.

Like any great house that has seen more than its share of tragedy, Liberty Hall's past casts its impressions on the present. Mrs. Varick appears to haunt the place still, trying to help its denizens and to point out her forgotten grave. She first appeared a few years after her death, after the graves were moved. She is described as kind and calm, dressed in a gray house dress and small of stature. Nicknamed the "Gray Lady," she favors her old bed-room and the staircase. But she has appeared and acted through-out the house—sometimes performing helpful chores, at other times slamming doors in the middle of the night. She occasionally makes beds, and tucks overnight guests in at night. Caught on film descending the staircase, she is usually smiling when she appears. Those who have experienced her apparition rarely seem to be frightened by her.

The same cannot be said of whatever walks the garden. It may well be the hapless Spanish singer who is seen racing through the garden on hot humid nights, her mouth "frozen open in a sound-less cry of terror." There seems to be no historical reason for the British soldier, dressed in the uniform of the War of 1812, who peers from outside through ground-floor windows into the living room. A deserter, perhaps? But the war did not reach into Ken-tucky. His identity must remain one of the secrets of Liberty Hall, where Kentucky history truly lives on.

Liberty Hall Historic Site
218 Wilkinson Street
Frankfort, KY 40601
(888) 516-5101
libhall@dcr.net

Antoine's Restaurant in Louisiana Sometimes Offers Supernatural Events a la Carte

The state of Louisiana is truly a world apart. Named after Louis XIV, the "Sun King" of France, back in the sixteenth century, it remains the most Francophone state in the Union. Instead of counties, the Pelican State has parishes; instead of the common law, Louisiana boasts Civil Law, based on the *Code Napoléon*. New Orleans was founded in 1718, and, although losing its status as capital to Baton Rouge, remains the largest city in the state.

Steamy, subtropical, and swamp-ridden, the countryside of southern Louisiana was settled in the late eighteenth century by the Acadians, French-speaking refugees from Nova Scotia. In recent years their cooking and music have become hugely popular. But they are primarily a rural people. New Orleans and certain other places in Louisiana were inhabited by the Creoles, descendants of the original French or Spanish settlers who may or may not be part black. The folklore of both Cajuns and Creoles is filled with strange tales: ghosts and witches, to be sure, but also the *Loup Garou*, the werewolf, and the *Feux Follet*, or will-o'-the-wisp. Stories of voodoo and pirates add a lot more to the gumbo of *bizarrerie* in the state.

From the time of the American purchase of Louisiana, Creole influence in New Orleans has slowly waned. The French Opera House burned down in 1919 and was never rebuilt, while the last daily French newspaper in the city ceased publication in 1926; the *Athénée Louisianais*, the major organization defending French culture, founded in 1876, soldiered on until sputtering out of existence sometime in the 1980s. New Orleans is definitely an English-speaking city.

But not all of the past is forgotten. Mardi Gras is as thoroughly celebrated as under the French and Spanish regimes. And seemingly every home in the old *Vieux Carre* (the French Quarter) is haunted. French influence remains powerful in the realm of food and such old-line restaurants as Galatoire's and Antoine's—still run by the Creole families who founded them—even now reign over the city's culinary scene. Antoine's in particular may be regarded as the temple of Creole food—and this is fitting, seeing that it is the oldest restaurant in the Quarter or anywhere else in New Orleans.

In 1840, a young immigrant from Marseilles, Antoine Alciatore, opened a pension and restaurant on St. Louis Street. After a successful five years, he summoned his fiancée from New York (where he had spent two fruitless years before coming to New Orleans). She and her sister arrived, and the wedding took place shortly thereafter. All three threw themselves into the work of cooking and hospitality. Antoine's Restaurant survived the Civil War and resulting occupation of the city. The Creole aristocracy made it their favorite establishment, and the place outgrew its location. In 1868, Antoine's moved to the spot on St. Louis Street where it stands today. Six years after, Antoine took ill. Not wanting his family to see him deteriorate—and wishing to die in his native land—he returned to Marseilles, leaving the restaurant in the hands of his wife. Sure enough, within a year he was dead.

Antoine's son, Jules, apprenticed under his mother for six years; then she sent him to France where he worked in the great kitchens of Paris, Strasbourg, and Marseilles. He returned to New Orleans in 1887, when his mother put him in charge of the restaurant. Jules invented Oysters Rockefeller, whose sauce remains a closely guarded secret. Jules in his turn married Althea Roy, daughter of a planter. They had two children: Marie Louise and Roy Louis. Born in 1902, Roy Alciatore headed the restaurant for almost forty years until his death in 1972. He kept the place going through Prohibition and World War II, opening the 1840 Room, a replica of a fashionable private dining room.

His sister, Marie Louise, married William Guste. Their sons, William Jr., former attorney general of Louisiana, and Roy Sr., became the fourth generation of the family to head the restaurant. In 1975, Roy's son, Roy Jr., became proprietor and served until 1984. He was followed by William's son, Bernard "Randy" Guste, who heads the restaurant in fine style today.

In addition to Oysters Rockefeller, Antoine's has given the world many other famous dishes, such as *Pommes de terre souffles*— delicious puffed potatoes—and *Pompano en papillote*—fish in a parchment bag cooked in a special wine sauce.

Antoine's has hosted the duke and duchess of Windsor, Elizabeth Taylor, Lillian Russell, Julia Roberts, Neil Diamond, Tom Hanks, Jack Dempsey, Tom Cruise, Bobby Jones, Ben Hogan, Joe Montana, Walt Disney, Bill Gates, five American presidents, two British princesses, German, Russian, and French princes, and innumerable other celebrities. So much a part of the city's life is the establishment that local author Frances Parkinson Keyes set her novel *Dinner at Antoine's* at the restaurant.

The restaurant has fifteen dining rooms, some of them tucked away in corners, designed for the most private and intimate dining. In recognition of the "Krewe of Rex"—second oldest of the semi-secret organizations who run New Orleans' Mardi Gras, and whose king reigns over the festivity—Roy Alciatore created the dining room called "Rex." Its walls are covered with photos of Mardi Gras royalty and memorabilia, including crowns and scepters of many years long past.

The Japanese Room owes its name and existence to the turn of the twentieth century Japanese fad. Jules Alciatore decided to create a grand room in Japanese style, in keeping with the craze. All of the decorations, down to the hand-painted walls and ceilings, reflected Japan. Many large banquets were held there until December 7, 1941, when the Japanese bombed Pearl Harbor. Roy Alciatore closed the room, and it stayed that way until gloriously reopened in 1983.

The Mystery Room owes its name to Prohibition. Cocktails were obtained from a certain room at Antoine's. When drinkers were asked where they got their cocktails, the stock reply was, "It's a mystery." It is still called the Mystery Room today, placed at the end of an interesting corridor. The room is dotted with souvenirs of famous restaurants around the world, as well as Groucho Marx's beret.

Yet another dining chamber is the 1840 Room. Decorated in the style of the period, its warm red interior boasts photos of successive generations of the Alciatore family. Among other rooms, there are the Hermes, where five American presidents have dined, and the Roy Alciatore on the second floor, named for the former proprietor.

Altogether, it is a charming place in every way, replete with tradition, history, elegance, and *very* good food. This author does not mind saying that it is his favorite restaurant in New Orleans—or for that matter, in the United States. But for all the pleasure one takes in visiting there, the restaurant is not immune to supernatural activity.

For many years, Henri Alciatore, "M'sieu Henri," was the maître d'. Cousin to the Gustes and descendant of Antoine himself, he fulfilled his role with grace and panache. But during his time at Antoine's he noticed a number of strange goings-on. One night in 1997, he observed what he took to be a busboy in white entering the Japanese Room. He tried to follow him, only to find the room locked—from the outside! M'sieu Henri entered the room to find it empty. At another time, while carrying records upstairs, Alciatore saw a vague, slightly glowing figure up the staircase, which quickly disappeared.

One waiter thought he saw Alciatore himself entering the Mystery Room. Following him in, as he thought, he found the room empty: Henri was actually at the front of the restaurant at his usual post. Since that time the waiter will not go into the room. Even the main dining room (featured in the Oliver Stone film, *JFK*) is not secure from the unearthly. One night, a cashier glanced into the dining room, and noticed a man in tuxedo standing by the first table. The cashier blinked, and the man was gone.

If you ever visit New Orleans, dinner at Antoine's is a must. You will find M. Guste and his staff attentive, and the cuisine excellent. But look around carefully, and keep your wits around you. Not all your fellow diners may be there in the same way that you are!

Antoine's Restaurant
713-717 Rue Saint Louis
New Orleans, LA 70130
(504) 581-4422
Fax: (504) 581-3003
info@antoines.com

A Maine Sea Captain's Mansion Boasts a Female Ghost

Tucked away in the northeastern corner of the United States, the state of Maine remains apart from the rest of the country in a number of ways. It was inhabited by two main Indian nations: the warlike Micmac, of eastern Maine and New Brunswick, and the more peaceful Abnaki. Only three tribes of the Abnaki Confederacy still reside in the state: the Maliseet (who do not have a reservation), the Passamaquoddies (about 1,500 residing on two reservations), and the Penobscots (about 1,200 strong on Indian Island in the Penobscot River at Old Town). These tribes had an interesting folklore, some of which survives. It mingles in an interesting manner with their Catholic faith: the Passamaquoddy are firm believers in the *Megumwasuck*, a race of native fairies that guard Catholic churches from profanation, zealously punishing those who commit sacrilege.

Lying midway between the cores of New England and New France, Maine has had a split personality between Anglophone and

Francophone that has lasted until today. Although the first English town in the state was established by the Plymouth Company at Popham in 1607 (the year Jamestown, Virginia, was settled), it did not survive the first few winters, leaving Jamestown the distinction of being America's first permanent English-speaking settlement. Attempts by Massachusetts settlers to establish towns were most often foiled by climate, deprivation, and Indian assault: only about six towns remained at the opening of the eighteenth century, although these were sufficient for His Majesty's Province of Massachusetts-Bay to claim the area.

But this claim did not go unchallenged: Micmac and Abnaki alike were allies of the king of France, and zealous Jesuit missionaries like Fr. Sébastien Râle had converted them to Catholicism. Thus Maine became a battleground during the long series of French and Indian Wars throughout the first half of the eighteenth century. But in 1763 the Treaty of Paris ended all French claims to the territory. Massachusetts offered one-hundred-acre lots free to anyone who would settle there, and the population doubled from 12,000 to 24,000 between 1743 and 1763. By 1799, the population of Maine grew to over 150,000.

Most of the early Maine towns were scattered along the coast or up the major rivers, a demographic that persists today. Being for the most part Yankees from Massachusetts, these early "down-Easters" came equipped with all the strange beliefs of their Puritan homeland. Every village had its Congregational church, and fear of witchcraft and the devil himself was far from unknown.

As a part of Massachusetts, Maine was far from immune to the political vagaries of its southern owner. In 1765 a Falmouth (now Portland) mob seized tax stamps, while attacks on customs agents increased. In 1774, a group of men burned a shipment of tea stored at York. After Lexington and Concord, hundreds of Maine men joined the rebel ranks. In reprisal, later that year British warships shelled and burned Falmouth. Maine men accompanied Benedict

Arnold in the failed effort to capture Quebec; an attempt to seize the British-held fortification at Castine in 1779 led to the most disastrous naval defeat of the war for the rebels.

Following the Revolution, settlers who disliked their subservience to Boston called for separation from Massachusetts. But the wealthy (and politically dominant) merchants on the coast resisted this until the War of 1812 proved that Massachusetts was unable or unwilling to protect the people of the District of Maine against another round of British raids.

Congress established Maine as the twenty-third state under the Missouri Compromise of 1820, allowing Maine to join the Union as a free state, and Missouri as a slave state; this move preserved the numerical balance between free and slave states in Congress. Portland was selected as the state capital, but in 1832 the capital was moved to Augusta. Modern Maine was well underway. In addition to the Acadian descendants clustered in the far north of the state, during the late nineteenth and early twentieth centuries Quebecois immigrants poured into southern Maine, turning such towns as Lewiston and Biddeford into French-speaking bastions. But such towns as Kennebunkport retained their Yankee flavor.

Kennebunkport was founded soon after the Plymouth Colony. In 1653, the town was incorporated as Cape "Porpus" under the government of Massachusetts. Emptied by Indian raids in 1689, the town was resettled early in the 1700s and renamed Arundel in 1719. It retained this name until 1821, when it was given its present name of Kennebunkport.

From the beginning of the nineteenth century, shipbuilding joined seafaring as a major industry for the town. One of the major families devoted to this trade was the Lord clan, the first of whose famous members was Lieutenant Tobias Lord (1748–1808). He began building small vessels on the Mousam River in Kennebunk around 1780. Marrying Mehitable Scammon in 1772, and Hepsibah Conant in 1781, he fathered at least four sons: Samuel, George, Tobias, and Nathaniel.

Son Nathaniel (1776–1815) was also a maritime businessman. Living most of his life in Arundel, Nathaniel married in his turn Phoebe Walker (1781–1864) in 1797. They had nine children: Mehitable Scammon, Daniel Walker, Lois Walker, Phoebe, Charles Austin, Nathaniel, Betsey Watts, Susan, and Lucy Jane.

All went well for the Lords until the War of 1812. The Royal Navy blockaded the Maine coast, and half the state was soon occupied by the British. Concerned about the effects unemployment would have on his shipwrights, and still possessed of a large fortune, he put the men to work building him what would be the most impressive house in the area. The famous architect Thomas Eaton was chosen to design the house, and it rivaled the finest Federal period homes found in Massachusetts towns like Salem and Newburyport. It was claimed at the time that the house was so well built that should Kennebunkport fall victim to a flood, the house would sail like a ship.

By the summer of 1814, the house was completed. But Nathaniel would not enjoy it for long. He took sick that winter, dying at last on February 24, 1815, at age thirty-nine. Nevertheless, for the next 150 years the Mansion stayed in the family. Nathaniel's grandson, Charles Clark, president of the New York and New Haven Railroad, made major renovations in the late 1800s. The house remained with the Lords until 1972, when it was sold and turned into a boarding house for elderly ladies; the following year it was listed in the National Register of Historic Places.

In 1978, corporate refugees Bev Davis and her husband Rick Litchfield, who had sought a small business that they could run together, found the Captain Lord Mansion. Although, as mentioned, it was serving as a home for senior ladies, it was licensed to serve as a "bed and breakfast." The new owners allowed five of the seven seniors to remain as residents for the next two years while they made extensive renovations.

Located in a residential area filled with seventeenth- and eighteenth-century Colonial and Federal-style homes, at the head of a village green overlooking the Kennebunk River, the Captain Lord Mansion boasts sixteen rooms laid out in Federal Style: lace-canopied four-poster beds, antique furniture, plush carpets, nineteenth-century art, and fireplaces. There is also a large carriage house on the property that has served as a sail loft and an artist's studio in times past.

But all of this beauty conceals an otherworldly secret: despite its charm, the mansion is said to be haunted. A woman, garbed in early-nineteenth-century clothes, appears and vanishes into the Lincoln Room. Originally called the "Wisteria Room," the name was changed since the wisteria plant is said to symbolize "Remembrance of the Dead," and apparently such remembrance is not really necessary there. It is claimed that the ghostly lady has also been seen on the spiral staircase leading up to the eight-sided cupola on the roof, and that she slams doors elsewhere in the house. Who is she? It is said that she may be Nathaniel's wife, Phoebe. But unless she says so, who knows? Perhaps she'll tell you!

The Captain Lord Mansion
P.O. Box 800
(Corner of Green and Pleasant Streets)
Kennebunkport, ME 04046
(207) 967-3141
Fax: (207) 967-3172

Edgar Allan Poe's House
in Maryland Offers Feminine—
if Undead—Companionship

Maryland was unique among the thirteen original American colonies, in that it was founded as a refuge for Catholics. It was the brainchild of George Calvert, the First Lord Baltimore. Eventually, however, the Protestants took control. Nevertheless, while westernmost Maryland developed a culture similar to neighboring Pennsylvania, the gentle valleys watered by tributaries of the Chesapeake became plantation country—a land of big houses, gracious living, and slavery.

As was customary in such areas, many plantation houses offer legends of ghosts, and the folklore of old England and Africa mixed and merged. Whispered tales of the "Snallygaster," just to name one strange Maryland creature, go back to colonial times. A sort of cross between a bird and a reptile, the creature snatched wayward children and barnyard poultry. Its name comes from the German *schnelle geist*, or "fast ghost." Marylanders painted perfect sevenpointed stars on their houses and barns to ward it off.

But the state's major towns have their weird tales, most especially Baltimore. The city owes its origins to the need of nearby farms and tobacco planters for a convenient port and customs house. Led by the famed Carroll family, local landowners petitioned Maryland's governor to create one, and on August 8, 1729, the bill that incorporated Baltimore as a town was signed into law. The new site attracted shipwrights and merchants, and by 1768 it had grown large enough to become the seat of Baltimore County.

The Revolution and the War of 1812 were hard on Baltimore; many of her best citizens were loyalists and had to leave after the first conflict, while the city sustained an unsuccessful British assault during the second. But Baltimore continued to grow, both in terms of population, and as a center of culture. By 1825, Baltimore had become the second largest city in the United States. As for culture, Baltimore shares with Richmond, Virginia, a claim on one of the greatest American writers who ever lived—Edgar Allan Poe.

Renowned for his strange tales and poems, Poe, together with Washington Irving, Nathaniel Hawthorne, James Fenimore Cooper, and Henry Wadsworth Longfellow, proved that Americans could produce literature the equal of Europe's. Such tales as *The Fall of the House of Usher, The Murders in the Rue Morgue,* and *Berenice*, alongside poems like "The Raven" and "Ulalume," have immortalized Poe among readers of uncanny literature. It is fitting then that some of legend-haunted old Baltimore's oddest tales should be connected with him.

Poe's great-grandfather, John Poe, brought the family to Baltimore in 1755, dying a year later. John's son and daughter-in-law, David and Elizabeth Cairnes Poe, raised seven children. David was active in persecuting local Loyalists, and so was rewarded with the title of "Assistant Deputy Quartermaster"—local purchasing agent of military supplies for the rebel forces. Helping Lafayette during the Virginia and Southern campaigns, he received the courtesy title of General. Elizabeth for her part was very active in making clothes for the troops.

General Poe's son, David Jr., became an actor in 1803, a few years later marrying an English actress, the widowed Elizabeth Arnold Hopkins. While the pair were performing in Boston, their son Edgar was born on January 19, 1809. Orphaned at age three in Baltimore, he was taken in (though not legally adopted) by Mr. and Mrs. John Allan in Richmond. There he was baptized Edgar Allan Poe. In 1815, the Allan family moved to England on business. There, Poe was enrolled at the Manor House School in Stoke-Newington, a London suburb (demolished in 1880, the school's site is now a fine wine bar, the Fox Reformed). In that establishment he learned Latin and French, while the gothic architecture and histor-ical landscape of the area affected his imagination permanently.

Poe attended the University of Virginia in 1826, fell out with Mr. Allan, and entered the army. Three years later, after his dis-charge, he arrived at the Baltimore home of his widowed aunt, Maria Poe Clemm. This was located in what is now called Little Italy, just east of the Inner Harbor. He then entered West Point, but after his expulsion he returned to Baltimore in 1832. Maria Clemm was now living at 3 Amity Street in west Baltimore, with her daughter Virginia Eliza, her son Henry Clemm, and Elizabeth Poe, Edgar's grandmother. Poe moved in, and turned from poetry to short stories. His best-known tale from this time is the horrific *Berenice*. In 1835, Elizabeth Poe died. Poe moved back to Rich-mond; the next year he sent for Maria and Virginia Clemm, whom he soon married, although she was only thirteen. Poe never re-turned to Baltimore to live for any extended period of time.

Although Poe never returned to live in Baltimore, he retained his affection for the city, often visiting friends and passing through on business. The rest of his career was spent in more or less short residences in various cities. In New York City (1837), then Philadel-phia (1838–44), and again in New York (1844–49), Poe attempted to carve out a literary career, alas with little success. Virginia's death in January 1847 devastated Poe, but he labored on. In the summer of 1849 he returned to Richmond, gave lectures, and was once more accepted by a fiancée he had lost in 1826. He returned to Baltimore, and was found unconscious on a street there. He died in a local hospital, and to this day everything from alcoholism to rabies has been suggested as the cause for his death at age forty. What is certain is that he was interred in Lot 27 of Westminster Burying Ground at Fayette and Greene Streets, near the graves of his grandparents and his brother.

What was arguably the happiest time of his life, then, was spent at the Amity Street house with his grandmother, aunt, and two cousins. The house was built around 1830 in what was then the country, a few blocks south of the new Baltimore and Ohio train station (now a museum). After the Clemms decamped for Richmond, the small building housed many different people over the ensuing century. In the 1930s the surrounding buildings in the area were demolished to make way for a public housing project. The Poe House, too, was scheduled for razing—an irony, given that the development was called the Poe Homes. Public outcry, fortunately, forced the housing authority to spare the site. The Edgar Allan Poe Society took over the house, opening it as the Edgar Allan Poe House in 1949. Thirty years later, the society approached the city of Baltimore, asking them to restore the house. After expending $90,000, the Commission for Historic and Architectural Preservation (CHAP), a city agency, took over maintenance of the site.

It is a five-room brick duplex, with uneven wooden plank flooring and three brick-lined fireplaces; there are also glassware and china belonging to Mr. Allan. Poe's bedroom is on the top floor, perched above narrow, winding stairs. On display at the house are also Poe's telescope, sextant, a lap desk he used at the University of Virginia, and a full-size color reproduction of the only known portrait of Poe's wife, Virginia, painted at her death in 1847. A set of illustrations made by Gustave Dore in 1884 for Poe's "The Raven" graces the second floor.

In such an atmosphere, the observation by actor Vincent Price (who acted in a number of Poe-inspired films produced by American International Films in the '50s and '60s), that "This place gives me the creeps!" while on a visit to the house in 1977 makes sense. For, as one might suspect, something appears to walk at the Poe House. Doors and windows are often seen to open and close without help. Back in 1968, a neighbor called the police after seeing a light moving around the closed building late at night. The responding police themselves saw a candle-like light move from the first floor of the house, through the second, and up to the attic. But when they entered the house, the police could find no one.

According to Jeff Jerome (curator of the house since 1977), no one knows who the spirit or spirits are supposed to be. Even though most of the activity takes place in the bedroom of Poe's grandmother, who died in it in 1835, many others have lived there down through the years. Nevertheless, many people have been tapped on the shoulder in the room. Radio station personnel broadcasting from the house in 1980 heard voices and other noises. A female ghost is said to touch visitors, open and close windows and doors, and whisper at people.

The residents of Poe Homes tell their own stories about the Poe House. Local children are told that Poe's ghost will "get them," while a November 1985 *New York Times* article declared that local street gangs were afraid of the house and left it alone. More recently, an article in the *Baltimore Sun* (September 18, 1999) reported on how the neighbors felt about the Poe house. A local man stated that in August 1999 he looked through the window to see a shadowy apparition sitting at a writing desk; while others have also reported this sight, Poe actually wrote in the attic. Years ago, during a blackout in the neighborhood, locals reported to the police that lights in the house stayed on all night.

Also on display are a number of cognac bottles, each left with three red roses at Poe's grave on the night of January 19, his birthday. Westminster Church has a number of weird stories connected with it, none bearing on Poe. But between midnight and dawn on that night, every year since 1949, a mysterious man in black hat, black overcoat, and white scarf has appeared to toast the author on his birthday and leave his strange gifts. A crowd usually gathers outside the churchyard's brick wall to watch the weird proceedings.

According to Curator Jerome, the roses left behind at the grave honor Poe, his wife, and his aunt. But since Poe apparently never mentioned cognac in his writings, the reason for its inclusion in the ritual is unknown.

In any case, even if you never make it to the graveyard for the annual visitation, be sure to see the Poe House when you visit Baltimore. After all—the sweet old lady who taps you on the shoulder may well know more about Poe than anyone living!

Edgar Allan Poe House
203 North Amity Street
Baltimore, MD 21223
(410) 396-7932
Fax: (410) 396-5662

At Longfellow's Wayside Inn in Massachusetts, a Daughter of the House Will Not Leave

In many ways, Massachusetts is *the* most American state. Although the oldest settlement is in Florida, the oldest English-speaking town is in Virginia, independence was declared in Pennsylvania, New York boasts the largest city, and the capital of the country is at Washington, it is Massachusetts where, in many ways, the national mentality was formed. The mythic power of the "first" Thanksgiving (although that rite was probably done at El Paso, Texas), the witch-trials at Salem, and the outbreak of revolution at Lexington and Concord hold the American imagination in much the same way as the Calvinism of the Puritans holds the American psychology.

They were a stern bunch, the first settlers at Plymouth Rock and Boston; religious they were, but they outlawed Christmas and Easter. The devil was all around them, and if denied the traditional European religious means of dealing with that unwelcome guest, they made up all sorts of ways of their own. Of course, this had a tremendous effect on their folklore. As H. P. Lovecraft points out in his *Supernatural Horror in Literature*:

> The vast and gloomy virgin forests in whose perpetual twilight all terrors might well lurk; the hordes of coppery Indians whose strange, saturnine visages and violent customs hinted strongly at traces of infernal origin; the free rein given under the influence of Puritan theocracy to all manner of notions respecting man's relationship to the stern and vengeful God of the Calvinists, and to the sulphurous Adversary of that God, about whom so much was thundered in the pulpits each Sunday; and the morbid introspection developed by an isolated backwoods life devoid of normal amusements and the recreational mood, harassed by commands for theological self-examination, keyed to unnatural emotional repression, and forming above all a mere grim struggle for survival—all these things conspired to produce an environment in which the black whisperings of sinister grandams were heard far beyond the chimney corner, and in which tales of witchcraft and unbelievable secret monstrosities lingered long after the dread days of the Salem nightmare.

Frightening as that image is, the passage of time softened it somewhat. New England is beautiful, especially in autumn. Over time the furious faith of the Puritans made way for the gentler creeds of Unitarianism and Transcendentalism (just as strange as what preceded them, to be sure, but far less intimidating!). A gentle nostalgia came to co-exist in rural Massachusetts with the early horrors, and immigrants from all over Europe added to the calming effect.

That said, there remains a somewhat eerie atmosphere to New England lore. Stories of ghosts abound, left over from the Indian Wars, the Revolution, and sundry more localized tragedies. Strange cults have traditionally emerged from the Massachusetts psyche, while a half-veiled yearning for "the good old colony days, when we lived under the King," vies with a firm pride in the state's role in the war for independence.

Sudbury, in its turn, is surely the quintessential Massachusetts town. Founded in 1639 by one hundred settlers and three hundred cows, it lives up to the image, with its common, its white meeting-style "First Parish" (Unitarian), its Town Meeting, and its community celebrations of Independence Day, Halloween, and Thanksgiving.

Very early on, the town began licensing businesses. In 1642, one Thomas Noyes was authorized to charge fare for a town ferry across the Sudbury River that separated the eastern section of the town from the western. Four years later, the first blacksmith was brought to the town by committee. From its incorporation, Thomas Walker held the only liquor license in Sudbury. As a result, the Black Horse Tavern, which had opened on the Boston Post Road in 1683, was illegal until Walker's death nine years later—at which time it received the license thus vacated.

In 1716, house and license were bought by a Marlborough man named David Howe—a distant relative of the great English family. Son and grandson of innkeepers in his native town, he and his wife Hepzibah made a success of the inn, which they renamed Howe's Tavern. By the time of his death in 1746, the coach traffic to and from Boston and Worcester guaranteed further growth. David's son Ezekiel was so well-to-do that he was elected a militia officer by his fellow townsmen. As the 1760s waned and the 1770s drew on, in common with many of the better off in Massachusetts, he began to resent the attempts of Parliament in London to coax the colonies into paying a small percentage of their expense. The inn became a center of the discontented: in 1768, the people of the town voted to boycott British imports. Those who would not join the boycott would be punished, and militia officers loyal to the Crown were purged.

On April 19, 1775, fighting between the militia and the regulars broke out at Lexington and Concord, when the latter attempted to seize the weapons and powder being stockpiled for future rebellion. Sudbury sent the largest contingent of "Minutemen"—346—from neighboring towns to Concord. Ezekiel Howe was in their number.

He did quite well after the war, continuing to expand the inn, as did his son, Adam, when he inherited it in 1796, and Adam's son Lyman, who took over in 1830. Assisting Lyman in running the place was his sister, Jerusha, called the "belle of Sudbury." Showing that the hatred of the Revolution had passed, she became engaged to an Englishman. He returned home to get his family's blessing on the match, but never returned. Jerusha lived the rest of her life at the inn, playing her pianoforte.

But during the 1840s, young Henry Wadsworth Longfellow visited the inn, partly drawn by its connections with his relative, General Wadsworth. He met many other interesting folk there, and thus began an association with the inn and its owner that lasted until Lyman died in 1861. Like Jerusha, he had never married, and the place was inherited by relatives with no interest in innkeeping. They would rent the hall out for dances, and some of the rooms out for long periods of time. But the good old times had passed, seemingly forever.

In tribute to the tales he had heard there, Longfellow wrote a series of poems, published in 1863 as *Tales of a Wayside Inn*. These were written as a set of stories told by a group of diverse friends at the inn. Lyman was cast as the teller of "The Landlord's Tale," which opens with the lines once known universally by American school children: "Listen my children and you shall hear, of the midnight ride of Paul Revere."

Ironically, it was this tribute to the irrecoverable that led to the inn's rebirth. In 1897, Malden wool merchant and antiquarian Edward Rivers Lemon bought the inn as "a retreat for literary pilgrims,"

renaming it Longfellow's Wayside Inn. He and his wife, Cora, operated the tavern until his death in 1919. Four years later, she sold it to
automobile manufacturer Henry Ford. Ford moved the one-room
Redstone School to the grounds in 1925, built the Grist Mill in 1929,
and the Martha-Mary Chapel in 1940. He also created the non-profit
status that the Inn operates under today.

Thus, once again, Longfellow's words of description are accurate:

> As ancient is this Hostelry
> As any in the land may be,
> Built in the old colonial day,
> When men lived in a grander way,
> With ampler hospitality.

Entering the inn, the Old Bar Room is on the right. One of the original rooms of the two-room house, it was used for working, eating
and cooking. In 1716, it became a bar. On the left is the parlor, immortalized by Longfellow:

> Then all arose, and said "Good Night,"
> Alone remained the drowsy Squire
> To rake the embers of the fire,
> And quench the waning parlour light.

There are ten rooms to stay in, all individually decorated with antiques, and equipped with private bath, air conditioning, and telephone. There is also a sitting room reserved for houseguests, and
breakfast is provided. The bar and the dining rooms are all welcoming to the public, and in addition to typical Yankee fare, one may be
treated to a "coo-woo," a powerful concoction of gin and ginger
brandy, touted as the first American cocktail.

But, of course, there is more. It is said that poor Jerusha remains in the inn where she lived out her life. Male guests have felt

her presence in Room 10, her old bedroom, lying against them in bed. She has been heard playing her piano. Her distinctive citrus perfume has been smelled as well.

All in all, the Wayside Inn is a warm and enjoyable place. It makes sense that its resident ghost should be so as well.

Longfellow's Wayside Inn
72 Wayside Inn Road
Sudbury, MA 01776
_(978) 443-1776_
Fax: (978) 443-8041

A Ghostly Couple Stays On
in Their Old Home in Michigan

Michigan's first contact with Europe came through the French trappers, priests, and soldiers who traveled along the Great Lakes, down from Québec. Centered at Detroit, Fort St. Joseph, and St. Ignace (on Mackinac Island), they built a trading empire among the local Indian tribes that lasted until 1763, when by terms of the peace treaty ending the French and Indian War, Michigan came under the British Crown. Despite Pontiac's Rebellion, the Brits held on to the area after the end of the American Revolution twenty years later. Until 1796, Michigan remained functionally a part of the new province of Upper Canada (Ontario); Detroit even sent delegates to the province's first parliament in 1792.

After the American takeover, settlers poured in. At first primarily New Englanders, the new arrivals were soon joined by more French-Canadians, Poles, Irish, Germans, Scandinavians, and many others. Each of these brought their own folklore, to add to the Indian and French legends that abounded throughout the region. The fishermen and other nautical types on the Great Lakes added their own tales of ghost ships, weather portents, and strange maritime disappearances and beasts.

Typical of Michigan settlements is Traverse City. Under the French and British, it remained solely in the hands of the local Ottawa Indians, who became quite wealthy from trading. The French named the area *la Grande Traverse* after the five-mile shortcut between either side of the mouth of Grand Traverse Bay. In 1839, a Presbyterian Minister, Reverend Peter Dougherty, established a mission for the Indians. Three years later, he built the first frame house on Old Mission. In 1846, the first American settlers arrived in the area. This led, five years afterwards, to the mapping out of Traverse City. In 1860, a regular weekly steamer service was established between Traverse City and Chicago, providing both a market for the area's new cherry farms and a venue for ever more settlers.

As the city grew, it acquired the trappings of town life; in 1881 the new Northern Michigan Asylum was established. Shortly afterwards, the Bower's Harbor Inn was built along Grand Traverse Bay on the Old Mission Peninsula, where Dougherty had first set up shop. Local legend maintains that the house, set among majestic oaks and pines, was built by one Captain Bower as a home for his ill wife. The story goes that a nurse hired to care for the woman had an affair with the captain; his wife supposedly hung herself in an elevator shaft installed for her use.

In reality, the house was erected by Chicago millionaire J. W. Stickney and his wife, Genevieve. Having made a fortune in lumber and steel, the pair built a baronial mansion with high ceilings and dramatic design. A fortune was spent decorating the house; one of its features was a gilt-edged mirror that made the plump Mrs. Stickney appear thinner. As the Stickneys aged, they installed an elevator to bring them effortlessly to the mansion's upper floors.

In contrast to the dramatic events of the Captain Bower legend, the Stickneys lived and died quietly in the house (although it is rumored that Mrs. Stickney became somewhat deranged before the end). After their deaths, the historic building changed hands repeatedly; eventually, in 1959, it was converted into a restaurant called the Bower's Harbor Inn.

In 1974, Grand Rapids restaurateur Howard Schelde discovered and bought the inn. The place already had the reputation of being haunted: lights turned on and off, glass broke, and objects moved by themselves. But the change in ownership did not slow down these activities—quite the opposite.

The odd happenings were and are attributed to Genevieve Stickney. So famous did they become that they were profiled on the television show *Unsolved Mysteries*. On one occasion, a customer ran out of the second-floor room where Genevieve's trick mirror was stored. Apparently, while looking into it she saw the reflection of a woman dressed in nineteenth-century clothes appear behind her. She turned around, only to find herself alone. A number of other ladies have since reported the same phenomenon.

While the standard rapping sounds have continued, and locked doors open and close on their own, Genevieve's is not the only apparition to be seen: J. W. himself occasionally appears in the old elevator. Although it has been out of service for years, it has the unpleasant habit of starting up by itself, and moving slowly from one story to another.

From time to time, after the manager turns off all the lights, locks the freezer door, and closes for the evening, he finds every light in the place lit and the freezer door unlocked and standing open. Nor is that the only light display—some claim to have seen the fireplaces lighting themselves. The food is delicious—but you may get more than you see on the menu.

Bower's Harbor Inn
13512 Peninsula Drive
Traverse City, MI 49686
(231) 223-4222
Fax: (231) 223-4228

The Author Himself Is Haunted in a Minnesota Restaurant

As with the rest of the states drained by the Mississippi, Minnesota's first European occupants were French traders, priests, and soldiers. The first permanent settlements clustered around what remains the center of the state—the Twin Cities of Minneapolis-St. Paul.

The cities are a microcosm of Minnesota as a whole; French, Germans, Scandinavians, Poles, Irish, and many other groups are settled in, and still maintain their national traditions and even churches. While the two cities are not renowned for their cuisine (mention Minnesota and those in the know will have frightening thoughts of *lutefisk*, a sort of Norwegian seviche) they do boast a number of fine old steakhouses. The names to conjure with in Minneapolis are Murray's and Manny's; but in St. Paul, it is the Lexington.

Back in the 1920s, the building housed a speakeasy. But, in 1935, it opened as a legitimate restaurant under its current name.

Since then, it has been a favored dining spot for St. Paul's elite. The chandeliers, old paintings, and leather furnishings in the dining area give it the feeling of a private club. The Lexington's Sunday brunch is legendary, while the dinner menu's pasta, New England-style crab cake, chateaubriand, peppered swordfish, and prime rib give one as delicious a meal as may be hoped for. For dessert the Lexington's strawberry crisp stands out. Moreover, the curving mahogany bar reminds one of the days when newly liberated drinkers happily drank to the end of Prohibition. It is one of the few remaining watering holes where I have been able to find a seven-layered pousse-café.

It is also one of the few places where I myself have been exposed to a ghost. Back in 2000, I was dining there with a local friend, Ben. We were seated at a table, one of whose sides (where my pal was ensconced) was part of a wall-length banquette, while my side featured a chair, whose left rear leg was flush against a wooden screen. This little detail is important for what follows.

As we ate, I told my friend that old restaurants and hotels are invariably haunted. He laughed, saying that he found that hard to believe. I explained that in such places the staff is often reluctant to speak about such things, unless they think that you already are aware of the haunting. He challenged me to prove this.

Although I had no prior knowledge of any haunting at the Lexington, I asked the waitress when she returned with our orders, "So . . . what's all this about the ghost?"

"Oh," she said, with a furtive look. "You know about that?"

"What have you heard?" I countered.

"Well," she replied, confidentially, "some nights, when it is a little less crowded than now, but not much, and a little later—but not much later . . . we hear stuff."

"What kind of stuff?"

"There are offices above us, and sometimes we'll hear furniture being thrown around up there. But when you actually go up to look—there's nothing. The furniture is all in place, everything's fine."

"Ah," I answered, trying to look wise. After the waitress left us, Ben and I resumed our conversation. Just then we heard noises just like the ones the waitress had described. Looking at my friend, I said, "Oh, come on!" I jumped up and sprinted up the stairs.

In the room above, restaurant employees were moving tables, desks, and chairs. I laughed in relief. They looked at me quizzically, and I said, "Ha! Thought you were the ghost!" The five or so staff looked at me oddly, and one said, "Well, it is true we sometimes hear stuff flying around up here. But tonight, as you see, it's just us."

Reassured, I returned to our table, and told Ben, "False alarm! No ghost, nothing at all! I guess it's a fake!" No sooner did I say this, than the rear left leg of my chair was heavily kicked, and I pitched forward. After I recovered my composure, Ben solemnly advised, "Um, Charles, I think you should wait until we leave to make fun of the ghost!" Good advice, to be sure, for anyone. But the Lexington will not disappoint, even if your chair-leg remains unkicked.

The Lexington
1096 Grand Avenue
St. Paul, MN 55105-3043
(651) 222-5878

Mississippi's Natchez
Has a Tavern Still Tended
By the Shade of a Servant Girl

Mississippi is the prototypical Deep South state. In common with the rest of the states drained by the river whose name she bears, Mississippi was first settled by the French, followed in succession by the Spanish, the British, and, at last, the Americans. Thinly settled outside the Gulf Coast and the Natchez area until the United States took over, after the Choctaw and Chickasaw were for the most part deported to Oklahoma, the state filled up with Anglo-American settlers and their slaves. In common with the rest of the South, the folklores of these two peoples provided an eerie background to life. There were and are, of course, regional variations—the people of the Delta have quite a different culture to those of the Gulf Coast, heavily influenced by the French and Spanish as these latter are.

But Natchez, the oldest European settlement in the state and on the river (having been founded in 1716, two years earlier than New Orleans), has an atmosphere all its own. With the rest of what was called then West Florida (the "Florida Parishes" of Louisiana, the southern reaches of Alabama and Mississippi, and the Florida panhandle east to the Apalachicola River), Natchez passed into British hands in 1763. As a result of the Revolution, the town became a refuge for loyalists fleeing persecution at the hands of the rebels, a situation that did not change when the colony passed under Spanish control in 1779. As a result of the treaty of 1798, Spain evacuated the northern reaches of West Florida, withdrawing toward the coast.

In that year, Natchez became the first capital of the Mississippi Territory, and in 1817, capital of the state (an honor she lost to Jackson five years later). As the largest port on the river north of New Orleans, the end of the Natchez Trace (which brought goods and settlers from the East), and the center of cotton-growing country, Natchez grew rapidly. On the Hill, planters and merchants built huge mansions that remain in number, size, and elegance one of the wonders of America. The area along the beginning of the trace filled up with stores and hostelries. But down by the river, Natchez-under-the-Hill emerged as a festering, crime-ridden collection of warehouses, brothels, wharves, and warehouses. Its colorful population of river-rats, roustabouts, gamblers, and the like created their own legends of mayhem and murder, in sharp contrast to the refinement and elegance of the Hill. Of course, the two sections were tightly linked by economic reality, however much they might despise one another.

One of the most notorious booze-houses under the hill was King's Tavern. The building was erected in 1769, and is now the oldest structure in Natchez. At first used by a blacksmith, it was bought by one Richard King in 1789, and turned into a tavern. A stagecoach stop for the Natchez Trace, King's Tavern became a bustling locale. But after more modern transport took over, the tavern became a private residence. Today, however, it is once more a restaurant specializing in prime rib and steaks. Favored by locals and tourists alike, its modern atmosphere could not be more different from its seamy days as a hot spot of Natchez-under-the-Hill.

One inhabitant, however, apparently remains from those early days. Richard King hired a sixteen-year-old servant girl, Madeline, as a waitress and maid for his establishment. Apparently, King's morals were no stricter than his customers'; he quickly made her his mistress. But Mrs. King did not appreciate the arrangement. No one is sure of what happened, but within a year, Madeline had disappeared. The locals suspected murder, but nothing could be proved. Did King kill his paramour? Did his wife do it? Or was there some other, even less savory event? No one knows, but soon after Madeline's departure, overnight guests at the tavern began feeling a strange, sad presence. During renovations in the 1930s, three skeletons were unearthed in the building's cellar, one that of a young girl clasping a jeweled dagger.

Since then, dozens of employees and guests have reported strange phenomena. Glowing orbs are said to pass by, and doors generally hard to move will swing open by themselves. If employees say, "All right, Madeline," they shut again. Faucets spout hot water without assistance. A few years back, a reporter was busy videotaping the restaurant's downstairs. His friend who had come to help him was supposed to be taping upstairs, assisted by a waitress. Overhead he could hear their muffled talking, and the floor creaking as they walked. But looking out the window, he saw his friend and the waitress walking around. Predictably, there was no one upstairs.

While the tavern is open for dinner nightly, there are no promises as to when or how Madeline will make herself apparent. But it seems that she continues to greet the favored few as she has done for over two centuries.

King's Tavern
619 Jefferson Street
Natchez, MS 39120
(601) 446-8845

A Tragic Family of Suicides
Haunts Their Missouri Mansion

Missouri is yet another French-founded state, whose area formed the second most important part of the Louisiana Purchase, after the Creole State itself. But the French fur traders from New Orleans who founded the city of St. Louis in 1764, and named it for Louis IX, crusader king of France, settled in territory Louis XV had ceded to Spain the year before. Built on a high bluff just eighteen miles south of the confluence of the Mississippi and Missouri rivers, St. Louis occupied a perfect site from which to trade with Indians in the fur-rich lands to the west. Other settlements soon followed: St. Charles, Ste. Genevieve, Portage des Sioux, Florissant, Potosi, and Old Mines (where French is still spoken). Although France regained her rights to St. Louis and the west in 1800, Napoleon sold the Louisiana Territory to President Thomas Jefferson in 1803 without ever taking possession.

Jefferson sent Lewis and Clark from St. Louis to chart the new Louisiana Territory in 1804. At that time, more than one thousand

French, Spanish, Indians, and free and slave blacks, lived in the city. Soon, St. Louis became the last stop for mountain men, trappers, and settlers heading to the newly opened frontier, gaining the city the title of "Gateway to the West." The first steamboat arrived in St. Louis in 1817, commencing a new era of commerce and travel along the Mississippi River. Joining the original settlers were people of many nationalities, especially Irish and Germans. The Germans in particular would change the nature of St. Louis forever, and impress on the city a character that still remains.

Of these latter immigrants, one of the most important was John Adam Lemp, a native of Eschwege (in the modern German state of Thuringia), who arrived in St. Louis in 1838. He set up a grocery store—but one with a difference: Lemp sold home-brewed lager beer, after the recipe his father had taught him in the Old Country. He aged his beer in the caves under the city. Two years after his arrival, Lemp abandoned groceries to go into brewing full-time, opening a brewery at 112 South Second Street. His efforts bore fruit, and he died a millionaire.

His son, William J. Lemp, took over the brewery and in 1864 built a new plant at Cherokee Street and Carondolet Avenue. Soon the new brewery covered five city blocks—by 1870 Lemp was by far the largest brewery in St. Louis, and the Lemp family was one of the wealthiest and most powerful in the city. In keeping with their new status, William Lemp decided that the family required a fitting residence. In 1876, he purchased a home near the brewery complex. Built by Jacob Feickert, Julia Lemp's father, in 1868, it was probably financed by William. He purchased it both for a residence and an adjunct brewery office. Already impressive, the house was transformed by its new owner into a veritable palace.

In 1884, a radiator system was installed and the grand staircase was replaced by an open-air elevator (the only remaining trace of which is the decorative iron gates in the basement restaurant). To the left of the main entrance is the former brewery office, with its decorative mantle of Italian marble. On the right is the parlor, equipped with a hand-painted ceiling and carved mantles made of African mahogany. Behind this room is an atrium; here the Lemps kept exotic plants and birds. The main bathroom of the house is a glass-enclosed, free-standing shower William discovered in an Italian hotel and brought back to St. Louis for his personal use, and a barber chair, as well as a sink with glass legs. To the rear of the house are three massive vaults used to store the great quantities of art objects collected by the family. On the second floor are the bedrooms, and on the third are the former servants' quarters. The wine and beer cellars, laundry, and kitchen were located in the basement. A tunnel from the basement entered the cave Adam Lemp used for his beer production, and which was later used by the family for entertaining. The entrance, however, is now sealed; the spiral stairs were cut away to prevent anyone entering.

At first, this luxurious home hosted nothing but the many parties and good times enjoyed by the Lemp clan. The culmination, perhaps, of these occurred in 1897, when William Lemp's daughter, Hilda, married Gustav, son of Frederick Pabst, patriarch of the Milwaukee brewing family. Frederick was one of William's closest friends.

But dark times were in store for the family. Their first great tragedy occurred when Frederick Lemp, William's favorite son and heir apparent to the brewery presidency, began to sicken, perhaps from overwork. He died of heart failure and other causes in 1901, at the age of twenty-eight. William was devastated. He became reclusive, walking to work only through the now-blocked tunnel to the brewery from the basement. On January 1, 1904, Frederick Pabst died. After this second blow, William gave up caring about the brewery, though he still went to work each day. On February 13, 1904, he ate breakfast, mentioning to a servant that he felt unwell. After his meal, he went upstairs to his bedroom and shot himself in the head with a revolver.

William J. Lemp, Jr. succeeded his father as president in November of 1904. Resolving to put his father's death out of his mind, he hired many more servants, built country houses, and spent wildly. Five years earlier he had married a woman with similar financial habits, Lillian Handlan, the daughter of a wealthy manufacturer. The new Mrs. Lemp was nicknamed the "Lavender Lady" due to her habit of wearing lavender clothes. Although the union produced one child, William J. Lemp III, the couple were later divorced in a 1906 trial that captured local headlines. But Lemp's troubles that year were not solely marital. Nine local breweries combined to form the Independent Breweries Company, and his mother died in March after a painful bout with cancer.

World War I was unkind to breweries everywhere, but lavish spending and neglect of the brewery's equipment left the Lemp Company behind. In March of 1920, yet another tragedy occurred when William, Jr.'s sister, Elsa Lemp Wright, who had reconciled with her estranged husband a short time before, shot herself in the mansion. Her husband heard the report of the gun as he was returning to their bedroom from his bath. Since he did not report the death for some hours, all sorts of speculation arose as to what "really" had happened. Her brothers William and Edwin went to the house as soon as the news reached them. When William arrived and was informed of the event, he simply replied, "That's the Lemp family for you."

Prohibition had already spelled the end of the brewery, which William Lemp, Jr. closed without notice to his employees, finally selling it to the International Shoe Company in 1922. These events depressed him further, and on December 29, 1922, he shot himself in the former brewery office. This surprised everyone, as he had just put his estate in Webster Groves up for sale, announcing plans for a prolonged European stay.

William Jr.'s brother, Charles, continued to live at the house after his brother's suicide, as did William Lemp III. The latter was only forty-two when he died of a heart attack in 1943. The other surviving Lemp brother, Edwin, in the meantime had entered into seclusion at his Kirkwood estate in 1911.

Charles never had been much involved with the brewery, preferring to work in banking and real estate. After his nephew's death he became ever more reclusive, and dwelt in the old mansion with his two servants. As with Howard Hughes, he acquired a phobia of germs, wearing gloves to avoid any contact with them. Although his brother Edwin often encouraged him to leave the tragedy-haunted place, Charles refused. On May 10, 1949, he became the fourth member of the family to die by his own hand. Unlike the rest of them, however, he left a signed suicide note reading: "In case I am found dead blame it on no one but me."

The following day, after his brother's cremation, Edwin Lemp took his brother's remains and buried them out on his farm. Although he appeared to have escaped the family curse at his estate, the years following his brother's death found him growing stranger. Rather than becoming a recluse in the family tradition, however, Edwin became afraid of being alone. Hiring a full-time companion, he entertained frequently. At last, in 1970, he died of natural causes at age ninety, the last of the Lemps.

Edwin had sold the mansion, so filled as it was with sadness, after his brother's death in 1949. It was turned into a boarding house; with the surrounding neighborhood it deteriorated. But a rebirth was in store. In 1975 Dick Pointer and his family purchased the old house, eventually turning it into an elegant restaurant and bed and breakfast. Its menu is classic, featuring such entrees as Beef Wellington, French Pepper Steak, Steak Diane, prime rib, Steak Charles, and Chicken a la Orange. But the delicious cuisine, the change in ownership, and the many happy diners cannot change the fact that something is not quite right with the Lemp Mansion.

After its transformation into a boarding house, strange knocks and unseen footsteps were heard in the old place. So well known were these phenomena in the neighborhood, that rooms were rarely full. When the Pointers bought the mansion, they found that it had some permanent tenants. During the renovations following their purchase, workers claimed that they were being watched, tools were vanishing, and they were hearing odd sounds. Many quit, rather than work in such conditions.

Since opening to the public, glasses are seen to lift off the bar and fly through the air without help. Employees have heard strange noises, and even seen apparitions. These are not strictly in-house occurrences, since restaurant-goers and overnight guests have re-ported doors locking and unlocking without assistance, the piano in the bar playing by itself, disembodied voices, and now and then the apparition of the "Lavender Lady."

So renowned has the place become that the November 1980 issue of *Life* magazine named the Lemp Mansion as "one of the most haunted houses in America." As might be guessed by the menu, its current owner, Paul Pointer, keeps up the high standards that the Lemps enjoyed in life. But he admits, "People come here ex-pecting to experience weird things, and fortunately for us, they are rarely disappointed." So if you are in the St. Louis area, and have a yen for Steak Diane, you ought to stop by the Lemp Mansion. You may well be served spirits, even if you don't take any alcohol.

The Lemp Mansion Restaurant
3222 DeMenil Place
St. Louis, MO 63118
(314) 664-8024
www.lempmansion.com

Montana's Chico Warm Springs Hotel Is Still Dominated By Its First Owner

Montana is aptly called "Big Sky Country." Alongside the Rockies, which give the state its name, it also boasts wide prairies in its eastern half and such wide rivers as the Yellowstone, the Columbia, the Missouri, and the Gallatin. Even today, it is a sportsman's paradise, retaining the wild charm displayed in such movies as *A River Runs Through It*. In early times, Montana's soil was filled with big game—elk, deer, buffalo, and much else. Not surprisingly, many tribes settled there, both before and after the coming of the Europeans. Blackfoot, Crow, Salish, Pend d'Oreilles, Kootenai, Assiniboine, Gros Ventre, Ojibwa, Cree, Sioux, and Northern Cheyenne all entered the state, the last four arriving from the north and east under pressure from white settlers. The Sioux and Northern Cheyenne won the last major victory against the newcomers, the Battle of the Little Big Horn, in 1876. This was the site of "Custer's Last Stand."

That event ended any serious threat from the tribes, in a process that began with the arrival of the first Europeans in the late 1700s. These were French and Scotch trappers in the employ of the Hudson's Bay Company. Coming to hunt, rather than settle, the intrepid folk settled among the Indians, fathering children among them. This was the origin of that mixed-blood people who would play such an important role in the history of Montana, the Dakotas, Oregon, Washington, and the Canadian West—the Métis. The legends of all of these peoples are rife with stories of magic, strange beasts, and ghosts.

But after the largest part of Montana came under American sovereignty with the Louisiana Purchase of 1803, all of this was set to change. The Lewis and Clark party stayed in the state in 1805 and 1806. They were the first to explore the Bozeman area in the southwest section of Montana, and they blazed the Oregon Trail. This road in time would lead thousands of settlers across Montana from the east, looking for a new life in the Oregon country. As yet, there was little to cause them to stop permanently in Montana. But U.S. Army posts were erected to give the travelers protection against the local Indians. Again, many ghost stories resulted from the clashes between the two peoples.

During the Civil War, gold was discovered at what is now Virginia City. As in California a few years before, this meant settlement. A northern spur from the Oregon Trail opened up at Landrock, and passed over into Virginia City. Called the Bozeman Trail in honor of Georgia native John Bozeman, it functioned for three years until the Sioux and Cheyenne, fearful of the onrush, closed the road.

Nevertheless, settlers stayed in the Gallatin Valley to farm and trade. On July 7, 1864, Daniel E. Rouse and William J. Beall platted a town named Bozeman; it was chosen to be the Gallatin County seat in 1867.

One Nelson Story settled in Bozeman, driving 3,000 head of cattle in from Texas, despite the opposition of the army. This was the beginning of Montana's powerful cattle industry. Much concerned with the culture of the rapidly building state, Story supported the creation of Montana State College (now MSU), and the Ellen Theater, in downtown Bozeman. This was paralleled by developments around Montana, as the increasing number of new settlers demanded the amenities of civilized life. The coming of the Northern Pacific Railway to Bozeman in 1883 meant that ever more people—tourists as well as residents—could enter the area. This they did, discovering the area south of Bozeman, the Paradise Valley. They soon found the thermal hot pools so beloved of moneyed nineteenth-century travelers. It was only a matter of time before smart folk began to open luxury resorts in the area.

So it was no surprise, when, on June 20, 1900, Bill and Percie Matheson Knowles opened the Chico Warm Springs Hotel, declaring that its springs could cure "rheumatism, stomach and kidney troubles, and all skin and blood diseases." While Percie didn't "hold with" drinking, nevertheless her husband built a saloon and dance hall at the site. So popular did the place become that it played host to President Theodore Roosevelt. Teddy slept there prior to visiting Yellowstone National Park, thirty miles farther south.

Percie's dislike of alcohol was doubtless reinforced by Bill's death on April 22, 1910, of cirrhosis of the liver. Percie and their twelve-year-old son, Radbourne, carried on. Closing the saloon she held responsible for her husband's death, the widow turned the place entirely into a health resort. Two years later, she brought Dr. George A. Townsend to the hotel. For the next thirteen years, Townsend enjoyed great success with local and visiting patients; a hospital wing was added, and the pools were enlarged. But Dr. Townsend retired in 1925, and that was the end of Chico Hot Springs' career as a hospital.

Radbourne finally moved away, and business fell off. Faced with increasing hardship and loneliness, Percie went senile, being confined to her room in the hotel. At last, she was admitted to the state mental hospital in Warm Springs, dying after four and a half years there in 1941. Two years later, Radbourne died, and the place went on the market. Owners came and went, and Chico Hot Springs swung back and forth between vacation getaway and health resort—a duality that, as we have seen, has plagued it since its opening. But in 1976, Mike and Eve Art moved on to the property from Cleveland, having bought it three years before.

Under its current regime, the resort has once again become popular among celebrities, attracting such notables as Peter Fonda, Jeff Bridges, and Dennis Quaid. But the newcomers do not seem to have chased certain prior occupants from their old haunts. Apparently the tragic Knowles clan—particularly Percie—has not given up residence, even if they no longer hold the deeds.

Apparitions of a lady resembling Percie's photographs have been seen many times around the old hotel. Filmy, white, and varying in degrees of distinctness, these manifestations have appeared almost everywhere at different times. But apparently, Percie's favorite locales are Room 349 and its environs (where she was confined during her period of senility, and where her jasmine perfume is often smelled, and her rocking chair always returned to the place by the window where she used to sit); the kitchen, where in addition to seeing her, employees have reported intense cold and the clattering and smashing of invisible pots and pans (the visible ones are rarely affected); the small bar by the dining room; and the piano in the lobby. She does not speak, but those who have seen Percie declare that while her expression is usually blank, they are sure that she is aware of them. To her also are attributed by the staff the vanishing and return of various objects, very often when they are needed.

What of Bill Knowles? He has been seen at least once, enjoying a quiet drink with his wife in the darkened dining room. A security guard observed them, and thinking that they were the owner's daughter and her boyfriend, passed on. But when he looked back into the room from the opposite end, there was no one there, although the two chairs were pulled out and there were a couple of glasses on the table. The next night the cocktail waitress insisted that everything had been cleaned up and set in order when she left.

Phones ring at night, with no one on the other end; the employee's radio in the kitchen has blared loud music, even though the power switch was in the off position—the plug had to be pulled for the radio to stop. A disembodied moaning voice has been heard in the lobby, and doors slam on the third floor—even when no one is staying up there.

But Percie and Bill are not the only entities at work in the old hotel. The annex, an area above the bar where many of the staff live, also hosts a number of odd happenings. Employees have reported being confronted in their bedrooms by a tall bearded figure; so frightened are they by this apparition that many report being paralyzed. Some actually claim to have been tossed around by him.

Many other bizarre happenings have been reported from Chico Hot Springs. But while they do not detract from the excellent cuisine and service, the luxuriant accommodations, the beautiful scenery, or the warmth of the springs themselves, they do add a spirit all their own to the place. Remember, the best time to experience such events is in winter, late at night. But from all accounts, the unearthly might visit you there at any time.

Chico Hot Springs Resort and Day Spa
#1 Chico Road
Pray, Montana 59065
(800) HOT-WADA or
(406) 333-4933
chico@chicohotsprings.com

Ghostly Sights and Sounds
in a Nebraska University Theater

Nebraska is the quintessential Prairie State. Its flat surface is broken only by such rivers as the Platte, the Loup, the Republican, and other central Nebraska waterways. The Arikara, Pawnee, Omaha, Ponca, Oto, Sioux, Arapaho, and Cheyenne hunted buffalo and raised corn, beans, and squash. They also told their stories of gods and heroes.

In the eighteenth century, French and Spanish explorers and fur traders first entered the area. Even though the area passed under American sway with the Louisiana Purchase of 1803 (with Lewis and Clark traveling up the Missouri River the following year), the Indians remained dominant for another three decades. In 1819, the U.S. Army established Nebraska's first military post, Fort Atkinson, while Bellevue, established on the Missouri River in 1823, became Nebraska's first permanent American settlement. Fur traders began using the Platte River for transport in the 1820s, and in 1830 the first wagon train passed through on its way to the

Rockies. Many more would follow. Missionaries to the Indians began their work in the 1830s as well.

Even so, until the establishment of Nebraska Territory in 1854, the state was reserved as Indian country; no white civilians were allowed to settle permanently there. Omaha and Bellevue struggled to be the territorial capital; Omaha won initially, but in 1867 the capital was moved to Lancaster, now known as Lincoln, when statehood was achieved.

After entering the Union, Nebraska was flooded by Czechs, Swedes, Swiss, Irish, Germans, Danes, Poles, French-Canadians, Dutch, and many other groups, all bringing their own folklores. These in turn mixed and melded with the general eerie lore of the frontier. But perhaps no town in the state is so haunted as Lincoln; even the capitol building, home to the country's only unicameral legislature, is claimed to host ghosts as well.

Founded on a dry lakebed, the site of Lincoln was much resorted to by Indians and early Americans for salt. One of the first of these was Captain W. T. Donovan, who had been sent to prospect by the Crescent Salt Company. Settling on the west bank of Salt Creek in 1856, he named his claim Lancaster after his hometown in Pennsylvania. Within three years, the area boasted enough people to become a county. The new county seat was in turn named Lancaster in tribute to Donovan for his help in selecting it.

Because the people who lived south of the Platte River had difficulty crossing the water, and yet had more senators in the territorial legislature than those on the north side, it was voted to move the capital seat to Lancaster, just after the Civil War. In homage to the late President Lincoln, Lancaster was renamed in his honor. It became the capital city of Nebraska at the same time Nebraska became a state on March 1, 1867.

Three years later, in keeping with Lincoln's new status as a capital city, the University of Nebraska was chartered there. Since then, NU has piled achievement upon achievement. In 1909, it became the eighteenth member of the Association of American Universities, and was the first institution in the American west to grant the Ph.D. degree. Here the world's first undergraduate psychology laboratory was born, as well as the discipline of ecology. Deep interest in literature and the arts was the catalyst for *Prairie Schooner* literary magazine, the University of Nebraska Press, and the Sheldon Memorial Art Gallery and Sculpture Garden. As regards athletics, more Cornhuskers have been awarded the title "Academic All American" than student-athletes of any other university. Not to be left behind, the school has long had a highly regarded theater program, centering on the Temple Building.

Erected in 1906, the Temple Building was the first campus building built outside the fence that surrounded the original four-block campus. The first such building at a state university paid for by private funds, it was the gift of oil magnate John D. Rockefeller, friend of then Chancellor E. Benjamin Andrews. William Jennings Bryan, who considered Rockefeller's oil money to be tainted, led a storm of protest by populist Nebraskans wary of philanthropic plutocrats.

· Nevertheless, using the Howell and Studio Theaters, today the UNL Department of Theatre Arts has three production programs: "University Theatre, the academic year main stage with faculty directors, faculty/upper-level student designers, and student actors; Theatrix, the academic year second stage completely run by students; and the NE Repertory Theatre, a regional professional summer theatre."

But old theaters and old colleges both often have reputations for being haunted. This double-whammy has apparently hit the Temple Building. The story goes that back in the 1940s, a student who was preparing for a performance of *Macbeth* tumbled to his death from the overhead rigging. Of course, professional actors have long held a superstition regarding this play: it is considered to be bad luck, plain and simple. Whether performed, quoted, or even just named, "the Bard's Play" or the "Scottish Play" (so called by old theater hands to avoid invoking the curse) will bring death, ill fortune, and poor box office to anyone ensnared in its wiles.

However that may be, since the student actor's unfortunate plunge, odd occurrences, mostly centering on the stage, are said to occur at the Temple Building whenever the play is performed. Some have heard a noise followed by a crashing sound from the stage; upon checking it out, they find that no one is there, nor is anything out of place. Moreover, the misty figure of a worker dressed in old-style clothes has been seen there.

But the fun is not confined to the theater stage. Back in the 1970s, the student's apparition was reported in the basement studios of the local university television station, KUON-TV. More recently, a ghost was seen in the light booth by several witnesses, after which it suddenly faded away. There have also been reports of strange thumping sounds coming from the attic. It may well be, as in so many other theaters, that the show really does go on. See what you can find out yourself, the next time *Macbeth* opens at the Temple.

University of Nebraska
Temple Building
12th and R streets
Lincoln, NE
(402) 472-2072
Ticket Office: (402) 472-4747
www.unl.edu/rep
www.unl.edu/TheatreArts/

A Dead Mother and Child Wander the Halls of the Nevada Governor's Mansion

When one thinks of Nevada, one thinks of Las Vegas. But the sprawling desert gambling capital is actually a relatively minor facet of a strange and varied state. Before the advent of no-fault divorce, Nevada's lax marriage laws made it a haven for the divorce-inclined; in the immortal song, *Shuffle Off to Buffalo*, the lyrics say: "If she knew what we know, she'd be on the road to Reno." The 1938 Federal Writers' Project Guide to the State speaks of the "divorcée colony" in that storied "Biggest Little City in the World."

Except for the mountain areas around Lake Tahoe (where I myself was once snowed-in in July), and the extreme south fronting on the Colorado River, Nevada is very arid; as part of the Great Basin, alongside neighboring Utah, the area was named by early explorers as the "Great American Desert." Although the Washoe Indians in the Tahoe area had a relatively comfortable lifestyle prior to the coming of the Europeans, the Shoshone,

Goshute, and Paiute in the flatlands earned the nickname "digger Indians" from the incoming settlers due to their exiguous existences. Nevertheless, they filled their hot and punishing environment with legends.

Not surprisingly, it was the mountainous area that first received permanent American settlement in 1851. At first, Nevada was part of Utah Territory. Reflecting the ongoing strife between Mormons and "Gentiles" in the areas farther east, both sides set up shop in rival settlements near present-day Carson City. The Mormon town was fittingly enough called "Mormon Station" (today's Genoa). Their rivals, miners and traders for the most part, set up Gold Canyon (now Dayton). Three years later, in honor of Kit Carson, the whole area was organized as Carson County of Utah Territory.

As things worked out, however, the miners were fated to triumph. Gold was discovered at the head of Six-Mile Canyon in 1859. The two miners who made the find were convinced by fellow miner Henry Comstock that it was on his property; the famous Comstock Lode entered history. Virginia City grew up near this area; the gold was surrounded with sticky blue-gray mud—this to be silver ore worth over two thousand 1859 dollars a ton. Miners from all over the world flocked to the Comstock, as they had to California a decade before. The story of pain and avarice was similar as well, giving birth to both ghost towns and ghost stories.

There was simply no way—especially after the Civil War began—that the federal government would entrust control of the bonanza to the Mormon territorial authorities in Salt Lake City. So on March 2, 1861, the Territory of Nevada was formed. Pro-Confederate elements within the territory were suppressed, and the gold and silver of the Comstock filled the thirsty coffers of the Union. Despite lacking the necessary population for statehood, Nevada was a stronghold of Union and Republican Party loyalty. Congress duly gave its approval, a constitutional convention met in Carson City on July 4, 1864, and Nevada was admitted to the Union on October 31; its electors were able to vote for Lincoln in the presidential election the next month.

But the Comstock benefited not only the federal government, but also a few fortunate businessmen as well. Fortunes were made, and mansions filled with imported furniture from Europe and the Far East graced Virginia City. Nevada was not the only beneficiary, however: San Francisco profited also. The millions made on the Comstock built the mansions of Nob Hill, and started the fortunes of such luminaries as William Ralston and Charles Crocker, (founders of the Bank of California), Leland Stanford, George Hearst, John Mackay, William Flood, and many others. The miners' palaces of Virginia City, as well as her hotels and saloons, witnessed many unpleasant events that would leave their echoes as hauntings.

One other group besides Indians and miners brought strange tales to Nevada in their wake. This was that mysterious nation, the Basques. Speaking a unique language and boasting a bizarre folklore of their own, the first Basques in the state were nomadic shepherds who left California in search of pastures in the early 1870s. Such towns as Elko and Winnemucca enjoy their presence today.

Carson City was founded as a community in 1858. Pioneer Abraham Curry set aside ten acres expressly for the construction of a capitol, three years before the formation of Nevada Territory. His prediction paid off: Carson City was designated both the territorial capital and the county seat of newly formed Ormsby County. Three years later, Carson City was chosen state capital at the constitutional convention and remains so today.

Although the capitol was soon built, both territorial and state governors lacked a permanent residence: for over four decades, they lived wherever they could find a place. Finally, in 1907, State Assembly Bill 10, the "Mansion Bill," was passed to secure a permanent site for an official gubernatorial residence. Mrs. T. B. Rickey

sold the land to the state for ten dollars. Designed by Reno architect George A. Ferris, the mansion was first occupied in July 1909
by Acting Governor Denver Dickerson and his family, and opened
to the public for its first open house on New Year's Day, 1910. The
governor's daughter, June Dickerson, was born in the mansion in
September 1909, the only infant ever to be born there. It is a classical revival building, with Georgian and Jeffersonian motifs. Stairs
and metal balustrades were added in 1969. Additional buildings
were added to the grounds in 1998.

As with any executive mansion in the United States, the
Nevada governor's mansion has seen many dramatic episodes—the
sort that often spawn ghosts. But for the most part, it has been a
tranquil place, unaffected by the excitement that buffets such latter
day centers of mayhem in the state as Las Vegas, Reno, and the former Mustang Ranch. It seemed to have escaped paranormal activity, and probably would have continued its placid existence, except
for one rather small event, which occurred in what we like to think
of as the halcyon days of the 1950s.

It was not a murder or suicide, a duel, or thwarted love that
started the ghostly ball rolling in the quiet governor's mansion. No,
it was a gift, an otherwise unremarkable antique mantel clock. It
seems that the inoffensive timepiece came complete with a ghost.
The parlor doors began opening without any apparent help, and a
cold, mobile "presence" began to be felt throughout the mansion.
Eventually, a housekeeper saw a woman and her eight-year-old
daughter wandering through the rooms and hallways; a ghostly
pair, in fact. No one knows who they are, or how they came to be
associated with the clock.

Through most of the year, the mansion's living denizens and
their staff are the only ones to confront the specters. But one day a
year, you may have your chance. Fittingly, that ghostly date when
the place is open for tours is Nevada Day, which is observed on the
last Saturday in October. But, as you may remember, the actual

date is Halloween, and sometimes that last Saturday falls on that spooky holiday. That would probably be the best time to seek out the lady and her daughter.

But if you feel yourself safe from this particular haunting 364 days a year, bear in mind that what happened to the home of His Excellency of Nevada might happen to you. Be sure you know the history of every antique you acquire. You don't know what may come with it.

Nevada Governor's Mansion
606 Mountain Street
Carson City, NV 89706
(775) 882-2333

A New Hampshire Murder
Lives On in a Restaurant

A lthough Massachusetts was the cradle of New England, New Hampshire is today more of a bastion of old Yankee ways and customs than the Bay State. While the tides of immigration that swept the Northeast from all over the world left the state far from untouched, the newcomers picked up a great deal of the local customs and attitudes. Many a Manchester French-Canadian or Portsmouth Italian would heartily agree with the motto, "Live Free or Die." This outlook has made the New Hampshire government resist the allure of a state income tax, leading many a refugee from "Taxachusetts" to flee across the Merrimack in order to preserve his income from the grasping commonwealth authorities in Boston.

But the same rocky soil prevails on both sides of the border, and the Indian inhabitants were likewise similar. The Abenaki in the north and the Pennacook in the south of the state were Algonquian in speech, and the latter nation also existed in Massachusetts. Many of their place names survive today, as do some of the legends with which they invested their land. Allied early to the French, most were forced to retreat into Quebec in 1723, where their descendants live among the Abenaki of St. François. But a few remained, and there are now reorganized bands of both tribes in New Hampshire.

The first English attempt to colonize dates back to 1623, when, under an English land-grant, Captain John Mason, in conjunction with several others, sent colonists to establish a fishing colony at the mouth of the Piscataqua River. This was the origin of the towns of Rye and Dover. Again, as distinct from Massachusetts, colonization was not the result of refugees from English rule, but as part of a well thought-out plan by King James I. Although Puritans would come north to settle and the Congregational become the established Church, loyalty to the Crown would remain stronger in New Hampshire up to the Revolution.

Portsmouth, Hampton, and Exeter quickly joined the list of New Hampshire towns, and the whole became a Royal Province in 1679. But nineteen years later, much to the disgust of most of the inhabitants, it was given over to Massachusetts, an arrangement that lasted until 1741. In that year, King George II restored New Hampshire's independence, appointing a local man, Benning Wentworth, as Royal Governor. Wentworth remained in his position until 1766, being succeeded by his nephew, John. He in turn governed the province until forced to flee by the rebels in 1775, leaving an enormous legacy (including Dartmouth University) behind him. He was appointed governor of Nova Scotia, and remains revered as a hero in that province even today.

The period of the French and Indian Wars and the Revolution, as well as the typical New England legacy of witchcraft, piracy, and the like, gave rise to a whole body of weird lore. As might be expected, some of this remains in the modern city of Nashua.

The name means "land between two rivers" in the Pennacook language. The city was originally chartered in 1673 as the town of

Dunstable. It was founded by Jonathan Tyng, whose frame house was located in the section of the town that now bears his name. At that time, Dunstable included Nashua, and the New Hampshire towns of Hollis, Merrimack, Hudson, Pelham, Litchfield, Milford, and Brookline, as well as the Massachusetts towns of Tyngsboro, Dunstable, Groton, Pepperell, and Townsend.

Most of the town's earlier settlers came from Boston and vicinity. But when news of Indian massacres, in King Philip's War, reached the town, many of the residents left. Some returned, however, after the war's end in 1677, finding their homes undisturbed. They were not so lucky in 1691, when Indians allied to the French raided the town. Subsequent attacks occurred in 1703. By this time, Dunstable was a town of Massachusetts.

Prior to New Hampshire's resurrection in 1741, a dispute broke out over ownership of Dunstable. Both Massachusetts and New Hampshire appealed to the Privy Council in London. On March 5, 1740, King George II awarded the upper valley of the Merrimack River to New Hampshire, dividing the original township of Dunstable in two. Dunstable, New Hampshire, was given a Royal Charter in 1746 (which document is preserved in the Nashua Public Library). The name of Dunstable was retained until 1836, when it was changed to Nashua.

The very year that New Hampshire regained its independence, a farmhouse was built that today is called the Country Tavern Restaurant (although it has incorporated the barn as well). With its exposed beam construction and antique furnishings, it takes the diner back to colonial days. Although the bill of fare is not exactly "authentic," it is delicious, boasting such delicacies as Cajun seafood chowder, lobster salad, coconut chicken salad, onion soup, blackened chicken with melted cheddar, and lemon pepper chicken.

But the same menu that lists these eatables also tells (on the back) the tragic story of Elizabeth Ford. Married to a sea captain, she and her infant child were murdered by her jealous husband, who had returned after a year at sea. The baby was buried under a tree on the property, while the mother was thrown down a well.

This grisly end has, not surprisingly, apparently led her to return to her home. Her operations in the restaurant have been featured on the television shows *Hard Copy* and *Unsolved Mysteries*.

On a somewhat less dramatic level, she is said to play the poltergeist: salt and pepper shakers, water pitchers, and even diners' dishes move without visible aid, while cups and saucers fly across the room. Doors open and close on their own, glasses are knocked off the shelves, and women diners claim to feel the sensation of fingers going through their hair.

But Elizabeth has also been seen, most often at a window of the barn section. There she is seen looking at the tree where her infant is said to be buried. Usually described as being about five-foot-seven with white gown and long white hair, Elizabeth is generally opaque, rather transparent. But her concern is apparently not restricted to her own child. She visibly interacts with customers' children; on one occasion it is said that Elizabeth came to the aid of a woman lunching with her young son. Having gotten his hands on a steak knife the lad was about to cut himself. The ghost warned the woman of the danger. Another time, a living dog was actually seen following her floating apparition. Appropriately, the ladies' room is considered one of the rooms most frequented by the very ladylike spirit. At the Country Tavern, the menu may not be what you would have eaten there in the eighteenth century. But there does seem to be at least one genuine colonial on hand.

Country Tavern Restaurant
452 Amherst Street
Nashua, NH 03063
(603) 889-5871

The Tragic Story of
New Jersey's Last Royal Governor
Echoes On in His Home

For people whose only knowledge of New Jersey amounts to whatever they can see from Manhattan, the Garden State is little more than a *Saturday Night Live* joke. But there is much more to Jersey than Hoboken. From Cape May to the Pine Barrens to the Ramapo Mountains, there are all sorts of strange and mysterious things to be seen. A crossroads of history and cultures, New Jersey packs a lot of punch into a small area.

The original people were primarily members of the Lenni Lenape or Delaware Confederacy, except the far south of the state, where Nanticokes strayed in from the Delmarva Peninsula. Algonquian speakers, these peoples had legends about every rock and river, seemingly, and their own pantheon of gods and devils.

The first European settlements in the state were those of the Dutch on the western side of the Hudson, along with one on the Delaware at Fort Nassau. The year after the English conquest of New Netherlands (New York, New Jersey, Delaware, and part of

Pennsylvania), New Jersey was included in the grant of Charles II to his brother James, the Duke of York, in whose honor New York was renamed. The same year James made the province over to two of his friends, Lord Berkeley and Sir George Carteret. Sir George having been governor of the Channel Island of Jersey, the province was named New Jersey. The next year Sir George began colonizing his new property, sending over his nephew, Philip Carteret, as governor. Arriving in New Jersey with a band of settlers, Carteret named the first town Elizabethtown, for Sir George's wife. More came later from New England, particularly New Haven; Puritans, they founded Newark and neighboring towns.

A form of government was prescribed in the so-called "Concessions," granting religious liberty to Englishmen in the new colony, as well as governance carried on by a governor, council, and an assembly of twelve chosen by the people. No taxes were to be laid without the consent of the assembly. The first of these met in 1668, adopting draconian laws modeled after those of Puritan New England. After a session of but five days it adjourned, and met no more for seven years. In 1670 many of the settlers refused to pay rent, maintaining that they had received their lands directly from the Indians, or else Governor Nicolls of New York before Sir George or Lord Berkeley arrived on the scene. The non-payees rebelled, elected an illegal assembly, and appointed James Carteret, Sir George's illegitimate son, as governor. But when James's father refused to back him up, the rebellion collapsed. It did have the effect, however, of frightening Lord Berkeley into selling his interest in the province to two Quakers, John Fenwick and Edward Byllynge. But Byllynge went broke, passing his share to trustees. Most prominent of these was the famous Quaker colonizer, William Penn, founder of Pennsylvania.

In 1676, New Jersey was divided into East Jersey, retained by Sir George, and West Jersey, encompassing the Quaker lands. Between these halves was a straight line from Little Egg Harbor to the

Delaware Water Gap. West Jersey's capital was placed at Burlington, and East Jersey's at Perth Amboy.

In 1680 George Carteret died; two years later East Jersey was sold at auction to twelve men, one of whom was William Penn. Each of these sold half his interest to another man, and so East Jersey came to have twenty-four proprietors. This was the origin of the Proprietors of East Jersey, still surviving as a corporation.

The Duke of York came to the throne as James II in 1685. Much concerned with the threat to the English colonies from the French and Indians, the new king gave thought to uniting the most threatened colonies—Maine, Massachusetts, Plymouth, New Hampshire, Rhode Island, Connecticut (all of whom had suffered in King Philip's War), New York, and the Jerseys—into one, much stronger colony. This was the forerunner of various "plans of union" for the separate colonies that were subsequently advanced, culminating after the Revolution with the present constitution of the United States. To form this "Dominion of New England," he suppressed the charters of those colonies, leaving, however, all previous land grants to individuals in place. In 1686, he appointed Sir Edmund Andros. But when the king was overthrown in 1688, the Dominion collapsed and the territories comprising it—not least the Jerseys—fell into anarchy.

The Carteret heirs, the Quakers, and New York all claimed the two colonies. Nevertheless, in 1702 New Jersey became a Royal province. Queen Anne gave her governor of New York jurisdiction over New Jersey (although the latter retained a separate assembly), which arrangement continued until 1738, when the two colonies were finally separated. Part of the new scheme of government, however, required that Burlington and Perth Amboy should be co-capitals, with the assembly meeting alternately in either town, and the Royal governor maintaining homes in both.

Perth Amboy's history dates back to 1651. In that year, August Herman purchased the site of the town from the Lenni

Lenape Indians. Incorporated in 1683, settlers began to call the land Ambo or Amboy Point, and finally Amboy. When, three years later, the settlement became the capital of East Jersey, Perth was added to the name in honor of one of the proprietors under the Royal grant: the Earl of Perth. In 1715, Perth Amboy received a Royal charter from King George I.

As a result, Perth Amboy boasts the oldest city hall in continuous use in the United States. It was established in 1685 when the first courthouse was built; in 1713, a new structure was built on the same site. This burned in 1731, and was rebuilt yet again about 1745. Still another fire claimed that building in 1764. At last, in 1767 the present city hall was built, containing court chambers, rooms for the Provincial Assembly, the Governors Council, and the City Corporation.

The governor also needed a local residence, however. The proprietors of East Jersey built the Proprietary House in 1762–64 for Governor Sir William Franklin. Designed by master architect John Edward Pryor, the Proprietary House was and is a grand Georgian-style house, truly fit for the king's representative. Of course, it was hard to lure Sir William away from his home in Burlington at Green Bank. This was not due to any overwhelming love of that town, but rather because it was only a few miles from Philadelphia, the Governor's birthplace and continued residence of his celebrated (although illegitimate) father, Benjamin.

Although his mother's identity is unknown, William was raised by his father and Ben's maid, Deborah Read. He accompanied his father on several missions, including those to England, where he completed his education, and was admitted to the bar. While there he met and courted Elizabeth Downes, a daughter of a wealthy Barbados sugar planter, marrying her on September 4, 1762. They had one son, William Temple. Due to his father's then-popularity at court, when the Franklins returned from England in 1763, William carried a commission as His Majesty's Governor of New Jersey.

Initially, relations between father and son remained close, but they deteriorated over the years as rebellion loomed and Benjamin became ever closer to the rebels. By 1774, William's reluctance to leave Burlington had evaporated, and he looked at the spacious home built for him as a refuge. Refusing to break his oath to the king, the governor was grateful to put some space between his father and himself.

Trying to maintain the legal government in a province where the majority remained loyal but the wealthy and their militia favored rebellion, William Franklin found himself and his wife under house arrest at the Proprietary House in January of 1776. The pressures upon him to either resign his commission or swear allegiance to the new regime (or both) daily mounted, as did the implied threats against his wife. He gave his parole that he would not leave the province. Attempting to salvage the situation, in June he issued a proclamation as governor of New Jersey, summoning a meeting of the legal legislative assembly. But both he and his captors knew that a loyalist majority would be returned. For this act he was arrested by order of the provincial congress of New Jersey, and removed to Burlington; his wife was left behind under continued arrest. Soon afterward he was sent to East Windsor, Connecticut. Elizabeth was subjected to continued harassment, until at last William Temple Franklin (who had allied with his grandfather) was able to obtain permission for her to pass through to British-occupied New York. Worn out by the treatment she had undergone during her imprisonment in her once luxurious home, she died without ever being reunited with her beloved husband.

William, in the meantime, remained strictly guarded in Connecticut, until, at last, in November 1778, he was exchanged and allowed to go to New York. Serving for a short time as president of the Board of Loyalists of New Jersey, he left for London in August of 1782. He died there in 1813.

His old house in Perth Amboy underwent many changes. After the Revolution, it became a private home; in 1809 it was transformed into a resort hotel, called the Brighton House; in 1883 it was turned into a rooming home for retired Presbyterian ministers, called the Westminster; after that the grand old house became a flophouse. Fire, vandalism, vacancy, and depression all left their marks.

But new hope dawned for the Proprietary House in 1967, when the property was taken over by the state of New Jersey. Restoration and preservation measures were undertaken by the Proprietary House Association, which is an independent nonprofit organization made up of concerned local citizens. With little funding the house is slowly regaining much of its former glory. Boasting a fine tearoom, it is open for visits. It also hosts a number of regular community events, including the annual re-creation of the arrest of Governor Franklin on June 9, 1776.

The tragic events of the Franklins' lives at the Proprietary House seem to have left a certain aftermath. Employees have seen a boy who appears to be pointing to the third floor, although no one claims to know why. It may have something to do, however, with an occurrence on that very story. Two employees of the Verizon company a few years back went up there to repair some phones. There they met a lady in a white dress. When they asked her for some information as to the layout of the phone system, she vanished in front of their eyes. The pair fled downstairs, declaring to the staff that they would never set foot in the building again. Is it Elizabeth Downes Franklin, still guarding the grand home she was so proud of in life, despite the tragedy that overtook her there? Perhaps. Apparently she gives a tickle to the cheek and a clap by the ear to staff members of whom she approves.

And what of her ill-starred husband? It is said by a former managing director that Sir William's influence can be felt, most strongly around the anniversary of his arrest. She claimed to have seen him on one or more occasions in her office on the ground floor, as well as to have heard him.

Nor are these three the only spirits who appear to dwell in the house. What are we to make of the glowing orbs of light photographed in the tearoom and the servants' quarters? It's anyone's guess, of course, as to what or who they might be. What is certain is that the fare served in the tearoom is delicious, and the tour with its insight into a key story of our history is well worth attending. And who knows? Any expression of sympathy to the losers in that long-ago conflict might well bring an expression of supernatural gratitude.

Proprietary House
149 Kearny Avenue
Perth Amboy, NJ 08861
(732) 826-5527

A Murder of a Son By His Mother
Keeps Things Stirring
in a New Mexico Restaurant

If ever there was a mysterious place, it is surely New Mexico, the "Land of Enchantment." From the artists' colonies in Santa Fe and Taos, to the restricted doings of the *Penitentes*, that strange brotherhood of grace and blood, to Indian *Kachinas*, to tales of wandering saints and witches, to the UFOs of Roswell, New Mexico has an incredible amount of weird lore packed within its boundaries. I went to college at New Mexico Military Institute in Roswell, before that city in the "Staked Plains" acquired its reputation as a center for alien landings; the Institute, like so many places of higher learning, had its own ghost stories which had nothing to do with visitors from outer space.

But the roots of New Mexico's odd aura lie in its distant past. Even today, the Cliff Dwellings of the Anasazi people evoke feelings of both sadness and awe—awe at the size and organization of these first Pueblos, and sadness at their unexplained abandonment. Yet some of their descendants, at least, doubtless dwell in the nineteen pueblos remaining in New Mexico today. When the Spanish arrived in 1540, the Pueblo Indians were about the best organized on the North American continent, just as their Navajo and Apache enemies were about the most successful nomads.

Although Vásquez de Coronado and his men ranged over much of the southwestern United States, discovering the Grand Canyon, and ranged deep into Kansas, there were no signs of the fabled "cities of gold" of which previous explorers had heard rumors. At this stage, there was no pressing reason for the Spanish Crown to invest money and men in this remote region, when so much of Mexico remained untamed.

But over the next four decades, Spain slowly and methodically settled northern Mexico. In 1582, Fray Bernardo Beltrán and Antonio de Espejo arrived in the area of the modern state, dubbing it "la Nueva Mejico." Inspired by a zeal for souls, the leaders of this expedition reminded the Viceroy in Mexico City that the region contained many people in organized settlements, ripe for conversion to the Catholic faith. In 1595, the wealthy Juan de Oñate, whose father, Don Cristóbal, had helped Cortés conquer Mexico, was commissioned to subdue New Mexico. Three years later, Oñate's expedition assembled at Compostela, Mexico; made up of nearly two hundred soldier-colonists, many with wives and families, nine Franciscan priests, several hundred Indian servants and allies, and thousands of head of livestock, the column slowly advanced toward the Rio Grande. In April 1598, it arrived at modern El Paso: Oñate took possession of the province in the name of King Philip II of Spain. Northward they traveled, calling on each village to swear allegiance to the king and his God. On July 11, 1598, the Spanish renamed a Tewa Pueblo, San Juan de Los Caballeros and established the first Spanish capital of New Mexico. The capital moved a few months later to Yunque, which was renamed San Gabriel. San Gabriel remained the seat of government until it was moved again to the newly found villa of Santa Fe in 1610. Spanish settlements were established along the Rio Grande, from Socorro in the south to the Taos Valley in the north. But in 1680, twenty-one Franciscans and more than four hundred colonists were killed in a mass uprising; the remainder of the three thousand colonists fled to El Paso del Norte, the southernmost settlement in the province. Along with them fled many loyal Indians, founding the tribal settlements around Las Cruces and El Paso that survive today.

A decade later, Diego de Vargas Zapata Luján Ponce de León was appointed Governor of New Mexico. In 1692, he peacefully reconquered New Mexico, an event observed annually in September at the famous Fiesta de Santa Fe. The next year, a renewed rebellion was put down, and in 1696 a larger one erupted. But by 1700, the Pueblos were reconciled to Spanish rule.

But while Spaniard and Pueblo would be united henceforth, New Mexico was an island under siege by various Indian nomads—the Comanche, the Apache, the Ute, and the Navajo.

Despite the constant fighting on the frontier, through the eighteenth century, a unique Hispanic culture developed in New Mexico, especially in the north. Alongside the Pueblos, the Hispanos evolved their own folkways, preserving much of their Spanish heritage (to this day their language is an extremely antique dialect of Spanish) while developing artwork and folk belief of their own. On the one hand, folk carvings of the saints—*santos*—were done in a distinctively New Mexico style, and such devotions as the shrine of Chimayo grew up, complete with miraculous healings and divine apparitions. At the same time, stories of *brujería*—witchcraft— abounded, as did tales of ghosts and *duendes*—fairies.

Although Mexico gained its independence from Spain in 1821, and took New Mexico along with it out of the Spanish empire, little changed in New Mexico immediately. But eventually, the new regime's open-door policy led to an influx of Americans along the Santa Fe Trail. Fur traders and merchants of many nationalities came to New Mexico; many married into Mexican families, becoming influential in local politics and commerce. They were in fact the forerunners of yet another titanic change for New Mexico.

War broke out between Mexico and the United States in 1846. After three months on the Santa Fe Trail, General Stephen Watts Kearny entered Santa Fe on August 18. Although he had shown some guile in persuading the Mexican governor to flee without fighting, a revolt was being planned by the locals. The opening shot was fired on January 19, 1847, when Charles Bent, the recently appointed governor, and several other local officials, were killed at Taos. The northern New Mexico insurrection known as "The Revolt of 1847" had begun. By February 3, the revolt was suppressed, and in 1848 the Treaty of Peace gave New Mexico to the United States. The 1853 Gadsden Purchase brought the United States Tucson, Arizona, and the small settlement of Mesilla, New Mexico, at the southern end of the future state, near El Paso.

Although Coronado, Oñate, and de Vargas all passed near or through the site of Mesilla, it was settled only in 1850, after the American takeover. Subject to Apache raids, the area only became secure after the U.S. Army established Fort Fillmore the following year. Having become the fort's supply center in 1854, Mesilla flourished. It was a major stop on the Chihuahua Trail, extending from that Mexican city to Santa Fe, and on the Butterfield Stage Route from San Antonio to San Diego. Anglos from the east settled there in large numbers, and merchants arrived to provide them with goods. The plaza witnessed many celebrations, and fine adobe buildings were erected all over the burgeoning town. Brief occupation by the Confederates during the Civil War did little harm to the village.

After the war, Mesilla resumed its position as commercial and transportation hub for the region, as well as outfitting miners and ranchers. Ever more people made their way through the town, and by the 1880s Mesilla was a social center as well. *Bailes* (dances), bullfights, cockfights, and theatrical plays brought folk from Chihuahua and Tucson. Many of the west's badmen flocked to the town to party and fight: Billy the Kid was sentenced to hang here.

But the good times were about to end. The railroad bypassed Mesilla for Las Cruces in 1881, and soon after the status of county seat fell to Las Cruces as well. The bars and hotels on the plaza became much quieter, although the little church of San Albino continued just as before. Mesilla went to sleep, retaining much of its nineteenth-century atmosphere. On September 10, 1957, the Mesilla Plaza was declared a state monument of New Mexico, which honor was followed in January 1982 by listing on the National Register of Historic Places. With its gazebo in the center, the Plaza hosts such activities as the *Cinco de Mayo* and *16 de Septiembre* fiestas, as well as the *Dia de Los Muertos* (Day of the Dead) celebration that occurs the first part of November, and Christmas Eve, when the plaza is bedecked with thousands of *luminaries*. But one of the most intriguing buildings on the plaza is the Double Eagle Restaurant.

Housed in a large, 150-year-old adobe building, the Double Eagle is filled with art, sculpture, antiques, and imported crystal chandeliers. But elegance is not the only nineteenth-century survival the restaurant retains. The restaurant's name comes from the gold twenty-dollar piece; a ten dollar piece was called an "eagle." First built in the late 1840s, the building has seen all of the history that has engulfed Mesilla.

The first owners of the building were the Maes family. The family was in the import-export business. Operating a trading company based in Santa Fe, the Maeses moved to Mesilla to escape the American takeover. Of course, the Gringos soon followed, but the family was by that time reconciled to their rule. Señora Maes considered herself a great lady, and planned an advantageous match for her teenaged son, Armando. But Armando had already lost his heart to one of their maids, Inez. Although they enjoyed the connivance of the other servants in hiding their love from Armando's mother, they feared her wrath, should she ever find out—justly, as it happened.

Eventually, Armando's mother figured out what was going on, and ordered Inez out of the house, dismissing her from the family's service. But, as is so often the case, young love found a way—on this occasion, tragically. Returning unexpectedly from a trip, Señora Maes found the lovers entwined in her son's bedroom. Horrified, she attacked Inez with her sewing shears, stabbing her in the heart. When Armando tried to defend his lover, he found himself stabbed before his mother realized what she had done. Stunned, she called out his name. But the couple died, and Señora Maes never spoke again.

The house passed through a succession of hands; in 1984, it was restored on a lavish scale by C. W. "Buddy" Ritter, a fifth-generation Mesillan and the current owner. Ritter commissioned designer John Meigs to fill the restaurant with antiques. Although named after the gold piece, the name "Double Eagle" is reminiscent of the badge of the imperial family of Austria, the House of Habsburg—one member of which, Emperor Maximilian, attempted an ill-fated reign over Mexico, which ended in his execution by firing squad in 1867. He and his empress, Carlotta, are commemorated at the Double Eagle with dining rooms named after them. The fare available in the restaurant—Tournedos Maximillian, shrimp scampi Chardonnay, raspberry seed sauce turkey sandwich, Mesilla chicken—is truly fit for an imperial kitchen.

The "Imperial Bar's" backlights are French *Corones*, boasting Lalique shades from the 1890s. In the Maximilian Room are French baccarat chandeliers, seven feet by three feet; each contains more than one thousand hand-cut glass crystals. The solid gold ceiling is hand-gilded with 18- and 24-karat gold leaf. There are twenty gold-leafed French mirrors in Greek Revival style. Lavish as they are, though, it is the Carlotta salon that seizes our attention.

This was the room in which Armando and Inez met their doom. An oil portrait of the empress holding a small white Maltese dog dominates the room; after her husband's murder, Carlotta went mad, living until 1927 in her native Belgium. But the more immediate tragedy of the Maes family is represented by two oval portraits of Señor and Señora Maes. There are also two uphol-stered Victorian armchairs in the room. Although few ever use them, the cut velvet fabric has been worn in the shape of human bodies; one is larger than the other, but both would be considered small by modern standards.

Since the chairs are rarely used, no one can tell why the vel-vet—which is recent—has grown worn. But that is not the only mysterious event in the Carlotta Salon. Although the motion detec-tors are always put on at closing, in the morning wine glasses are found broken, and tables have changed their location. Names are heard being whispered and strange perfumes smelt. A photograph is believed to have been taken of the ghosts and is displayed on the wall. Who knows? You may have an unseen dining companion!

Double Eagle
On the Plaza
Mesilla, NM 88046
(505) 523-4999

An Uptown Mansion
with a Sad History Features
Famous Ghosts in New York

New York is certainly one of the most exciting states in the Union. Of course, for many outsiders (and, perhaps, for many residents of New York City) the city that bears the same name as the state as a whole is all there is worth noting in New York. Not so. From Yonkers to Lake Champlain, and west to Niagara Falls and beyond, upstate has a lot to offer the visitor. Even so, to a great degree the tail *does* wag the dog.

From the first settlement by the Dutch, New York has acquired a wealth of strange lore—much of it popularized by the first internationally known American author, Washington Irving; the *Legend of Sleepy Hollow* is one of innumerable such tales told around firesides (and forced on school children) for generations. As a native-born New Yorker, it is one of the things this author is proudest of.

Renowned in these legends were the manor lords of New York, such as the Van Rensselaers, the Van Cortlandts, and the Philipses. Granted huge tracts of land by the Crown, these baronial clans attempted to reproduce feudalism in the New World. In 1693, Frederick Philipse, a Dutch-born carpenter who had made his money both through his trade and a wealthy marriage, was given a manor by royal charter. Called the "Manor of Philipseborough," it encompassed the present town of Yonkers and 150 square miles of land; he was also given the patent of Fredericks-borough, or Sleepy Hollow, which comprised 240 square miles. He built on these properties two great manor houses and, at Sleepy Hollow, the Old Dutch Church later made famous by Washington Irving. In token of his wealth and position, Philipse was a member of the governor's council for more than twenty years, and a friend of all the royal governors from Sir Edmund Andros to Lord Richard Bellemont.

His descendants ruled the Philipse estates happily until the Revolution. Great-grandson Frederick Philipse III, however, was to be the last lord of the manor. Born in New York in 1746, Frederick graduated from King's College (now Columbia) in 1773. In keeping with family tradition, he became a member of the assembly; he also gave a great deal to charity. Living more lavishly than any of his ancestors, Frederick initially tried to maintain neutrality in the political upheavals leading up to the Revolution. When independence was declared, however, he knew that he had to choose sides. On November 28, 1776, Frederick joined over two hundred other prominent New Yorkers in signing a "Declaration of Dependence," indicating their continuing faithfulness to their sovereign, George III. General Washington ordered Frederick arrested. He and his family fled to the British-held city, and his lands and homes were confiscated and sold. Although the Crown eventually gave him £62,075 in compensation, he was forced to flee to England when the city was evacuated in 1783, and died there, broken-hearted, three years later. Both his homes survive today, however, and are open to the public.

His sister, Mary (1730–1825), also inherited a great deal of wealth from their father. Well-educated, she was also beautiful, with laughing dark eyes and dark hair; although she was strong-willed, she was also very kindly. Staying with her sister and brother-in-law (Colonel Beverley Robinson) in their New York City home in 1756, she met a young Virginia colonel, George Washington. At twenty-four, Washington was on his way to Boston to meet Governor Shirley, after fighting the French and Indians in the Ohio country. Mightily attracted to the young heiress, he stopped by again on his way back. He spent as long as he could with her before he returned to the front; but he was unable to propose to her before he did so. Shortly thereafter, he heard that Colonel Roger Morris, his companion-in-arms and confidante on the bloody field of Mononga-hela, won Mary's hand. The couple was married in 1758. After fighting under James Wolfe at Quebec, Morris settled down with his wife in lower Manhattan in 1764.

But as the son of a British architect, Morris was desirous of try-ing his hand at building. The next year, he and his wife erected a palatial summer home in the north of the island, which they dubbed "Mount Morris." Located in what is now Washington Heights (then called Harlem Heights) at the corner of 160th Street and Edgecomb Avenue, it was and is a Palladian-style four-story house with a balcony and a basement. Before the wall of trees and buildings seen today grew up around the mansion, Mount Morris offered spacious views of downtown Manhattan as well as of New Jersey and Westchester.

All was well for the young couple at first, and in fairly rapid suc-cession the marriage produced four children. But as with her brother, the events of the revolution would overtake Mary's domes-tic happiness. At first, the rebels seized control of New York City. Colonel Morris re-affirmed his allegiance to the King, and their house was confiscated. It became Washington's headquarters in the autumn of 1776, while Mary's property holdings, including a large estate in Putnam County, were likewise seized. The Morrises fled to the Philipse holdings in Westchester County, until the British de-feated Washington and took Manhattan. General Sir Henry Clinton used Mount Morris as his headquarters in turn; the Morrises and their children were forced to leave for England in 1783; but because the children had not been condemned as traitors, they were able to sell their reversionary interests in their mother's property to John Jacob Astor for £20,000. Added to this, the British government also gave £17,000 in compensation for Morris's losses. Mary, her sister Mrs. Robinson, and the wife of Reverend Charles Inglis (Rector of New York's Trinity Church, and first Anglican Bishop of Halifax after the evacuation in 1783) were the only women accused of treason during the Revolution. Morris lived on in England until his death in 1794; Mary outlived him for another thirty-one years, dying at the age of ninety-six and being buried by her husband's side near Saviour-Gate church in York.

Mount Morris, in the meantime, was sold as a tavern once the war was over. Called the Calumet Inn, it became a fashionable stopping place on the post road to Albany when New York was the nation's capital. All the leading figures of the day stayed there—including President Washington.

But this brief period of prosperity ended after the federal capital moved on. The Calumet Inn fell on hard times. But it was purchased in 1810 by another couple keen on returning it to its former status as a domestic showplace. Stephen Jumel was a French wine merchant; his wife Eliza (or Betsy) Brown or Bowen (both variants are recorded) was an American. When young, she had been a prostitute in Providence, Rhode Island. Gaining in knowledge, she made her way to New York, where she earned a reputation as a stage actress and courtesan. Described as "a beautiful blonde with a superb figure and graceful carriage," she gave herself to such worthies as Thomas Jefferson, Aaron Burr, and Alexander Hamilton. It has been said that she was one of the causes of the duel between them, and that she smuggled secret political information from Hamilton to Burr.

However that may be, she left the political round to become the mistress of Jumel; she lived with him for several years in his mansion at Whitehall and Pearl Streets. After they were married, the Jumels lived in France, where they were popular figures at the Court of Napoleon I. In 1810, after they bought Mount Morris, they restored and refurbished it with fine furnishings in the latest Parisian styles. Five years later, the couple offered Napoleon a refuge; but the wily Emperor declined the favor.

In 1826, Mme. Jumel returned to America, while her husband remained in France. Armed with power of attorney over her husband's fortune, she increased it while dividing her time between Paris and New York. The couple returned to live in the mansion together in 1828. When Stephen died in 1832, following a fall from a carriage, he left his wife the wealthiest woman in America. Although his death was ruled accidental, rumors remain to the effect that she let him die while he lay wounded.

But after a year as a widow, Eliza married her old flame, the now disgraced Aaron Burr, in the octagonal parlor of the mansion. Diarist Philip Hone wrote on July 3, 1833, "The celebrated Colonel Burr was married on Monday evening to the equally celebrated Mrs. Jumel, widow of Stephen Jumel. It is benevolent of her to keep the old man in his later days. One good turn deserves another."

A year later, Eliza filed divorce proceedings against Burr. She claimed that he had squandered her money on Texas land settlement deals and committed adultery "at divers times with divers females." Burr was seventy-eight years old; his soon-to-be ex-wife was twenty years younger. The divorce became final on the day of his death, September 14, 1836. Ironically, her lawyer, Alexander Hamilton, Jr., was the son of her other former lover, whom Burr had killed in the famous duel.

Mme. Jumel continued to live in her sumptuous house on Harlem Heights, but as the years passed her looks and her sanity alike vanished. At last, still immensely wealthy, she died in 1865. Subsequent owners, the Earles, sold the house to the city of New York in 1903; it opened as a public museum the next year.

Today, the Morris-Jumel Mansion is operated by Morris-Jumel Mansion, Inc.; together with the surrounding Roger Morris Park it forms part of the Jumel Terrace Historic District. The mansion has eleven restored period rooms including the octagonal drawing room, a dining room glittering with nineteenth-century ceramics and glass, and Eliza Jumel's chamber, with a bed that is said to have belonged to Napoleon. The house was extensively restored in 1994, and despite its tragic history, is one of the jewels in the crown of the city of New York. But it is not only docents and visitors that wander there.

On January 19, 1964, a visiting class arrived ahead of the museum's curator. Waiting outside, the children became unruly. A blonde woman dressed in a purple gown came out onto the second floor balcony and yelled at them, telling the children firmly to "Shush!" She then turned and walked through a closed solid wood door. When the curator arrived, the students began complaining about the woman letting them stand outdoors in the cold instead of letting them into the mansion to wait.

On another occasion an enthusiastic teacher, anxious to see the whole house, ran upstairs to the top floor, which is generally closed to the public. Seeing a Revolutionary soldier step out of a painting, she fainted from fright. Another teacher on a subsequent visit suffered a fatal heart attack having been confronted by a ghost in the mansion. A maid said to have thrown herself out a window over an unhappy love affair with a member of the Jumel family has also been seen haunting the third-floor servant quarters. Still other visitors report meeting the ghost of Aaron; an angry Stephen Jumel has also made himself known.

Morris-Jumel Mansion
1765 Jumel Terrace
New York, NY 10032
(212) 923-8008

A North Carolina Battle Between Diehard Foes Lives On

N orth Carolina—the Tarheel State—has long billed itself as "a valley of humility between two mountains of conceit," in reference to the neighboring and (reputedly) more aristocratic states of Virginia and South Carolina. Certainly, her colonial capitals of Edenton, Bath, and New Bern could not compete with Charleston or Williamsburg in elegance (although Tryon's Palace, the accurately reconstructed Royal Governor's residence in New Bern) shows that the king's representative among the Tarheels had little to be ashamed of.

Even so, great plantations were fewer and hardscrabble farms more numerous in North Carolina. It was poorer country, and the province and then state's ports, such as they were, did not handle anything like the volume of trade that came in through Norfolk and Charleston. But for all that, North Carolina's European history goes further back even than Jamestown, Virginia's settling in 1607. Roanoke Island was the site of Sir Walter Raleigh's abortive attempt at colonization in 1587. After producing the first English child born in the New World (Virginia Dare), the settlers vanished, never to be heard from again. Local legend holds that they were absorbed into the nearby Croatoan tribe; whether or not this is true, the Lumberton Indians, descendants of that people, still use a number of surnames found in the "Lost Colony" of Roanoke. Even more mysterious is the tale that a ghostly white fawn—said by locals to be the spirit of Virginia Dare—still roams the island.

The Outer Banks of North Carolina are an isolated, beautiful, and (in hurricane season) perilous place. Despite the encroachments of tourism since World War II, however, there are still pockets of the locals, descendants of fishermen from Dorset whose accents and beliefs reflect their region of origin.

The North Carolina Low Country was settled by English, Swiss, and African slaves, all of whom left their mark on the area's folk beliefs. The Up Country, further inland, was populated by a wide variety of groups, most notably Highland Scots, whose weird lore is legendary. The Appalachians, of course, welcomed the Ulster Scots we have seen in other states of that mountain range.

The American Revolution hit North Carolina in much the same way it did the other thirteen colonies. The province may not have had the same number of wealthy magnates as their more "conceited" neighbors, but they did have some. These welcomed the revolt as a chance to seize complete control. Not surprisingly, many of their less-well-to-do brethren rallied to the Crown in response. The Revolution degenerated into a bloody civil war, and perhaps no place in the state was bloodier than Moore County.

Settlements had begun appearing around 1739. Although the first traders, hunters, and farmers were primarily English and Ulster Scots, they were joined by Germans, French Huguenots, and Pennsylvania Dutch about a decade later. Then, in the 1770s, Highland Scots moved up the Cape Fear River basin and settled in the area of modern Aberdeen and Southern Pines. Although the

Sandhills, as the area is called, featured poor soil, it was rich in longleaf pines. The new arrivals set to work felling trees for naval stores—particularly for the Royal Navy.

The Deep River winds through the area, eventually curving in a horseshoe bend. High above this spot on a hilltop stands one of the oldest big houses in North Carolina Up Country, the "House in the Horseshoe." Built around 1772, it is also called the Alston House, after its builder and first owner.

Philip Alston was the son of Joseph John Alston and Elizabeth Chancy Alston, both natives of Halifax County, North Carolina. John was an extremely wealthy man; at his death his estate comprised more than one hundred fifty slaves and more than one thousand acres of land. Of this largesse, however, Philip's father left his son only those slaves he already possessed. Despite this setback, the younger Alston married the wealthy Temperance Smith (another Halifax native); her dowry included a large tract of land on the Roanoke River, which greatly increased her new husband's wealth.

So equipped, in 1772 Alston purchased four thousand acres north and south of the bend in Deep River. Soon afterward he built the magnificent house that still stands on its original site; he then built the palatial House in the Horseshoe. By 1777 his holdings would total 6,936 acres and a number of slaves. Alston was both the richest man and the biggest political power in the area, and so, not surprisingly, joined the Revolution. As a Lieutenant Colonel in the militia, he was in charge of suppressing all those loyal to the king in his region. As the loyalists were, in the beginning, mostly unarmed, this was an easy job. But it would not remain so.

Despite their lack of weaponry, organization, and support from regular troops of the Crown, as the war continued the loyalists eventually acquired all three—though never enough. But one of the loyalist leaders who emerged in the Up Country was one David Fanning.

As Alston was typical of Tarheel rebel leadership, so too was Fanning of the loyalists. Born in poverty on October 25, 1755, at the settlement of Birch (or Beech) Swamp, Amelia County, Virginia, David Fanning spent his early life in North Carolina. Being orphaned at the age of eight, he was bound to Needham Bryan (Bryant), a county justice who paid for his education. When Fanning was eighteen, he moved to Raeburn's Creek in the western section of South Carolina, to farm and trade with the Indians. When the war broke out, he was a company sergeant in the Upper Saluda militia of South Carolina. So divided was the area and the unit, that in July 1775 the company mustered "to see who was friends to the King and Government, and . . . who would Join the Rebellion."

Since the Up Country militia tended to support the Crown, the Council of Safety in Charleston sent a mission to persuade them to rebel. At first a truce prevailed; but when the rebels arrested a prominent loyalist and the rumors spread that the rebel Council was inciting the Indians to attack the loyalists, a struggle ensued. Under Major Joseph Robinson the loyal militia, including Fanning, besieged the rebels at Ninety-Six. On November 22, the latter surrendered the fort and its artillery. So frightened by this were the rebel leaders in both Carolinas that they mounted a large-scale rebel invasion into the South Carolina Up Country, defeating the loyalists at Big Cane Brake in December. Fanning fled to the Cherokee, with whom he had traded and who remained loyal to the king.

He returned to the Up Country after the rebel leadership published an amnesty for loyalists who did not fight against them. But when a group of rebel troops robbed him of his trade goods and roughed him up, he returned to rallying the king's friends. The rebels imprisoned him in January of 1776—the first of fourteen stretches in captivity over the next three years. Sometimes he was released; most often he made daring escapes, in a foreshadowing of his future adventures. But by 1779 the difficulties of his existence had shattered his health. Fanning returned home and agreed to remain neutral and even to guide rebel units through the woods upon request.

All this changed in 1780, when the soldiers of the Crown re-entered the province of South Carolina, taking Charleston on May 12. Fanning and other loyalists organized themselves into the "bloody scout," assisting the regular and provincial troops of the King over the next several months. Fighting between rebels and king's men became increasingly brutal, with atrocities committed on both sides; but by the end of October, the loyalists had lost the initiative. Faced with this reality, Fanning fled to North Carolina, and began recruiting followers to support an expected advance north by Lord Cornwallis.

As planned, in February 1781 Cornwallis raised the royal standard at Hillsborough, North Carolina, calling for local support. Fanning answered the call, even though the previous month the British general had informed him that he could not give him officer's rank. Even though Fanning recruited five hundred men, all but fifty were sent home due to an almost total lack of arms and provisions. But on July 5, he was appointed by Major James Henry Craig as colonel of the loyal militia of North Carolina's Chatham and Randolph Counties. For several months Fanning and his men conducted raids "in the interior parts of N. Carolina," the conflict continuing without pause after Cornwallis departed for Virginia in May.

His unfailing optimism and his personality made him popular among his men and his party; but in the next few months he was to prove himself both dashing and ruthless. Through his rapidity and secrecy he captured many prominent rebels, while hanging in reprisal those who had similarly dealt with loyalists. Fanning was here, there, and everywhere. On one occasion, he dashed into the village of Pittsborough, while court was in session; Fanning's militia carried off judges, lawyers, officers, and some of the citizens. Three weeks later, Fanning and Alston, respectively the fiercest proponents of their two causes, met at last.

Alston's men had been responsible for fighting loyalist irregulars in their local area. They captured Thomas Taylor, one of Fanning's lieutenants. Despite beating Taylor with musket butts, Alston and his crew left him to die. When Fanning discovered the murder, he swore revenge.

The House in the Horseshoe, then as now, was in an extremely defensible position. Alston felt completely safe, holed up as he was with thirty of his men on the morning of August 5, 1781; but his sense of security vanished quickly when Fanning and a much larger force rode up. The siege was on, and for five hours the bullets flew—many of the bullet holes remain in the walls. At last, Fanning decided to smoke the rebels out by setting the house on fire. A cart was duly filled with burning straw and set rolling against the wall of the house. Realizing that the attackers meant to burn down her home, Temperance Smith Alston quickly tied a pillowcase to a broomstick, and opened the front door. In exchange for the lives of those inside, Mrs. Alston offered surrender terms to Fanning.

However ruthless Fanning may have been with his enemies, toward the ladies—at least in this stage of his career—he was chivalrous. The Alstons left for another plantation of theirs in North Carolina, agreeing not to fight the forces of the king any longer. Alston sat out the rest of the conflict.

Not so for Fanning. Shortly afterward, at Hillsborough on September 12, he conducted a surprise raid with 1,220 loyal militia, took Governor Burke with his whole suite and more than two hundred prisoners. So hated was he by the rebels that he was specifically exempted from every offer of amnesty to loyalists, and after the war was one of three men excluded by name from the benefit of the general "act of pardon and oblivion" of offences committed during combat.

Fanning didn't care much, however, and continued the struggle long after the surrender of Cornwallis at Yorktown in October of 1781. By the spring of 1782, however, he decided to settle down, marrying Sarah Carr, a sixteen-year-old woman from Deep River, North Carolina. The couple arrived in June at refugee-filled

Charleston; in November, a month before the British evacuation of the city, they fled with other loyalists to St. Augustine, East Florida. But this haven did not last, as the Treaty of Paris ending the war returned the Floridas to Spain. After a short stop in Nassau in the Bahamas, the couple arrived in New Brunswick on September 23, 1784.

But happiness eluded him in his new home. He received very little money in compensation from the Crown; while he served in the House of the Assembly for ten years starting in 1791, and did a great deal of important work there, his switching of parties halfway through did little to advance his career. Worse, he was the first member of the New Brunswick assembly expelled for a felony conviction. The felony in question—rape of a minor—was undoubtedly trumped up: Fanning had made many enemies. At last, the governor pardoned and exiled him, and he died at Digby, Nova Scotia, in 1827.

Fanning's post-battle career was weirdly paralleled by Alston's. Although he had served as a lieutenant colonel in the state militia, a justice of the peace, and a state senator, Alston was constantly accused of corruption. He was twice indicted for murder (Thomas Taylor's was one of these, for which he was pardoned by the governor of North Carolina), removed as justice of the peace, and suspended from the state legislature. In 1789 he was imprisoned for the murder of a political rival, but in December 1790 Alston escaped from the Wilmington jail and fled North Carolina to Georgia. He was shot the next year through a window as he lay in bed; his family shortly afterwards sold his property (including the House in the Horseshoe) and left the state.

The Alstons and Fanning were very strong characters in their own right, whose paths crossed at a crucial time in American history. There was one more individual, however, to leave his mark on the house: Governor Benjamin Williams. Four-time governor of North Carolina, colonel under George Washington, member of the first board of trustees of the University of North Carolina, and member of the national congress at Philadelphia, Williams greatly expanded the house, adding two wings containing a kitchen and a master bedroom. He also turned the property into a slave-run cotton plantation. Dying in 1814, he is buried on the plantation grounds. His family owned the house until 1853. Several different owners succeeded one another, until 1954, when it was purchased and restored by the Moore County Historical Association. In 1955 the state acquired the site.

Despite all the drama that has taken place within its walls, the house remains fairly unchanged. It is a two-story frame plantation house with a gable roof, large double-shouldered Flemish bond chimneys, and a shed porch. The woodwork is fine, and the interior boasts late colonial and early Federal-period pieces.

It is a popular tourist stop. But as might be expected from the history of the house, it does not appear to be uninhabited—on a permanent basis. When I attended California State University, Northridge, I read a paperback book by a former occupant of the house. Describing events several decades old, the author made the place sound very eerie, indeed.

But even today, pitched vibrations, footsteps, and whispering in the fireplace have been heard, and an orb lifting high into the air has been seen.

House in the Horseshoe
324 Alston House Road
Sanford, NC 27330
(910) 947-2051

A French Nobleman Remains in His North Dakota Chateau

Nor th Dakota is one of our remoter states, best known to outsiders through the dubious medium of the film *Fargo*. But
there really is a lot to be seen there, from the Black Hills to the
Prairies. Of course, it is known as the birthplace of Lawrence Welk;
but there are also rather less conventional interests.

The first inhabitants were, of course, the Indians. When the
first Europeans arrived, the Dakota or Lakota (Sioux), Assiniboine, Cheyenne, Mandan, Hidatsa, and Arikara were encamped.
Groups of Chippewa moved into the northern Red River Valley
around 1800, while Cree, Blackfoot, and Crow hunted the western
buffalo ranges. As was typical among the first nations everywhere
in North America, they invested the landscape with tales of gods
and heroes, witchcraft and demons. But none of these stories prepared them for the arrival of their new neighbors.

The French had claimed all the lands drained by the Mississippi;
the area west of that river they named "Louisiana," after King Louis

XIV. But none up of them explored their claims as far as North Dakota until 1738, when the Sieur de La Verendrye reached the Missouri River from Canada while searching for a water route to the Pacific Ocean. Others were to follow; these would include La Verendrye's sons four years later.

Remote as the region was, the fur trade linked it to a worldwide economic and political system. In 1763, the Treaty of Paris gave all French lands drained by Hudson's Bay to Great Britain, including the country drained by the Red River of the North. To prevent their falling to the British, France had given Louisiana to Spain one year earlier; this area would be returned to France in 1800. Three years later, Napoleon Bonaparte sold Louisiana to the United States. This sale, known as the Louisiana Purchase, made western North Dakota American territory. The eastern part remained in British hands; fur and other trade there were firmly in the hands of the Hudson's Bay Company.

In 1812, Irish and Scots colonists led by the Earl of Selkirk founded Pembina, the permanent European settlement in North Dakota. Pembina would also serve as the center for a network of communities of *Métis*, the mixed French, Scots, and Indian people who arose from the HBC traders' marriages with native women. Not surprisingly, four years later at Pembina, Frs. Dumoulin and Provencher opened the first Catholic church in North Dakota; attached to it was the first school, taught by William Edge. The same year, the United States acquired eastern North Dakota by treaty with England. In 1823 an expedition led by General Stephen H. Long surveyed the official boundary between the United States and British North America at a point north of Pembina. Most of Lord Selkirk's colonists evacuated Pembina, and moved up the Red River to British territory. The Métis remained behind, however, serving as intermediaries between the new authorities and the Indians.

American traders, explorers, and military personnel in the Northern Plains became ever more numerous during the early nineteenth century, although relations between the newcomers and the Indians remained peaceful, due in no small part to the work of the latter's Métis cousins and Catholic missionaries. The Indians themselves became key players in the fur trade, centering on such trading posts as Fort Union and Fort Clark. In exchange for meat and furs, the Indians received guns, metal tools, cloth and beads, and other trade goods.

All of this interaction did little to change the folklore of the Plains people, Indian or half-breed. But the Americans came with an important legend of their own: that of Prince Madoc. Supposedly, in the twelfth century this Welsh Prince had brought colonists from his native land to Mobile Bay in Alabama (the D.A.R. erected a plaque there to commemorate this event). It was said that these Welshmen brought their cattle and implements to Kentucky; after some centuries of peaceful living, they were driven west by the Cherokee, and fled up the Mississippi to the Missouri River. Following it north, they met and merged with the Mandan Tribe in North Dakota. Although conventional historians have long discounted the story, even today it has vociferous defenders. George Catlin, the nineteenth-century chronicler of the Mandans, was a strong proponent of it, composing lists of words common or similar in the Welsh and Mandan languages. Various Mandan customs and legends were pointed out as proof of the tale, as was the appearance (lighter and taller than many of the neighboring Indian tribes) of many of them. In recent years, partisans of Prince Madoc have pointed to such anomalies as the discovery of Roman coins (still in circulation in medieval Wales) as further evidence.

Even if the story is true, the Mandan's Welsh blood did not save them from the damage contact with the Americans did to the Plains tribes. In 1837 smallpox virtually wiped out the Mandan at Fort Clark. They amalgamated with the neighboring Arikara and Hidatsa tribe, an arrangement that has lasted to the present at the three nations' reservation of Fort Berthold.

Even so, peace between Indians and Americans in North Dakota would last until the outbreak of the Civil War. The Santee Sioux of Minnesota revolted in a bloody uprising in 1862. Although this was put down by the U.S. Army, military columns searched the Northern Plains for fleeing Minnesota tribesmen. Although the three tribes and the Chippewa remained neutral, battles between the army and the Sioux at Whitestone Hill in 1863 and at Killdeer Mountain and in the Badlands in 1864 broke Sioux opposition. Many accepted confinement on reservations to avoid starvation. A chain of military outposts was established, beginning with Fort Abercrombie in 1857—a place today believed to be haunted. The great slaughter of the northern bison herds after 1870 caused the nomadic tribes of western North Dakota to submit.

It was from Ft. Abraham Lincoln, near Bismarck, that units of the Seventh Cavalry commanded by Lt. Col. George A. Custer left in 1876 to search for Indians who would not move onto reservations. The massacre of Custer's men at the Little Big Horn River in Montana, while it made household names of such figures as Crazy Horse, Gall, and Sitting Bull, did not affect the final outcome. Many Sioux fled to Canada to escape the Army; back in the states, the last Sioux finally surrendered at Fort Buford in 1881. The last gasp of independent Indian religion and politics came with the massacre of the "Ghost Dancers" in 1898.

But the Indian hold on the Dakotas was doomed long before. In 1861, Dakota Territory was organized by the United States Congress. Settlers began to pour in when the westbound Northern Pacific Railway was built to the Missouri River in 1872 and 1873. Along and near the rail line, new towns sprang up to serve settlers and crews. Fargo and Bismarck, as an example, both began as railroad communities. The Federal Homestead Law of 1862 impelled farming settlement after the first claim west of the Red River was filed in 1868.

More than 100,000 people entered the territory between 1879 and 1886. Most took up homesteads, although large, highly mechanized, well-financed "Bonanza" farms were opened by a wealthy few. Even though some of these, such as the Dalrymple and Grandin spreads, lasted into the twentieth century, most failed spectacularly. Nevertheless, thanks to this growth, on November 2, 1889, President Benjamin Harrison approved the admission of North Dakota to the United States.

From 1905 to 1920 (when rigid immigration quotas were enacted) a second settlement boom occurred, increasing North Dakota's population from 190,983 to 646,872. Although many were immigrants of Scandinavian (especially Norwegian) or German (such as the parents of Lawrence Welk) derivation, a group of Scotch-Irish-English descent comprised many of North Dakota's early business and political leaders. By 1915 more than 79 percent of all North Dakotans were either immigrants or their children.

One group that has, as we have seen, played a part out of all proportion to their numbers in North Dakota history, is the French. From the first explorers, to missionaries and traders, and then with the Métis, Francophones spearheaded every stage of the state's early development. The same would happen with the period of the "Bonanza" farms.

In 1883, Medora, North Dakota was already a bustling cattle town. The year before, there arrived in America a handsome, spirited French nobleman, Antoine Amadee, Marquis de Mores. Of Spanish descent, he was born in Paris in 1858, and graduated from the Military College of St. Cyr, where he was a close friend of the future Marshal Petain, in 1881. It was in the next year that he married the rich and charming Medora von Hoffman of New York, daughter of a German-American banker and nobleman. The duo resolved to return to the new marquis's homeland. The marquis made a hunting trip out west, and, with characteristic dash, decided to build a packing plant in the cattle country to capitalize on the advantage of avoiding shipping live animals to eastern abattoirs. Wealthy in his own right and backed by his millionaire father-in-law, de Mores came to the wild badlands to build the plant that was to be the center of operations for the Northern Pacific Refrigerator Car Company. De Mores bought the land around the plant upon which was to spring the town of Medora. St. Mary's Catholic Church, one of the oldest in North Dakota, and also the Von Hoffman house, which was built for Medora's mother and father, still stand in the town of Medora today.

The marquis's most striking legacy is the rustic but aristocratic twenty-six-room home that his neighbors dubbed "the chateau." Overlooking his town and enterprises, the frame home was ready for Medora Von Hoffman's arrival in spring 1884. Rich furnishings, oriental carpets, and fine accoutrements accommodated the family and their wealthy guests, including Theodore Roosevelt. The couple's two children, Athenais and Louis, as well as nurses, maids, and other domestic help, accompanied them to Medora. For three years, the family occupied the home seasonally, returning to New York during the winters. Among their pastimes were hunting, music, and art, common diversions of nineteenth-century aristocrats. Both Medora and the marquis were skilled hunters.

Unhappily, the marquis had only grass to feed his cattle, thus meaning his work was restricted to certain seasons. Easterners consistently undersold him, and one disaster after another struck both this business and the stage line he attempted to found. Many of his neighbors resented his nobility. With all of these troubles and scrapes with the law, in 1886 he closed his plant's doors and returned to Europe.

Three more years were spent in Tonkin, in French Indo-China, trying to promote a railroad. The irrepressible marquis once again accepted defeat and returned to France. From 1889 on, he was much involved in Royalist politics and Catholic social work, opening bistros to give workers free refreshments, food subsidies, and easy credit to the poor. He left France for Algeria in 1894, and was killed at the age of thirty-eight by Tuaregs on June

9, 1896; this was near El Aoutia in Tunisia, while he attempted to pioneer a way across the Sahara.

Nevertheless, the marquis's mark has remained strong on the town. St. Mary's Church, originally named the "Athenais Chapel," after the couple's daughter, was built for the marquis by her husband in 1884. It was presented to the village in 1920 by the de Mores family, and is still in use by the Catholic community. The statue of the Marquis de Mores, on Main Street, was erected by the family in 1926. It stands in a small plot that is part of de Mores State Park, three tracts comprising about 128 acres, deeded to the State Historical Society of North Dakota in 1936 by Louis, Count de Vallombrosa, eldest son of the marquis.

But now as then, the center of the de Mores legacy in Medora is the Chateau. It is now a historic house museum and contains many of the original furnishings and personal effects of the de Mores family. Here the drama surrounding the rise and fall of the family's prospects was played out. The marquis always intended to return at some point, but died without ever doing so. Many who visit the home report a feeling of being watched; some have encountered cold spots. Passersby have claimed to see lights on in the old home, long after it has been closed for the night. Could it be that the marquis made it back after all? Or is it the marquis himself, preferring the plains of North Dakota to the Tonkin jungles or the deserts of North Africa? Or is it someone else whose life was caught up in the ruin of the family, or who came there afterwards? We don't know; but what is certain is that a visit here will link you to a strange but intriguing chapter of North Dakota and United States history; and, it might just be a rather spirited visit.

Chateau de Mores
612 East Boulevard Avenue
Bismarck, ND 58505
(701) 328-6266

In Ohio, a Priest
Haunts His Church

Ohio, the "Buckeye State," although nominally under French
rule for over a century, received no permanent European settlers until after the area passed to the United States in 1783.
In 1749 a couple of Jesuit missionaries had settled near present-
day Sandusky, but they were forced to leave three years later
when their order was suppressed. In 1790 a colony of Frenchmen
settled at Gallipolis on the Ohio; Dom Pierre Joseph Didier, a
Benedictine monk, built a church. The colony broke up after a
few years, however, and the parish was not reestablished until
1852. Five years after Gallipolis's birth, Fr. Edmund Burke, a sec-
ular priest from Quebec, became chaplain of the U.S. Army post
at Fort Meigs, near the present site of Maumee. He remained
there until February 1797, ministering to the Catholic soldiers at
the fort, and trying to evangelize the local Ottawa and Chippewa
Indians. Catholicism would have to wait over a decade to get
firmly established in Ohio.

Of course, that was true of most of the United States after the Revolution. Before independence, Catholicism had been illegal in ten of the thirteen colonies. In the territories acquired by the British from France and Spain in 1763, it was confined to a few struggling settlements. But the assistance given by those two countries to the rebels made the freeing of Catholic Americans from legal disabilities imperative (even though the Declaration of Independence denounced the king for giving his new French subjects in Quebec and the Old Northwest religious freedom).

In any case, civilian settlements of any religion in the Ohio area were not possible until after the local Indians were militarily defeated and pushed out of most of the state in 1798. But across the Ohio in Kentucky, settlers had been pouring in from the east since the Revolution. Many of these were Catholics from Maryland. By 1800, a single priest had been sent to minister to them, one Fr. Stephen T. Badin, a refugee from the French Revolution. More were needed; Pope Pius VII decided that it was time for the Dominican Order to make its home in the United States. In 1806, Fr. Edward Dominic Fenwick, O.P., was sent to Kentucky with three other Dominicans to found a priory of his order. They settled in Washington County, where they founded St. Rose of Lima Priory.

In Ohio, by this time, settlers of many nationalities and faiths were coming in. Jacob Dittoe, a German Catholic, had settled near Somerset, Ohio. There he and about twenty of his countrymen had carved out farms from the wilderness. Dittoe wrote to Bishop Flaget of Bardstown and to Fr. Fenwick asking for priests. In response, en route to visiting Baltimore, Bishop Flaget and Father Badin crossed the Ohio River at Maysville, Kentucky, in 1812. There they encountered another German Catholic whose four children they baptized. On their way to Somerset the two clerics met the Dittoe and Fink families, for whom they celebrated Mass and heard confessions.

Since, by the autumn of 1816, several more priests had been ordained for Kentucky, Fr. Fenwick began spending more and more time in Ohio. In response, Jacob Dittoe and his Somerset neighbors built the first Catholic church in Ohio. Nothing grand, it was a one-story, log house with bare ground as a floor. Near this chapel was erected another log house of two rooms to serve as a rectory for the missionaries. It was blessed by Fathers Fenwick and Young on December 6, 1818.

Although both laypeople and priests were out in the depths of the frontier, and must have felt very isolated from the great world beyond, that world was aware of them. A truly royal gift arrived at the church: a chalice given by King Ferdinand VII of Spain. This was a sign of things to come. More Catholic settlers of various nationalities arrived: German, Irish, and Alsatians. They all worshipped at the church.

The numbers of Dominicans also grew, and in time St. Joseph's became an independent priory. In 1828, a new brick church with a steeple was built; in 1843 this church, too, was replaced with a Gothic church, equipped with a spire 160 feet high. A fire destroyed that one too in 1864—the present structure was built a few years later. Joseph Sadoc Alemany, O.P., one of the Dominicans, while in Cuba picked up the crucifix that hangs over the altar today. He eventually became the first bishop of Monterey, California, and then the first archbishop of San Francisco (and my high school, in Mission Hills, California, was named after him!).

Although St. Joseph's was reduced to a simple parish in 1925, it has hosted a Dominican parish until the present day. The church has witnessed many important and some peculiar historical episodes in its day, but one in particular was unearthly.

A certain priest died, and shortly after was seen roaming the halls of the now-demolished priory buildings. He would be seen standing at the foot of his erstwhile brothers' beds, and even in the sacristy while they were preparing to say Mass. The ghost then started extinguishing the candles at the altar. At length he did this so often that the priests were unable to keep them lit. The Dominicans feared that the dead priest must be guilty of some great sin; but eventually all the Masses were offered for which the decedent had accepted stipends but which he'd failed to offer prior to his death. The ghost was never seen again.

This is a not uncommon sort of haunting in Catholic circles. In his *Ghost Book*, Sir Shane Leslie tells the story of the pastor of St. Patrick's, Plumstead, in South London. After Fr. Arthur Staunton died in 1913, the other priests there were troubled every night for about a year and a half by strange noises in the rectory. The new pastor, Fr. Daniel McCarthy, felt that it was Fr. Staunton making the sounds, and that he wanted something to be done that he had left undone. Whenever McCarthy went on vacation, the sounds would stop, only to break out again on his return. Looking into the matter, he discovered the will of an old lady in the parish, which directed that after her death Fr. Staunton was to say ten Masses for her and her husband. She had died eighteen months before, at the time the noises were first heard. The Masses were said at once and the noises ceased. As Sir Shane concludes the account, "The ghost came back again on the following Christmas night and it was an expression of joy and thankfulness. The omission of the Masses was not through Father Staunton's fault as he was an invalid for a year before he died and had in fact survived the Testatrix by several months."

Just as the king of Spain's gift to St. Joseph's at its birth showed its connection to the Church around the world, so too does the resemblance of the parish's ghost to such as Fr. Staunton. But in 1994, thieves took four chalices from the church, including Ferdinand VII's. One can only hope that the perpetrators of this crime are being haunted even now. In any case, if ever you are in the area, stop by and say a prayer for the departed cleric. Who knows? He might do the same for you!

Saint Joseph Rectory
5757 State Route 383, N.E.
P.O. Box 190
Somerset, OH 43783
(740) 743-1317

The Spirits of the Old West
Live On in an Oklahoma Theater

When the Louisiana Purchase was acquired by the United States in 1803, it was thought that the wilderness beyond St. Louis in what is now Missouri was so wide and trackless as to remain forever unsettled. Of course, in 1763 George III had thought the same of the sprawling lands between the Appalachians and the Mississippi, which he acquired that year from the French. Both the king and President Thomas Jefferson had the same idea—turn the vast area just acquired into a permanent refuge for Indians driven ever westward by the pressures of settlement. George III refused to open his new lands to European settlement, and this was one of the contributing factors to the Revolution that cost him the crown of America.

Successive United States administrations were much more flexible, and steadily eroded the frontiers of the "Indian Territory" from the whole Louisiana Purchase north and west of Missouri and Arkansas, down to just Nebraska, Kansas, and Oklahoma. By

1860, only Oklahoma (less the Panhandle) remained as "Indian Territory." Most of the state was occupied by the "Five Civilized Tribes"—Choctaw, Chickasaw, Creek, Cherokee, and Seminole—who had been driven out of their homes in the southeastern states by Andrew Jackson (in defiance of the Supreme Court). The extreme northeast corner of Oklahoma, however, was in the hands of a number of smaller tribes who had been pushed out of Illinois, Indiana, Ohio, and New York.

To punish them for siding with the Confederacy (they were southerners, after all), the Five Civilized Tribes had the western half of Indian Territory confiscated from them. It was supposed to be given to still other tribes being expelled from their own homes, and much of it was. But the "Cherokee Strip" in the northwest of the state, Greer County in the southwest, and the central section around modern Oklahoma City, were opened successively to settlers. Then the newly arrived tribes were deprived of their lands. At last, in 1907, what remained of Indian Territory was amalgamated with the newcomers' Oklahoma Territory to form the modern state of Oklahoma. The last remnant of Jefferson's vision of a region completely given over to the tribes was snuffed out, 104 years after it was first dreamed.

But a new dream was being born as the old one was dying. As successive parcels of Oklahoma Territory were opened up to settlers, the famous "land rushes" were held. Settlers in wagons would line up at the border of the newly opened area, and as soon as a gun was fired, signaling the opening, the settlers literally rushed in, and staked their claims to whatever parcels of land they could. These dramatic episodes were dramatized by Tom Cruise and Nicole Kidman in the fairly forgettable film *Far and Away*.

Pawhuska, Oklahoma, is the capital of the Osage Nation. This tribe actually was already in Oklahoma when it was granted to the Five Civilized Tribes; but their current territory, Osage County, had to be bought back in 1871 from the Cherokee. The city owes its name to the famous Osage chief, Pahu-cka—"White Hair." He was given this name as a result of his part in St. Clair's Defeat in Ohio, in 1792. The young brave wounded an American officer who was wearing a powdered wig in accordance with the style of the time. As the Indian started scalping his quarry, the wig came off in his hand. While his would-be scalper stared at his quarry, the officer made off. Pahu-cka thus won both an unbloody scalp and a name for himself.

Unlike most tribes in the United States (at least, prior to Indian gaming), the Osage are far from poor. Since the tribe retained its mineral rights in the county, they became the richest people per capita in the world during the 1920s' oil boom. It is not uncommon to notice many of the Osage wearing diamonds in their ears.

Even before the oil strike, the Osage were always friendly to the newcomers. After they staked out their own county, they allowed Americans to visit, live, and work on their territory. Of course, not all of these have been welcome guests: Jesse James, Belle Starr, and Bill Doolin all hid out in the hills around Pawhuska. At various times figures from politics or Hollywood, such as Herbert Hoover, Tom Mix, Clark Gable, Bob Wills, and Ben Johnson have stayed there, as well as such oilmen as Frank Phillips and Jean Paul Getty. Back in the 1920s, the oil tycoons would sit under the "Million Dollar Elm" in Pawhuska, bidding for Osage oil leases that helped make their fortunes.

Curiously enough, Pawhuska boasts the first Boy Scout troop in the United States—predating the organization of the Boy Scouts of America. In May of 1909, Reverend John F. Mitchell, an Anglican missionary priest from England (who had worked with Lord Baden-Powell there, the founder of scouting), was sent to St. Thomas Episcopal Church by the Church of England. Reverend Mitchell organized a troop of Boy Scouts under an English charter, equipping them with English uniforms and manuals. A life-sized bronze statue in front of the Osage County Historical

Museum honors Reverend Mitchell and the nineteen charter members of the troop. When the BSA was organized, the Pawhuska troop joined the organization, receiving the title of Troop No. 1; this lasted until the Cherokee Area Council of Boy Scouts was formed in Bartlesville, Pawhuska. Renumbered Troop No. 33, the Pawhuska troop remains the original Boy Scout troop in America.

In the 1880s, travelers were numerous enough in town to require a proper hotel. The Pawhuska House Hotel was the result, an island of elegance in the Osage nation. But a community requires more than accommodation to be called a great city; it requires culture. In 1911, a Greek immigrant named George C. C. Constantine bought the building, transforming it into the elegant Constantine Theater. It was his dream to make his theater the grandest venue in the west. Unfortunately, over time, the grand old edifice fell into disrepair.

In 1987, a local group led by Eileen Monger began renovation. Now more than 90 percent complete, the Constantine boasts a live stage in Greek Revival style as well as a seating capacity of 589. It is listed on the National Register of Historic Places and with the National League of Historic Theatres. The theater now hosts wedding receptions, art exhibits, concerts, and much else. Group tours may be arranged with docents in period costume. But apparently they are not the only images of the past present. As with so many theaters, the Constantine is haunted.

Apparently, the hauntings fall into two groups. One seems to date from the days when the building was the Pawhuska House Hotel. The phantoms of old cowboys are heard fighting and hitting each other with their fists in the old theater; moreover, objects sometimes fly through the air. In a town where one of the Dalton boys was once sheriff, it can't be too surprising that some nights at the hotel were raucous, and some of that activity seems to linger. A few people report surges of uncontrollable anger in the building.

But there seems to be a gentler, feminine presence as well. This is said to be Sappho Constantine Brown, Constantine's beautiful daughter. While the restoration was going on, workmen heard phantom footsteps and saw an apparition of the girl. Her restful presence (in life she was a choir member at St. Thomas's Episcopal Church in Pawhuska) provides a striking contrast to her rowdy housemates.

So if you get anywhere near Pawhuska, be sure to go to the Constantine and take in a tour or a show. But if it's ghosts you're after, you'll be better off having a quiet evening with Mrs. Brown than a night out with those particular boys.

Constantine Theater
110 West Main
Pawhuska, OK 74056
(918) 287-4158

A Betrayed Public Benefactor
Wanders His Home in Oregon

European settlement came late to Oregon. In common with the adjoining sections of Washington, the Indians of the forested western part of the state had many strange legends, such as that of the Sasquatch, or Bigfoot, which story has survived among Indian and newcomer alike to the present day. Although Russia and Spain both claimed Oregon by virtue of maritime exploration, neither nation established settlements.

In 1806, however, a British trading post was set up by Simon Fraser of the North West Company, on today's Fraser Lake, near the Fifty-fourth parallel. John Jacob Astor's American Fur Company set up a post at Astoria, at the mouth of the Columbia River, in 1811. But hardly had it begun operations when the War of 1812 broke out; the Astorians received word the next year that a Royal Navy force was en route to take possession of the mouth of the Columbia. This news was brought by agents of the North West Company, who offered to buy Astoria at a reasonable value. Fearing confiscation if he delayed, the American factor accepted the offer, and the post was renamed Fort George by its new owners.

Astoria was restored to American ownership in 1818, and the United States and Great Britain agreed to a ten-year's joint occupancy of the "Oregon Country," as the region encompassing modern Oregon, Washington, southern British Columbia, and Idaho came to be called. Spanish claims in the nebulous southern area were eliminated a year later, when the boundary was fixed at the Forty-second parallel; and Russia in 1824 renounced all interest below 54'40. After its purchase of Astoria in 1813, the North West Company continued to control the fur trade in Oregon until 1821, when it was merged with its London-based rival, the Hudson's Bay Company. Soon thereafter American traders and trappers began to push westward beyond the Rockies into the rich domain of the British fur traffic. Their frequent clashes with the men of the Hudson's Bay Company together with the beginnings of organized immigration to the Oregon Country brought American Power increasingly to the fore. By the late 1830s many Americans were demanding in bellicose tones that Great Britain should relinquish all jurisdiction south of 54'40, and "Fifty-four forty or fight" proved a popular slogan in James K. Polk's presidential election campaign.

The treaty of joint control was in effect when Dr. John McLoughlin, destined to be the most powerful individual in the territory for twenty years, came down the Columbia to Fort George. Appointed Chief Factor of the Hudson's Bay Company in 1824, within a year he built Fort Vancouver on the north side of the Columbia River, a few miles east of the Willamette. Six-feet-two, beaver-hatted, already white-haired at forty, McLoughlin knew how to control his half-wild white trappers; he made beaver-hunting vassals of the Indians and for a long time succeeded in outdoing all competition—though many of his competitors were given places in the Georgian mahogany chairs at his table. With Fort Vancouver as capital, he was ruler of a vast domain stretching from California to Alaska and from the Rocky Mountains to the sea. In his period of office he employed many French-Canadians who, when their terms of service expired, settled on French Prairie in Marion County, where their descendants can be found today.

Until early in the 1840s there was no local government in the Oregon Country except that of the Hudson's Bay Company, which exercised feudal rights derived from the British Crown. McLoughlin enjoyed the protection of British laws in the conduct of his company's affairs, but Americans in the region were for the most part ignored by successive administrations at Washington. Despite his misgivings concerning the effect of their arrival on the business of the Hudson's Bay Company, Dr. McLoughlin had aided the newcomers with credit and counsel. In 1845, however, the Company forced him to resign, and his influence on the development of the area came to an end.

The issue of ownership of the Oregon Country was settled in 1846, when the two countries compromised on a boundary along the Forty-ninth parallel, and the Oregon Country between that and the Forty-second parallel on the south became undisputed American soil.

European occupancy of Oregon City, in an area that the Hudson's Bay Company did not want settled, was forced upon the company, because of the pending boundary settlement between the United States and Great Britain. "It becomes an important object to acquire as ample an occupation of the Country and Trade as possible," company officials wrote in 1828, "on the South as well as the North side of the Columbia River, looking always to the Northern side falling to our Share on a division, and to secure this, it may be as well to have something to give up on the South when the final arrangement comes to be made." Dr. McLoughlin was ordered to set up a sawmill at "the falls of the

Wilhamet (south of the Columbia) where the same Establishment of people can attend to the Mill, watch the Fur & Salmon Trade, and take care of a Stock of Cattle."

Three log houses were built on the site of Oregon City in the winter of 1829–30, and potatoes planted in the spring. The Indians, resenting this infringement of their territory, burned the houses. A flourmill and sawmill constructed in 1832 made use of the first water power in Oregon. Bad feelings quickly developed between encroaching American settlers and the already emplaced Hudson's Bay Company, and in 1841 a group of Methodist missionaries organized a milling company occupying an island below the falls, opposite the property claimed by Dr. McLoughlin; later they built on shore, directly on his property. In order to forestall this trespass, Dr. McLoughlin the following year named the town and had it platted. In 1846, of course, it passed with the rest of the southern Oregon Territory to the United States.

Born at Riviere-du-Loup, in the province of Quebec, on October 18, 1784, Dr. McLoughlin was of Irish, Scottish, and French descent. He began practicing as a doctor before he joined the HBC. From his headquarters at Fort Vancouver, the tall, white-haired gentleman with the cane had ruled in a kindly, paternal manner over the whole Columbia country. He ruthlessly but openly crushed competition in the fur trade, was generous to destitute immigrants regardless of their nationality, enforced prohibition of liquor among the Indians, and preserved peace between Indian and European. McLoughlin always treated his wife, Marguerite Wadin McKay, with great deference, even though she was part Indian. More than once he rebuked a colonist for "your manners before ladies," when the miscreant failed to remove his hat in her presence. But all of this ended when he resigned as factor.

Dr. McLoughlin moved to Oregon City after his resignation, paying his former employers $20,000 for the land that he had claimed in Oregon City on the company's behalf in 1829. But the change in government the next year meant that he had to start again. His British citizenship, Catholic faith in a Protestant country, and comparative wealth prevented his election to public office; the U.S. Congress ordered much of his property seized because he was an alien. Nevertheless, he remained a remarkably generous man, serving as the community's doctor, mayor, and investor. The doctor built himself a new career promoting the economic prosperity of the territory he had helped to establish. In gratitude for his help in building it, when a Catholic church was built at Oregon City in 1846 to serve as a cathedral for the region, it was named St. John the Apostle after his patron saint.

In 1851, Dr. McLoughlin took out American citizenship; his new fellow citizens elected him mayor of Oregon City. He and his wife were once again known for their hospitality and their support of the community. A supporter of small business as a means for helping emigrants become established, he loaned money for commercial ventures. Nevertheless, although the doctor owned sawmills, a gristmill, a granary, a general store, and a shipping concern, and donated land for schools and churches, he became cash poor. The community he had helped establish ignored him, and Dr. McLoughlin spent his embittered last few years operating his store while attempting to collect from those who had obtained seed and supplies from him during the time he was chief factor and then mayor.

Shortly after Dr. McLoughlin arrived in Oregon City, he built an elegant home at the south end of town, near the falls. It was and is a rectangular two-story structure with simple, dignified lines, characteristic of early Oregon architecture. The lumber used in construction was cut locally, but doors and windows were shipped around the Horn from the east. So too was much of Dr, McLoughlin's original furniture, which remains in the house. He died in the house on September 3, 1857; three years later his wife followed him to the grave.

At first, the doctor's residence went through neglect and abuse reminiscent of that which had haunted its builder. After Dr. McLoughlin's death, the home was turned into a camp for Chinese laborers and later a whorehouse. At last, in 1909, the much-abused old structure faced the wrecking ball.

At long last, however, local opinion woke up. The McLoughlin Memorial Association was formed; money was raised to move the house to a public park atop the bluff. Ironically, this lot was one of the places set aside by McLoughlin for public use when he laid out the town in the 1840s. In 1910, the home opened as a museum. Twenty-one years later, congress designated the McLoughlin House a National Historic Site, the first in the west. For many years, all went well in the happily restored old house, serving as a memorial to the doctor and giving him the recognition he so well deserved and had been denied in life.

This was to change. Dr. McLoughlin and his wife had been buried side-by-side next to the church named in his honor, and which he had done so much for. It is extremely important to Catholics to be buried in consecrated ground. But in the 1970s, someone had the bright idea of moving the graves of McLoughlin and his wife to the house's new location.

It was then that the doctor began to walk. Not only has his tall shadow, but also Dr. McLoughlin himself has been seen walking through the upstairs hall and bedroom of this old mansion; objects move without aid, while disembodied footsteps are heard on the stairway and upstairs. One staff woman, entering the front door, heard someone vacuuming upstairs; she saw a tall shadow come down the stairs, making heavy footsteps as it came. It swept around the corner, from the bottom of the staircase, into the dining room where a harpsichord played. The shadow ducked to enter the dining room. Every September 3, about 9:35 AM (the date and time of the doctor's death) his portrait above the downstairs fireplace is struck by the sun, and radiates a brilliant golden aura.

Nor is he the only revenant to stalk the mansion. Many people have seen the ghost of a female apparition out of the southeast second-floor window. Mrs. McLoughlin smoked pipe tobacco; while working in an upstairs bedroom, another lady on the staff smelled pipe tobacco. The fragrance followed her around as she worked, leading her to suppose that the lady of the house was supervising her actions. There are others who make their appearance, including a phantom dog that races through the first floor halls. The memory of the "Father of Oregon" is certainly worth honoring; perhaps his own wishes regarding his and his wife's last resting place ought to be as well. In the meantime, it would be well worth visiting his current haunts—and possibly stopping by St. John's Catholic Church to say a quick prayer for them as well.

The McLoughlin House
713 Center Street
Oregon City, OR 97045
(503) 656-5146

Haunting Stays in the Family at a Pennsylvania Ancestral Mansion

T he "Keystone State," as Pennsylvania is called, has a most intriguing history, which in turn has given birth to very strange folklore. It is of course renowned as the cradle of national independence. But there is far more to Pennsylvania's history than memories of Jefferson and Franklin. Granted in 1681 by King Charles II to William Penn, in repayment of the financial debt owed Penn's father by His Majesty, the state was founded as a refuge for unpopular religions—Penn was a Quaker, at the time a much-despised sect. In typical colonial fashion, the Appalachian sections of the Province were settled by Ulster Scots, the country farther east by Germans (Catholic, Lutheran, Mennonite, Amish, Moravians, and Reformed), and the capital—Philadelphia—and its environs by a dizzying complex of nationalities and beliefs. Due to its freedom of religion, Pennsylvania played host to the first Catholic church built legally in English-speaking lands since the Reformation: Old St. Mary's, erected in 1733 in Philadelphia. But less conventional faiths came to rest here also.

In June of 1696, a band of religious refugees from Germany reached Philadelphia by ship. In their homeland, they had been accused of heresy and occult practice. Their leader was a young scholar named John Kelpius. Their arrival date was St. John's Eve (June 23), a legendary night of magic in European folklore. Called the "Mystic Brotherhood," they ascended the highlands northwest of the city. With them they carried branches of St. Johnswort. They wove it into garlands, and then built bonfires, around which they danced and sang. When the moon was at its highest, the Mystic Brethren of both sexes cast their garlands into the fires, and then set burning logs rolling down the hillside. Normal enough customs in Europe at the time (and still surviving in some places there today), these activities seemed rather odd to the local Quakers. Kelpius and his followers were Pietist Christians, inspired by the visions of Jakob Boehme. But they also drew inspiration from the shadowy Rosicrucian movement, and practiced healing, magic, divining, and horoscope-casting. The weird side of Pennsylvania's history was well and truly started.

It has been rather unkindly said that Pennsylvania boasts two great modern cities, Philadelphia and Pittsburgh, separated by Alabama. While this is a bit of an exaggeration, the descendants of the Ulster Scots in the hills, and the Pennsylvania Dutch east of them (who, with the Cajuns of Louisiana and the Hispanos of New Mexico are unique as colonial-era groups who have more or less successfully maintained their own culture and language) retain a great deal of strange folklore.

The latter group is well known for a subset within their number, the modernity-resisting Amish. Amish and non-Amish Pennsylvania Dutch are very careful to protect their homes and barns with "hex signs." But these protections against evil are only the tip of the iceberg: Pennsylvania Dutch Country is rife with stories of witchcraft, ghosts, and magic. The area even has a magical handbook of its own: *Powwows; or the Long Lost Friend*,

first published in 1819 by one John George Hohman. A Catholic
born in Germany, his activities in Pennsylvania stretch from
1802 (when he arrived in Reading, Pennsylvania from his homeland) to 1857, though we are unsure of his actual birth and
death. He set up as a teacher and practitioner of folk magic, for
which there was a market among the Pennsylvania Dutch.
Hohman's book, despite the Indian name, is a very traditional
collection of European magic spells, recipes, and folk remedies,
combining Catholic prayers, magic words, and simple rituals in
order to cure simple domestic ailments and rural troubles. While
"Hex," as the Pennyslvania Dutch system of magic is called,
looks to this very pious book as its source, it has occasionally resulted in such blood-curdling activities as the Hex Murders of
1928, at Niemeyer's Hollow, near York.

It is a long way from rural witchcraft to the sophisticated Main
Line suburbs of Philadelphia. But for almost three centuries, the
town of Merion was home to the General Wayne Inn, long
renowned as the most haunted tavern in America; it was this
writer's first choice for inclusion in this book as Pennsylvania's
entry. But here we hit a more prosaic mystery. Many an old restaurant, hotel, or bar is renowned in its community as an institution.
Such places are often considered as much a part of the local landscape as the hills or the river. But in reality, such places are as
much money-making (or -losing) enterprises as a gas station or
beauty parlor. They operate to turn a profit; if they cannot, they
will close, and a bit of what makes the town, city, or hamlet unique
dies with them. So it was with the General Wayne: having opened
in 1704, it closed down in 2002. Saving someone buying and re-
opening it, the old hostelry and its history and legends are as dead
as the many ghosts that are said to inhabit the ancient building.
This author invites his readers, when making decisions about dining out, to divide their dinners and lunches in two: half for trendy
new establishments or chains like Denny's, the other for whatever

antique or historic places may grace their hometowns. It is not merely a way of gratifying the palate; it is also an investment in the future as well as the past of the local area.

In any case, a new site had to be selected; in this case it was an old private home, inhabited by the same family—the Meades and Esbys—since its construction in 1911. Now, many a grand home has been given over to state or local authorities and is open to the public. But such a place is a museum. When the family have gone, the building ceases to be a living home. Here too, support should be given to such places as are open to the public. Baleroy Mansion, the home of the descendants of Union Civil War General George Meade, is one such place. Open to the public on a limited basis, tours should be arranged by correspondence with the address given below.

Situated in the quiet and historic Philadelphia neighborhood of Chestnut Hill, Baleroy has acquired the title of "Most Haunted Home in America." Whether or not that is true, it has been featured on a number of television shows. George Meade Esby, great-grandson of the general as well as current owner and occupant, seems accepting, unafraid, and matter-of-fact about sharing his residence with unseen occupants—some of whom are decidedly nasty.

The Blue Room, for example, boasts priceless antiques and paintings, some of which were owned by notables like Napoleon. But in it rests the so-called "chair of death"; at least four unfortunates who have sat in it have died sudden and unexpected deaths. Mr. Esby believes it to be the domain of a dead lady named "Amanda." A cold blob of ectoplasm has been seen in the doorway leading from the Blue Room into the Reception Room; this, the owner and others believe, is Amanda. On the second floor, a rather nasty old woman has threatened visitors with her cane, only to vanish. A painting of Mr. Esby's younger brother Steven, hanging on the staircase, flew fifteen feet in front of guests.

It may be the profusion of antiques that is part of the problem, as some of them appear to have brought previous owners with them. Thomas Jefferson has been seen in the dining room, while a monk in a brown habit turns up in the bedrooms. Mr. Esby, while lying in bed, noticed that there was an indentation in the mattress next to him; just then, something grabbed him by the arm. When he turned on a light, there was nothing to be seen.

Mr. Esby moved into the house when he was six and his younger brother was five. Upon their arrival, the brothers ran to the fountain in the courtyard. Leaning over its edge, the older boy saw his own reflection. Young Steven's, however, was a skull. The lad died shortly after that. But apparently he has not left.

Workers on the house have seen Steven in an upstairs window while they were working on the fountain. Another worker saw a little blond boy; as he and his co-workers looked at him, he faded away in front of their eyes. Yet another worker's son, while working in the basement, heard a voice calling him by name. Although he answered, there was no response. He soon discovered that his father had been on the third floor, and that they were alone in the house. The son refused to work in the basement thereafter.

Mr. Esby has seen both his uncle and his mother in the house; moreover, there are loud footsteps, knocks at doors—but no one evidently responsible for any of it.

These are only a few of the strange goings-on at Baleroy Mansion, where items float through the air, and the sound of a phantom automobile graces the driveway. Mr. Esby reigns serenely over it all; if you write to the mansion and are admitted on tour, who knows who (or what) you might see?

Baleroy Mansion
111 West Mermaid Lane
Philadelphia, PA 19118

Rhode Island's Sprague Mansion Is Still Infested with the Strong Personalities Who Lived There

Rhode Island is the smallest state, to be sure; but it bears the longest name, being officially the state of "Rhode Island and Providence Plantations," a title that refers to the two nuclei of the area's first settling. There was much about those early days to set Rhode Island off from its New England neighbors, and indeed, from the other original colonies. Most obviously, there was the matter of religion: where Connecticut, New Hampshire, Maine, and Massachusetts were staunch supporters of Congregationalism as their established church, Rhode Island's founder was Roger Williams, a Baptist minister. As a result, although all religions (save Catholicism) were tolerated in colonial Rhode Island, as per Williams's beliefs, the Baptists played the same role there as did the Quakers in contemporary Pennsylvania: they helped set the tone and occupied some of the first places in society. This is why Brown University, alone of all the Ivy League colleges, has vestigial ties to the Baptists, rather than to the Episcopalians,

Congregationalists, Unitarians (who derived from the latter), Presbyterians, or Reformed.

Rhode Island's geography lent itself to shipping and smuggling; prior to the Revolution, merchant princes in Newport and elsewhere built homes that were incredibly stately by eighteenth-century standards, just as the great industrialists and bankers would do a century later. Those Narragansett Indians who survived the horrors of King Philip's War settled down alongside the Yankee farmers and continued to tell their tales of heroes, gods, and witches. The latter were a group the Yankees were familiar with. In terms of folklore, Yankee magic, Indian lore, tales of the Revolution, smuggling, piracy, and the sea created a heady mix.

It is no surprise, then, that Providence, Rhode Island, produced one of the greatest American horror writers: Howard Phillips Lovecraft (1890–1937). Steeped in his state's and New England's weird legends, he married them to his own imagination and created a world of fright still compelling today, more than a century after his death. Every Hallowe'en his fans gather at his grave in Providence's Swan Point Cemetery to commemorate his life and career.

Bizarre as H. P. Lovecraft's work was, however, the actual folklore of Rhode Island could be stranger, as he certainly knew. For example, the sage of Providence was aware that when he was two, the rural hamlet of Exeter suffered an episode of vampirism. One Mercy Brown, after her mother and sister died, expired herself. When her brother fell ill, their father was convinced that it was Mercy's doing. She was dug up, and found to be incorrupt and to have shifted in the coffin. Her heart was found to contain fresh blood. The shocked townsfolk burned the heart on a rock, and had her brother eat the ashes as a cure. This grisly medicine failed, and he died less than two months later. When *Dracula* author Bram Stoker died, newspaper accounts of Mercy Brown were found in his files. But Mercy was one of at least five such cases in New England's most tolerant state. It should be no surprise that the state is rife with tales of ghosts—revenants at once less menacing and easier to live with.

One of the best-known haunted houses in the state is the Sprague Mansion in Cranston. Cranston owes its origin to Roger Williams, who, in 1638, with twelve other proprietors, bought a tract of land called the "Pawtuxet Purchase." This would become the eastern part of present-day Cranston. In a short period of time, other settlers came, including William Arnold, whose son, Benedict, became the first governor of Rhode Island under the charter of 1663. The previous year, some settlers from Warwick bought the "Meschanticut Purchase," comprising the remainder of the town. Various conflicting land claims were resolved, and in 1754 Cranston was incorporated as a town.

Already, in 1712, the Sprague family had arrived. They would put Cranston on the world map. Already fairly prosperous through owning and operating a gristmill on the banks of the Pocasset River, in 1790 they built a house considered quite grand at the time. Two and a half stories, it featured a central chimney, low ceilings, gabled roofs, and simple woodwork. The home was expanded eastward by two bays in the early nineteenth century, in token of the success their newly expanded business brought them.

In 1807, William Sprague II converted his gristmill into a small cotton mill for carding and spinning yarn. Eventually, he and William III, his son, installed water-driven power looms; this allowed them to lower production costs and increase output. The Spragues' new business was dubbed the Cranston Print Works, and was the first in the United States to print calico. It was also the first to use chemical bleaching.

When William died in 1836, the two sons, Amasa and William III, took over the business. Although each brother was elected to the state legislature, Amasa ran the family business; William III served successively as a U.S. representative, governor, and senator. This ended when Amasa was murdered on December 31, 1843. He left the mansion to travel to Johnston, but he never arrived. The following morning, he was found beaten to death, almost within sight of the family home. Although John Gordon was suspected of the murder, was tried, and was hanged, evidence later came to light proving his innocence. This was the last execution in Rhode Island; the resulting outcry led to the abolition of the death penalty. To this day, the identity of the actual killer remains a mystery.

William III resigned from the senate and returned to Cranston to manage the company. Under his management, the company continued to prosper; when Amasa's son, William IV, came of age, he took over the company. By 1860, the Cranston Print Works was an industrial empire running from Maine to North Carolina.

Impressed with his own wealth, William IV decided to expand the home. In 1864, he built a two-and-a-half story, three-bay addition to the south. Topped by a belvedere, this addition was higher than the old house; entry to the original building is made through the landings of the new stairway. New rooms included a double parlor and dining room on the first floor, as well as two bedrooms on the floors above. Moreover, the new stairway was given a handsome mahogany railing. In each principal room was placed an Italianate marble fireplace. A large brick carriage house was erected on Dyer Avenue, and formal gardens were laid out behind the mansion.

The mansion became a showplace, and important people from all over the country came to curry favor with William IV. From the belvedere he and his family could survey their holdings: orchards; vineyards; woodlands; reservoir; a railroad; a horse-car company; the Cranston Print Works Manufacturing Company with its two villages of mill houses, school, community store; boarding houses; meeting house; post office; counting house, and a horse racing track. But these additions to the house were made while men were fighting and dying in the Civil War. He was a member of the Rhode Island State Militia and a United States senator—thus it was quite a stroke when he was seen leading a charge at the Battle of First Manassas. He was offered a commission as brigadier general in 1861; this he declined, however, because he wished to be a major general.

The year before he built his addition to the mansion, William IV married Kate Chase Sprague (1840–1899), ten years his junior and daughter of Salmon P. Chase. Co-founder of the Republican Party, Chase had been the candidate the wise money was placed on to be the party's nominee in the convention of 1860. His daughter was considered, at nineteen, the most beautiful woman in Washington; her gowns and hairstyles were the awe of men and the envy of ladies. She too believed that her widowed father would be president; she in turn would be the hostess of the White House. Of course, Abraham Lincoln won both nomination and election, but he asked Chase to be his secretary of the treasury. Immediately Kate Chase was seen as a rival by First Lady Mary Todd Lincoln. Miss Chase's bearing, creamy skin and hazel eyes, bronzed red hair, intelligence, and graceful manners made her much sought after, both as guest and host. Because Secretary of State William Seward's wife was ill, Kate was the premier cabinet hostess; loving this role dearly, she entertained diplomats and foreign celebrities from abroad at elegant suppers and "at-homes."

She was soon attracted to the gallant young senator/soldier from Rhode Island. In 1863 they married, and their wedding was attended by President Lincoln and his cabinet, foreign diplomats, congressmen, relatives, and many friends. It was said to have been the most magnificent wedding ever known up to that time in the United States: the wedding cost $250,000 in 1863 money, at least eighteen times that amount today. But the cotton manufacturer soon found that his new wife had very expensive tastes, as her father noted many times in his diaries. Nevertheless, at first they were very happy: on June 16, 1865, William Sprague V was born, immediately becoming the pride and joy of his grandfather, Salmon Chase.

But very soon, problems developed for the couple. Kate found William IV dull and uninspiring; he found her frivolous and feckless about money. At first, their tensions could be smoothed over; the ruin of the Southern elite after the war contributed to the family fortune; cheap cotton kept William Sprague's mills running at full capacity during the late 1860s and '70s. But as the '60s wore on, trouble began to emerge again. Then, in early 1870, Salmon Chase had another heart attack, which paralyzed his right side. Weak and very ill, he consented to move to Canonchet (a country estate outside Cranston the Spragues owned) to be under Kate's care. While there, William IV showed great concern and visited his father-in-law constantly. Although Chase was still very ill in 1871, his daughter saw his health improving and hoped that he would get the Democratic nomination. She believed that he was the only candidate who could unite the liberal Republicans and disgruntled Democrats. Once more, however, her father was passed over; this time the Democrats selected Horace Greeley to run against Ulysses S. Grant. Since even Greeley's friends admitted that he was eccentric, Kate could not believe that they would do this. By the time of the election, she had another baby girl, Portia. Chase planned to move from the Spragues' Washington mansion at E and Sixth Street to his own home in Edgewood.

Yet despite the political disappointments of his wife, William IV was not too upset; by 1872, he was the wealthiest man in North America. But his happiness all ended rather swiftly. In May of 1873, Chase spent what he called a "nice day" at Canonchet with his daughter, son-in-law, and their children. He seemed content enough; after leaving Canonchet he traveled to New York to be with his other daughter Nettie and her husband. While staying with them, he suffered another stroke. The Spragues rushed to his bedside, but the sixty-five-year-old Chase died. His death plunged Kate into despair; she apparently never recovered from this depression, and it lasted the rest of her life. The Spragues' marriage swiftly started to come apart.

Worse was to come: William IV lost almost everything in the financial panic of 1873. Lack of money and his wife's continuing emotional slide led to a scandal-ridden divorce in 1883. William V left home to try to make his fortune in Washington State. Instead, he killed himself in 1889, leaving a suicide note blaming his father for his being a failure. Kate, in the meantime, had retreated to her father's crumbling Washington, D.C. estate, the scene of so many of her past triumphs. There she died penniless and alone in 1899. William IV outlived his fortune and his happiness by many years, dying in Paris in 1912. He was buried at Swan Point Cemetery alongside his son; his wife was interred at Spring Grove Cemetery in Ohio.

After the Sprague fortune collapsed, their mansion was sold, being used at different times as a boarding house or foreman's residence. The old house was in danger of being demolished in 1967; the Cranston Historical Society acquired the property, established it as their headquarters, and opened it to the public. Housing furniture from the Carrington Collection of the Rhode Island Historical Society, the Sprague Mansion is the best-known historic structure in the city.

But as the scene of a tragedy worthy of Greek drama, it would be very surprising if some shadow of the past did not still lie upon the place. Sure enough, it does; the Sprague Mansion has been called the most haunted house in Rhode Island, an eerie distinction in an eerie state.

An apparition is often observed descending the main staircase; the first occasion was by a woman living there in 1925—thirteen years after William IV's death. Visitors to the wine cellar have reported a hand reaching out and touching them, although no one else was present; still others have felt cold drafts from nowhere in the cellar. Lights turn themselves on and off, while the sound of disembodied footsteps resounds in the doll room. A woman in black has been seen standing in the belvedere atop the mansion. In the ballroom, a young woman has been seen standing in front of the mirror. Wearing a long Civil War type gown, some have claimed that it is Kate Chase Sprague, reliving her time as belle of the ball—or is it her in the belvedere, mourning her beloved father's death? Who or what is the figure that has been seen on the back steps of the mansion, and what is it that has been spied in the carriage house? With so much sadness in the house, one has a wide cast to choose from. Mrs. Sprague? Either of the ill-starred Williams, father or son? Murdered Amasa? His killer? Any of the innumerable servants who shared the family's tragic lives? Who can tell? But perhaps, if you visit, you will find out. In any case, you will have been, for a short time, part of a story that is a true American tragedy.

Sprague Mansion
1351 Cranston Street
Cranston, RI 02920
(401) 944-9226

Suicide and Fear Bring Dead Tenants Back to South Carolina's Hampton Plantation

T he "Palmetto State," as South Carolina is called, boasts of its aristocratic origins, in sharp distinction to its humbler neighbor to the north. But unlike the north, where New Jersey, Connecticut, and Rhode Island were formed out of separate colonies that merged, the Carolinas originally were one. In 1663 King Charles II granted a charter to a group of eight English nobles, called the Lords Proprietors. In their sovereign's honor they called the land Carolina. In early April 1670 the first settlers arrived and established Charleston, named in honor of the king as well. In 1712 the province of Carolina was divided into North and South Carolina, each with its own governor.

Three groups comprised the majority of the earliest settlers of South Carolina: English from Barbados, French Huguenots, and African slaves. Germans, Irish, and Scots came in large numbers during the eighteenth century. The merchants of Charleston and the rice and indigo planters of the low country

cultivated an elegant way of life in their townhouses and plantation homes—a way of life dependent on slave labor. The slaves
who were settled in the low country maintained many African
words, customs, and beliefs—giving rise to a culture know in
this area as "Gullah," and in Georgia as "Geechee." Their folklore includes many tales of magic and ghosts, and, indeed, the
whole low country—among blacks and whites alike—is filled
with such beliefs. Remnants of the Indians of the area, mixed
with European and African blood, persist in the area under the
name of "Brass Ankles" and "Red Bones." The low country remains a mysterious area, while the up country conserves strange
tales of its own.

So it was during the buildup to the Revolution. But as in the
rest of the colonies, the Revolution was first and foremost a civil
war that divided families, and led eventually to bloodshed without
quarter on both sides. A whole host of ghost stories arose, as they
did from the Civil War.

These conflicts led to fortification of Charleston Harbor: a
palmetto log fort, later named Fort Moultrie, on Sullivans Island
fended off a British attack in June of 1776; but four years later a
fresh assault succeeded. Even the rebel governor, Charles Pinckney, swore allegiance to the Crown. With independence, Ft.
Moultrie became a stone fort, and in November of 1827, one
Private Edgar Allan Poe arrived there. Remaining until December of the following year, the future author of strange tales gathered material for a number of his works, the most popular being
"The Gold Bug."

Northeast of Charleston is the Santee country, a land of
rivers, swamps, and isolated towns and plantations. Alligators,
poisonous snakes, and mosquitoes made settlement difficult, and
early on the African slaves were a large majority of the population. By 1729, the largest settlement in the area, Georgetown, was
a busy seaport. In 1732, King George II accepted the proposal of

the locals to officially declare the town a port, and appoint a royal "Collector of Customs." As with the rest of the Carolina coast, shipping often fell prey to the more than two thousand pirates sailing up and down the seashore. Their exploits, treasure, and the ghosts of their victims (and their own ghosts) entered the area's store of legends.

Initially, naval stores, such as pitch, turpentine, rosin, and timber for shipbuilding, were the major exports, with deputies for the surveyor of the king seeking out particularly tall pines suitable to mast in ships of the Royal Navy, and marking them with the "King's Broad Arrow." But a new use for the land became apparent, when the "War of Jenkins Ear" cut the British empire off from its traditional sources of Royal Blue Indigo dye.

As the indigo plant grew wild all along the coastal plains of South Carolina, it made sense for the cleared land to be used for indigo planting. Blue being the most difficult color to produce in a dye, indigo would bring its cultivators huge fortunes. Soon, Georgetown and its environs supported an aristocratic society of plantation owners. One remaining relic of those days is the "Winyah Indigo Society" in Georgetown. Chartered by King George II in 1758 as a social and charitable organization, its present building was built in 1853.

By the end of the eighteenth century, however, indigo in vast amounts was being produced in India and the East Indies. The price fell, forcing the planters to look to other commodities. Their own area's natural swampiness suggested an answer—rice. The new crop caught on, brought in an awful lot of money, and saved the economy; not just in Georgetown County, but throughout the low country. With their aristocratic manners and interests, the same gibing question asked of the Louisiana French Creoles was now asked of South Carolina's nabobs: "How are they like Chinese? They eat rice and worship their ancestors."

This "brown gold," worked by armies of slaves, allowed most of the planters to make the transition to independence, and helped fund the struggle against the Crown. But in the next war the plantation owners would not do so well. The surrender at Appomattox resulted in the end of slavery and the beginning of a long slow death for the low country rice industry.

After that war, the planters did what they could to maintain their gracious homes. One such mansion that, in itself, sums up the whole area's history is Hampton Plantation, now a state park. The area was first settled by French Huguenots. About 1735, the oldest part of what is now Hampton Plantation was built by one Noe Serre II, and his wife, Catherine Challion. They in turn produced a daughter, Judith, who married one Daniel Horry. Leaving the plantation at his father-in-law's death, Horry in turn produced another Daniel, who inherited the place.

The home which came into his hands was a one-and-a-half story, central-hall building. After 1757, Daniel Horry II enlarged the house to its present size. Called Hampton by 1769, it was a working rice plantation. After his first wife died, he married a much younger woman, Harriott Pinckney. The daughter of Eliza Lucas Pinckney and sister of Charles Cotesworth Pinckney, Harriott came of a most remarkable family, and unwittingly catapulted Hampton Plantation into national prominence. With her, her mother entered the annals of Hampton Plantation.

Eliza Lucas Pinckney was the daughter of George and Anne Lucas. Her father was lieutenant governor on the British colony of Antigua. Her parents sent her to be educated at a finishing school in England, where botany captured her fancy; in 1738, her family moved to a plantation on Wappoo Creek, in South Carolina.

At age sixteen, Eliza put her knowledge of botany to use when she became the manager of three of her father's plantations when he was ordered to rejoin the British army. It was Eliza who introduced indigo to the province. Such a remarkable girl contracted a remarkable marriage: on May 27, 1744, she married widower Charles Pinckney, an attorney who was the former speaker of the Commons House of Assembly. At her husband's plantation on the Cooper River, Pinckney cultured silkworms and made silk, presenting the Princess of Wales with a silk dress. Eliza also had four children there: Charles Cotesworth in 1746, George Lucas in 1747 (he died in early infancy), Harriott in 1748, and Thomas in 1750. Three years after Thomas's birth, the family left South Carolina for London after Charles Pinckney became Agent General for the province. The Pinckneys returned to America in 1758, but Charles died there of malaria on July 12.

Eliza was grief stricken, but after a suitable period soldiered on, managing her husband's properties profitably enough to educate her sons in England and to provide an honorable match for her daughter. Life was happy enough, but as it did to so many families, the Revolution ushered in tragedy and fear. Daughter and wife of royal officials, her sons and son-in-law were active in the rebel cause, to which she acquiesced at some emotional cost. The cost was made tangible when her property was destroyed by British raids. She went to wait out the war with her daughter at Hampton plantation. She would remain there most of her life.

Daniel Horry II died in 1785, leaving a son, Daniel III, and a daughter, Harriet. His will left the use of the plantation to Harriott for her lifetime, although Daniel III was his heir. Six years later, great news came: President Washington would visit Hampton! The large Adam-style portico and pediment were added in preparation for the president's arrival. The two ladies greeted the general when he stopped by for breakfast on May 1, 1791. They "were arrayed in sashes and bandeaux painted with the general's portrait and mottoes of welcome." The next year, however, Eliza was taken ill with cancer. She left for Philadelphia for treatment, but died there in 1793. President Washington served as one of her pallbearers when she was buried in St. Peter's churchyard.

Daniel III predeceased his mother, and so Hampton passed to his sister. She in her turn had married Frederick Rutledge, of a very prominent Ulster Scot family in the state, one of whom had signed the Declaration of Independence. Up to this time, Hampton Plantation had been a relatively happy place, free of the unrelenting tragedies that have haunted so many of the houses we have been exploring. But, in the 1830s, Frederick and Harriot's son, John Henry Rutledge, overwrought because he was not allowed to marry the woman he loved, sat down in a rocker in the library, put a gun to his head, and shot himself. Nonetheless, the owners of Hampton continued to receive famous visitors. Audubon painted birds there; in 1843, Edgar Allan Poe wrote "The Gold Bug" at the place.

When Harriott died in 1858, Hampton passed to her son, Edward Cotesworth Rutledge, with the request that, as it "has been in our family for five generations," it not be sold out of the family. Edward complied with this request. But once again, history intervened in the destiny of the plantation. As Union troops neared the place, Edward hid a number of treasures on the property. They would not be recovered in his lifetime or that of his son.

In time, Hampton Plantation was inherited by Archibald Rutledge, eighth and last private owner of Hampton Plantation. By his time, the old place had fallen on hard times. Born in 1883, Archibald had apparently absorbed the literary associations of the place, as he pursued first an academic and then a literary career. In 1904 he became an English teacher at Mercersburg Academy in Pennsylvania, a post he would retain for thirty-three years. During that time, he visited his crumbling inheritance only on holidays.

When he retired from the academy, he went to work on two major occupations. One was the continuing of his writing, which would culminate in twenty-five books of poetry, and forty-five of prose, nomination for the Nobel Prize, and innumerable other awards, including being named Poet Laureate of South Carolina. His other work was restoring his home to its former splendor, with little help other than that of family and friends.

It was in the course of this endeavor, and while searching for the ghost who had been heard by the family for years, that Archibald made an exciting discovery. He was searching a passageway from the ballroom to the living room, when he found a secret sealed closet from the cellar. Archibald and a helper sawed into the closet from the cellar. Therein they discovered a small box with a folded house plan containing an X marked about thirty-five feet, angling from the house with a chest drawn on it.

Going outside he found that the location marked on the map with an X was near an old oak tree. Using a steel rod he probed around the tree until it hit something solid. Digging down four feet, Archibald discovered a sealed crock. Inside it was an 1861 copy of the *Charleston Mercury* newspaper reporting the firing on Ft. Sumter, together with other newspapers. These wrapped up 198 gold coins dating from 1795. The Rutledge clan had had a legend about Edward hiding money from Union soldiers during the Civil War.

Archibald was indeed successful in restoring Hampton. But a lifetime of searching never revealed the ghost. In 1973, the last master of Hampton Plantation left it to the state of South Carolina; it is on the National Register of Historic Places as well as a national historic landmark. Today the state operates it as a living history site, with many interpretative programs. The interior is unfurnished.

But the lack of furniture does not seem to affect the ghost. As it did when the Rutledges lived here, the ghost of Hampton Plantation is heralded "by a remarkably regular series of sounds," emanating from the bedroom over the dining room area. The performance begins with a quiet rocking sound, followed by three distinct raps, and at last the sound of a body being dragged from the northwest to the southeast corner of the room. In addition, sounds of a man's sobbing and a chair that rocks itself are reported in the library downstairs. Could it be that John re-enacts his suicide, while his father continues to mourn? Who knows? But what is certain is that a visit to Hampton Plantation would be well worth your time.

Hampton Plantation
1950 Rutledge Road
McClellanville, SC 29458
(803) 546-9361

The Hotel Alex Johnston
in South Dakota Offers
Many Haunting Amenities

L ike its neighbor to the north, South Dakota straddles the Black Hills, the Northern Prairies, and great rivers flowing into the Missouri. The Sioux and Arikara, after the coming of the horse (thanks to escaped mustangs from Spanish settlements far to the south) enjoyed a semi-nomadic lifestyle, and were able to chase the buffalo. For them, spirits—good and evil—inhabited the countryside, and some of their descendants believe the same to be so today.

The French claimed the state as part of Louisiana, as early as the seventeenth century. But no actual Gallic penetration started until the brothers Louis-Joseph and François la Verendrye arrived in 1743. As their father had, five years before, they were looking for the Northwest Passage. But the Black Hills blocked their path; as they began their return to Quebec, they buried a lead tablet, claiming the region for France, on a hill near Fort Pierre, placing some stones in a pyramid over the top. It was found by a group of high school students in 1913.

The brothers were the first of a torrent of French-Canadian, Spanish, and English traders who came to South Dakota. Although France ceded Louisiana to Spain in 1762 to save it from the British, most of its European inhabitants were still French. One of these was Pierre Dorion, who arrived in 1785. Probably the first permanent white settler, he married a Sioux woman, and built a home on the Missouri River near present-day Yankton. More of his countrymen followed him, while British traders proceeded up the Missouri and established a trading post among the Mandan in North Dakota. This is what passed to the Americans with the Louisiana Purchase of 1803.

The following year, Lewis and Clark passed through the state en route to the Pacific. They returned to South Dakota in 1806. Six years afterwards, Sacagawea (the only woman in the party) died at Fort Manuel in South Dakota. The Missouri River soon became a major artery of trade; the difficulty of navigating it upriver, however, earned it the nickname of "Old Misery." British and American traders built fur-trading posts, but the end of the War of 1812 left the latter in control. In 1823 a treaty with the Indians left the United States government in definite political control. Nine years later, the St. Louis-based American Fur Company built Fort Pierre in the center of the modern state. This was the start of Pierre, today the capital of South Dakota. Five years later, a smallpox epidemic affected the Arikara so badly that they left to join the similarly devastated Mandan in North Dakota.

Growing conflict between the Indians and the Americans led to the Treaty of Fort Laramie in 1851. The tribes promised not to fight one another, and to leave whites passing through unmolested; the government swore to prevent further settlement. Both sides broke the accord. Three years later, war broke out. As with every conflict, a whole new layer of ghost stories was forged, as atrocities left their mark on the spiritual atmosphere. The following year, the army built Fort Randall near modern Yankton.

Settlers began pouring in, and the towns of Yankton, Sioux Falls, Vermillion, Elk Point, and Bon Homme were founded. President Lincoln created Dakota Territory (comprising both the modern states of North and South Dakota) in 1861, with Yankton as the capital. At first, growth was slow; the year following territorial status, the Sioux revolt broke out in Minnesota; when it was suppressed many of the Sioux fled into Dakota. They were chased at intervals by the army.

After the war, many foreign settlers arrived from Germany, Sweden, Norway, Finland, Ireland, and the Czech lands, bunching together in ethnic enclaves. Since the prairies had few trees, the settlers used blocks of earth to build homes, calling them "soddies." Around the fire in the isolated houses, so different from what they had left behind in Europe, they told the weird tales of their far-off homelands, and concocted new ones based upon their strange surroundings.

Another conflict with the Indians led to yet another treaty. This one established the Great Sioux Reservation, encompassing all the land west of the Missouri River to the modern border of Wyoming, including the Black Hills—sacred to the tribes. Settlers would not be allowed in, although soldiers and scouts could be.

The first railroad came to Dakota in 1873 from Iowa, running to Vermillion and Yankton. Another ran from Minnesota to Lake Kampeska. Although there were no towns along that line, in Dakota Territory, railroads often preceded settlement. But the next year, a powerful inducement to settle would make itself known.

In 1874, the army sent Lieutenant Colonel George A. Custer to explore the hitherto little-known Black Hills. Custer brought one thousand soldiers, fifty Indian scouts, scientists, newspapermen, a photographer, and a band. Two of the men found gold in French Creek, which news the newspapermen immediately dispatched to the rest of the nation.

A few months later, twenty-eight men left Sioux City, Iowa, and slipped into the Black Hills illegally. Spending a hard winter in a log stockade on French Creek, they turned up only forty dollars worth of gold. Although the army escorted them out in the spring, the die was cast. At least eight hundred prospectors slipped into the Black Hills past the army the next year. They too found little gold, but their presence and Indian reprisals led to another war, and the slaughter of Custer and his men at the Little Big Horn.

One of the first settlements in the Black Hills was Rapid City, founded in 1876 by a group of disheartened prospectors who had failed to find gold. Named for the limestone spring stream that passes through the city, originating high in the Black Hills, Rapid City *rapidly* indeed became a center for commerce, culture, transportation, and education for the Black Hills and the entire high plains. Not only was it a major rail crossing, but the city also became the center for travel to such places as Mount Rushmore National Memorial, the Badlands National Monument, and Wind Cave National Park. Without a doubt, such a sophisticated outpost needed a grand hotel.

The visionary who finally built one was Alex Carlton Johnson (1861–1938), vice president of the Chicago and Northwestern Railroad, which had done so much to put Rapid City on the map. He had two inspirations in the design of the hotel: the Sioux, whom he had admired so greatly, and the Germans who had settled—many by his railroad—so much of the state. In a way, his hotel would be a concrete symbol of reconciliation between these two traditions. The result was to be a basically Germanic Tudor building featuring many Indian symbols and motifs—a uniquely American, and South Dakotan, ideal. In 1927 construction began on the hotel; it was the day before work began on Mount Rushmore. On July 1, 1928, the first guest registered; many more, including such celebrities as Jimmy Stewart (who had his own table in the restaurant) followed.

The elegant lobby would not, at first glance, look out of place in any grand hotel in Europe. But look more closely: in the lobby tiles are depicted the Sacred Four Directions, from whence the Sioux believed their four sacred powers to be derived. Thus the north (white) is the sign for the Cleansing Snow; east (red) is the home of the Morning Star, the home of Daybreak Knowledge; south (yellow) is the home of Warm Winds, rejuvenators of the land; west (black) is home to the "Thunder Being," who gives strength and power in time of trouble. Don't be dismayed by the display of what appears to be a swastika; it is actually a symbol used by Indians since prehistoric times.

In recent years, the independently owned hotel has been meticulously restored, using original photographs and plans, to its appearance in the 1920s. As a result of its authenticity, the hotel is listed on the National Register of Historic Places; it is a member of NTA and of the Association of Historic Hotels of the Rockies. The hotel is also the recipient of the first Governor's Great Service Award and Governor's Service Star. The Alex Johnson remains what it has been since its opening: a landmark of the downtown skyline, *the* place to stay in Rapid City, and one of the great hotels of America.

But as is so often the case with such places, although the elegance and glamour, the good food and excellent service, and the many good times had there are readily apparent, they must coexist with darker elements. It is claimed that sometime during the 1930s, a hotel manager jumped to her death from the roof. Certainly the top floor appears to have its problems. Currently used for storage, hotel workers have heard furniture moving around; lights will flicker on and off. An employee reported that a chair was flung down the stairwell at him from the top floor doorway; of course, no one was on the floor at the time. Several of the staff have quit because of the apparitions, such as the phantom woman on the eighth floor. Odd noises and disembodied crying have been heard and pianos have played on their own. In one guestroom, a ghost occasionally stands at the foot of the bed. Alex Johnson built the hotel as a gesture of reconciliation between Indian and European. Perhaps it serves a similar function for the living and the dead. When visiting Mount Rushmore, one ought to take the opportunity to try and find out!

Hotel Alex Johnson
523 Sixth Street
Rapid City, SD 57701
(605) 342-1210 or
(800) 888-2539
Info@AlexJohnson.com

A little Girl—
with a Few Disembodied Entities—
Haunts a Tennessee Theater

Tennessee falls into three very distinct portions: the mountainous east, the central plain, and the Mississippi River-attracted west. The diversity of the state goes back to Indian days, when the Cherokee controlled the east, the Shawnee the center, and the Chickasaw the west. The first Europeans to enter Tennessee were the Spanish in 1540 under Hernando de Soto. They saw no reason to stay, but in April of 1541 they camped near the present site of Memphis, raising the Spanish flag. Then they crossed the Mississippi out of Tennessee history.

In 1673, two English explorers crossed the mountains into Tennessee, only to have one of them killed on the second trip; that same year, two Frenchmen camped near Memphis and were treated well. Nine years later, La Salle and his men arrived at Memphis, built Fort Prudhomme, and departed after claiming the land for France. In 1693, Charles Charleville set up a trading post in an old Shawnee stockade at French Lick, half a mile from the bluff upon which the little frontier town of Nashville would be built nearly a century later.

Thus, long before there were any permanent settlements, France, Spain, and England all claimed the state. Although there were scattered incursions by various of the three nationalities, the French and Indian Wars effectively prevented any permanent settlement until 1769, when one William Bean built his cabin on Boone's Creek near the Watauga River; he was joined by several families from North Carolina, while other groups settled Carter's River Valley (1771) and on the Nolichucky River (1772). Collectively, they were known as the Watauga Settlements.

Although legally part of North Carolina, that province had provided little government for its towns on the other side of the Alleghenies, which neglect sparked the conflict called the "Regulators' War," the Regulators being western North Carolinians who rebelled against the lack of courts and other governmental bodies in their region. When the incident was crushed in 1772, many of the Regulators fled over the mountains to Watauga; but in any case, it was highly unlikely that the assembly in New Bern would take any action.

Given this power vacuum and their isolation, the people of the Watauga Settlements soon felt the lack of organized government. So in 1772 they formed the Watauga Association, electing five magistrates to make and administer law. This was the first independent government in North America. Nevertheless, the Wataugans had no legal title to the lands they occupied. Until March 17, 1775, the area was Cherokee country; on that date the newly created Transylvania Land Company purchased nearly 20,000,000 acres from the Indians. Immediately the Transylvania Company resold the Watauga territory to its settlers.

At the outset of the Revolutionary War, the Wataugans organized themselves into a military district that they named for George Washington. They then requested annexation to North Carolina, which was granted in 1777. Washington District became Washington County, encompassing the entire state. In 1779 Jonesboro was platted as the county seat. On October 7, 1780, Wataugans joined other rebels fighting the loyalists at King's Mountain—the only battle of the revolution in which Tennessee troops took part.

While this was going on, other settlers were pushing westward into Middle Tennessee along the Cumberland. Nashborough (today's Nashville) was founded in 1780. Isolated as the Watauga and Cumberland settlements were, they petitioned North Carolina for more aid—military and civil. But the North Carolinian authorities, partly as a gesture of good will, partly to avoid responsibility, immediately ceded the region to the federal government.

Annoyed by this news, delegates from Washington, Sullivan, and Greene counties met at Jonesboro and discussed becoming an independent western state to be called Franklin. In the same year (1784) a constitution, patterned after that of North Carolina, was adopted. Although North Carolina rescinded its cession, the "Franklanders," as they called themselves, refused to abolish their new state. Instead, a general assembly met at Greeneville in March 1785, choosing officers to act under Governor John Sevier. Although there were continual clashes between Franklin officials and those sent over the mountains by North Carolina, the "Lost State of Franklin" lingered until 1790. In that year congress accepted the second offer of cession from North Carolina, as well as from Virginia and Georgia, and created "The Territory of the United States South of the River Ohio," commonly known as the Southwest Territory. This new entity comprised modern Tennessee, Kentucky, and most of Alabama and Mississippi. The Territorial government operated for nearly six years, with its seat at Knoxville.

Kentucky became a state in 1792, and within four years of that occurrence Tennessee had more than a fourth of the population necessary to become a state. A constitutional convention met in

Knoxville on January 11, 1796, and petitioned congress for admission to the Union. Their wish was granted on June 1, 1796.

But these exciting events affected only the eastern and middle parts of the state. On Admission Day, the Chickasaw Bluffs, as the current site of Memphis was called, were firmly in the hands of Spain. Although the French had ceded paper control of the area to Great Britain in 1763, the Chickasaw were Spanish allies. They only became more so over the following three decades. In 1795 Spanish troops under Louisiana Governor Gayoso arrived, setting up a fort on the site of the old French Fort Assomption (built in 1739). Gayoso called his construction San Fernando de Las Barrancas, after the prince of Asturias, heir to the Spanish throne (and later King Ferdinand VII). He sent Benjamin Foy, a Dutchman and experienced Indian trader, to guard the fort and to keep in contact with the Chickasaw. Nevertheless, when the U.S. government sent troops to the Bluffs two years later, they found that the Spanish had retreated to the other side of the Mississippi.

It would take time to lure settlers to the area. At last, Memphis was founded in 1819 by John Overton, James Winchester, and Andrew Jackson. The trio created a river port halfway between New Orleans and the Ohio Valley; by the late 1840s, there were many trade-goods-filled flatboats and cotton-laden riverboats lining the riverbank. Front Street's Cotton Row attracted merchants eager to buy and sell the area's high-quality cotton. Despite the damage wreaked on all the river ports by the Civil War and Reconstruction, Memphis recovered. It even prospered during the early twentieth century, as its proximity to timber made it a center for the hardwoods trade.

But through it all, Memphis and its environs retained a separate identity from the middle and eastern parts of the state. Her cultural and economic ties to such places as New Orleans and Natchez ensured that while eastern Tennessee was pro-Union during the

Civil War, continuing to send delegates to congress and threatening to secede from the state, Memphis was firmly pro-rebel. While the mountaineers hammered away on their dulcimers for music, and Nashville nabobs enjoyed classical chamber works, Memphis looked south to New Orleans.

Thus it was that jazz came to Memphis. On Beale Street, black music men like W. C. Handy were pioneering the Blues. Four decades later, that tradition would influence a young man named Elvis Presley, who, after making a fortune, would settle down in Memphis at his Graceland estate.

But other, darker things made their way up the Mississippi as well. Beale Street was not only a center for the Blues, but for the shops of various "cunjur" men. Their craft developing from Louisiana Voodoo, the "cunjur" doctors of Memphis and West Tennessee in general ply a strange trade, indeed. "Cunjur doctors will sell you 'hands' or 'tobies' enabling you to detect witches and ward off their spells. Through cunjur you can cause rain, find lost property, wither the tongue of your gossiping neighbor, win your sweetheart's love, and drive your enemy insane or to the grave. It can force your debtors to pay you and your creditors to forget you, make your wife fecund or barren, cause the fish to bite, and the mosquitoes to forage elsewhere. The power of cunjur is as limitless as its user's desires."

With such a subculture, it should be no great surprise that one of the best-attested haunted public buildings in the country is in Memphis. But to see it, we will leave the dark world of "cunjur" behind, and instead attend one of the south's greatest theatrical venues, the Orpheum.

Originally built in 1890 as the Grand Opera House, the Orpheum sits on the corner of Main and Beale Streets. At its inception, it was called the grandest theater outside New York City. As a setting for vaudeville, the theater featured singers, musicians, and magicians galore. Becoming part of the Orpheum Circuit of vaudeville shows in 1907, the Grand was renamed the Orpheum.

All went well for the Orpheum for quite a few years. But in 1921 a twelve-year-old girl named Mary was killed in an accident in front of the theater. Two years later, a fire broke out during a show featuring a stripper named Blossom Seeley. The theater burned to the ground.

Nevertheless, in 1928 a brand new Orpheum was built on the original site at a cost of $1.6 million. Twice as large as her predecessor, the new theater, decorated in the style of François I, boasted (and boasts) tasseled brocade draperies, enormous crystal chandeliers, gilded moldings, and a Mighty Wurlitzer pipe organ. The auditorium, seating nearly three thousand, is decorated in shades of gold, red, and cream; it includes a huge stage, orchestra pit, balcony, and domed ceiling.

Although vaudeville was dying, cinema was coming into its own. All over the country, incredibly beautiful movie palaces were being built. Thus, it was not much of a stretch in 1940, when the Orpheum was purchased by the Malco movie theater chain. Malco ran first-run movies there until 1976, when the company decided to sell the building in the face of competition from multiplexes. Some even wanted to raze the old theater in favor of an office complex. But in 1977, the Memphis Development Foundation purchased the Orpheum; Broadway productions and concerts began coming back, and the theater had new life.

But the years had not been kind to the old place. The Orpheum was closed on Christmas in 1982 for a two-year, $5 million renovation. Restored to its 1928 grandeur, the theater was reopened in January of 1984. Since then, it has annually hosted two seasons of Broadway tours—more than any other theater in the country. Performers such as Cary Grant, Andy Williams, Johnny Mathis, Gladys Knight and the Pips, Kenny G, Chuck Mangione, Stacy Keach, Patti LaBelle, Robert Goulet, Dorothy Hamill, Harry Connick, Jr., Tom Jones, and the Vienna Boys Choir regularly grace its stage. Moreover, Ballet Memphis and

Opera Memphis are headquartered there. Twice, the Orpheum has come back from the dead.

But so, too, has its most regular patron. Mary, the twelve-year-old killed outside in 1921, apparently has also staged a comeback. For more than sixty years, patrons and staff have reported doors opening and closing by themselves, and hearing her giggling voice, and her feet tapping up and down the aisles. Moreover, she has been seen sitting in her favorite seat, C-5. She is courteous, however, never disrupting a performance. Yul Brenner saw her sitting in C-5, dressed in a twenties-style white dress, when he was performing in *The King and I* at the theater. Nor was he the only actor to notice her there; several cast members of *Fiddler on the Roof* noticed her as well, and also noted that she seemed to be enjoying the show.

But she is not confined to the auditorium: a woman patron and friends saw a twelve-year-old girl, in an old-fashioned white dress, dancing in the lobby. Before their eyes, she vanished. She also gives attention to the staff. A theater workman constantly felt her presence around him, describing it as "a cold, eerie feeling, like getting into a bathtub of cold liver." She also played pranks on the housekeeper, taking her tools, and putting them in the toilet.

But she is not the only phantom haunting the Orpheum. Workmen have seen a theater door fly open and then shut without any help. Trying to repair the theater's Wurlitzer late at night, a repairman decided that he needed a break. He locked up, and went to get some coffee. Ready to return to the uncooperative organ, he returned to find that the problem was already fixed.

One night the security guard locked a homeless man in the fifth-floor gallery by mistake. Suddenly, the guard heard a terrifying scream. Then came the sound of feet flying down five flights of darkened stairs, followed by the smashing open of the entrance doors. The homeless man never stopped running, and the doors were knocked off their hinges. Whatever he saw, it could not have been pleasant.

From time to time the alarm system goes off at night. On one such occasion, police arrived with canine units to investigate. The dogs refused to enter the theater; they lay down on the ground and refused to budge. Whatever spooked them, it was something invisible to their masters.

Today, the staff seems used to the presence of Mary, and whoever else may be there. The Orpheum is a great place for top-notch acts. But it may be an unearthly one you remember best!

_____

Orpheum Theatre
203 South Main
Memphis, TN 38103
(901) 525-7800

San Antonio's Menger Hotel
Is Filled with Historic Texas Ghosts

he "Lone Star State" has quite a reputation among its sisters in the Union. As of this writing, its former governor is President of the United States, and the popular view of Texans by those who don't know them is colored by memories of the old *Alamo* film. Texans are considered loud, obnoxious, poorly spoken—the most southern of southern caricatures. Unfair as that picture is, it is also inaccurate. While it's true that East Texas received a preponderance of its Anglo and African settlers from the south, after independence in 1836, many other folk—German, Czech, French, and so on—settled in ethnic enclaves, all of which still exist; all these groups—and their Anglo and African predecessors—had various strange beliefs and tales, many of which yet survive. But what is particularly neglected by the popular view is the Spanish side of Texas.

The Indians who inhabited Texas at the time the first Spanish explorers arrived in 1519 are all gone now; identifiable tribes—the Alabama-Coushattas and the Tiguas—came from out

of state; the former as refugees from the east after Texas independence, while the latter arrived in the seventeenth century
alongside Spaniards fleeing the Pueblo revolt in New Mexico.
The Cohuiltecans were absorbed into the general Hispanic population as a result of evangelization by the Mission Padres, the
Tonkawa were exiled to Oklahoma, and the Karankawa were, to
be blunt, exterminated. Neither Spanish nor Anglo-Texans had
any use for their cannibalism—they were the only tribe in North
America to practice it.

But while both Spanish and Indians had strange tales, one of the
strangest paved the way for eventual peaceful colonization—at least
in south Texas. In July of 1629, a delegation of about fifty Jumano Indians from Texas appeared at the Franciscan convent of old Isleta,
south of Albuquerque. They had come to ask for missionaries for
themselves and their neighbors, and showed some knowledge of
Catholicism. Asked who had instructed them, they replied, "the
Woman in Blue." Shortly afterwards, an expedition, led by the Franciscan Fray Juan de Salas, set out for the land of the Jumanos guided
by the Jumano chief. Reaching a spot in southwest Texas, the group
was received by a large band of Indians. They said that they had been
told by the Woman in Blue of the missionaries' approach. About two
thousand natives presented themselves for baptism and further cate-
chizing. Two years later, Fray Alonso de Benavides, former religious
superior in New Mexico, journeyed to Spain seeking the identity of
the mysterious nun. Under his questioning, Sor María de Jesús at
Agreda admitted that she had experienced some five hundred bi-
locations to New Spain and that she was indeed the Woman in Blue.

This remarkable woman was born in Agreda (near the border
of Aragon and Navarre) in April of 1602. She was the eldest daughter of Francisco Coronel and Catalina de Arana, and from childhood
had demonstrated both unusual piety and remarkable memory.
When Maria was sixteen, she convinced her father to turn the family castle into a convent for Franciscan nuns. Receiving religious

vows on February 2, 1620, she took the name María de Jesús. Her new order soon expanded beyond the castle, moving into the convent of the Immaculate Conception in Agreda. The nuns' habit was Franciscan brown with an outer cloak of coarse blue cloth.

Throughout the 1620s María de Jesús repeatedly lapsed into deep trances. During these interludes she dreamt that she traveled to a distant and unknown land, where she taught the Gospel to a pagan people. These trips took her to eastern New Mexico and western Texas, where she contacted several Indian cultures, including the Jumanos. She told her mystical experiences to her confessor, Fray Sebastián Marcilla of Agreda, who in turn wrote of these events to his superiors. They contacted the archbishop of Mexico, Francisco Manso y Zúñiga, who wrote the religious superior of New Mexico in May of 1628, requesting confirmation. The next year, the Jumanos arrived at Isleta.

But the work of María de Jesús was not confined to bilocation. She had a number of visions of the life of the Virgin Mary, which she recorded in her four-volume book, *Mystical City of God*; during her last twenty-two years, she actively corresponded with the Spanish king, Philip IV. Dying at Agreda on May 24, 1665, her story was published in Spain several years afterwards. While María de Jesús declared that her last visitation to the New World was in 1631, she was not forgotten in Texas—in 1690 a missionary working with the Tejas Indians was told about the event by his converts. As late as the 1840s, a "Woman in Blue" traveled the Sabine River valley helping malaria victims, and a similar apparition was reported as late as World War II. A picture of the event is displayed in the Cathedral of Fort Worth. But were these two later apparitions María de Jesús paying a return visit from Heaven, or two other living nuns following in her footsteps? We shall never know this side of the grave.

Despite the aid of the Blue Lady and the establishment of missions, exploration, and claims of sovereignty, Spain did not get around to actually colonizing Texas until 1716, with the foundation of San Antonio, the colonial capital. El Paso was in existence much earlier, of course, but it was part of New Mexico. Other settlements followed: Laredo, Goliad, Nagadoches, Refugio, Los Adaes (in present Louisiana), and elsewhere. Despite the recurring fights with nomadic Apaches and Comanches, Spanish Texas flourished. Franciscan padres had founded and refounded forty missions; the Royal authorities founded ten presidios extending from central Texas eastward to the site of present Robeline, Louisiana, and southward to Chambers County; civil municipalities ranged from Laredo to San Antonio and Nacogdoches; ranches and farms dotted the landscape. The majority of the population was probably mestizo, and reasonably well contented.

As a result, when the first war of Mexican independence broke out in 1810, the Tejanos vigorously resisted several attempts to detach them from the Crown. Only when Agustin de Iturbide proclaimed a Catholic Mexican Empire in 1821 would they accept independence. When he was overthrown, Texas docilely passed under the new republican regime—a regime that badly miscalculated, by encouraging settlement by Anglo-Americans from the United States. Soon, Hispanics were outnumbered by Americans. They threw off the government they had sworn allegiance to, winning their independence in 1836 (it is perhaps suppressed guilt over this incident that leads to similar fear by Anglos toward today's burgeoning population of Hispanics in the southwest). The new Texas Republic abandoned the old capital at San Antonio, establishing their seat of government first at Washington-on-the-Brazos, and finally at Austin, where it has remained ever since, through annexation by the United States, statehood, secession, and forcible reincorporation into the Union.

But San Antonio, since its foundation in 1718, has remained the spiritual capital of Hispanic Texas. Reminders of this status are everywhere, including the Royally endowed Cathedral of San Fernando, the Spanish Governor's Palace, and the chain of five missions extending from the Alamo out to the suburbs. Although under Anglo political control since 1836, San Antonio remains very much a Spanish-speaking city.

But another element took its place in San Antonio's culture and tradition alongside Hispanics and Anglos: the Germans. After the United States annexed Texas in 1845, Germans poured into the state, particularly after the suppression of the 1848 revolts in the Fatherland. One of their most enduring legacies is the King William Historic District, just south of the central business section. Laid out between 1853 and 1859, the area was named in honor of Wilhelm I, king of Prussia.

But there is another tangible reminder of German San Antonio, located on the Alamo Plaza: the Menger Hotel. William Menger had arrived in San Antonio from Germany in the early 1840s. He operated a brewery at the hotel's present site with Charles Phillip Degen. In 1857 he and his wife decided to expand their boardinghouse, so that his patrons could sleep off their drunkenness, thus avoiding falling off their horses en route to their homes. Guided by local architect John M. Fries, Menger built a two-story cut-stone building featuring classical detail; the foundations were laid on June 18, 1858, and the hotel opened on January 31, 1859. The hotel was so successful that a forty-room annex was soon added; Sam Houston made it his regular hotel in San Antonio. A tunnel ran to the adjacent brewery. Menger died at his hotel in March of 1871; his widow and son took over.

After Reconstruction ended and the railroad arrived in 1877, the Menger became the best-known hotel in the southwest. The cuisine offered in the Colonial Dining Room included such viands as wild game, mango ice cream, and snapper soup made from turtles caught in the San Antonio River. Soon the hotel was attracting contemporary celebrities. William Sydney Porter (O. Henry) mentions the hotel several times in his stories. In the winter of 1872–73 poet Sidney Lanier stayed at the Menger; there he wrote his sketch "San Antonio de Bexar." The military also patronized the place: in 1873 General Philip H. Sheridan and Secretary of War William W. Belknap stayed there, and President Ulysses S. Grant spent four days there in 1880. Robert E. Lee came as well. Richard King, founder of the famed King Ranch and a frequent guest, died in his room at the hotel in 1885. Travelers raced from the depot in order to be in time to check into the "eight rooms with adjoining baths." But not all the occurrences were pleasant: in 1876, a chambermaid, Sallie White, was murdered by her husband. The Mengers buried her at their expense.

In March of 1879 gaslights were installed. Improvements followed fast upon each other: an east wing was added in December 1881, and seven years later, a new lounge was opening, featuring such unheard-of luxuries as a solid cherry bar, cherry-paneled ceiling, French mirrors, and gold-plated spittoons. The hotel's specialty drinks, such as river-chilled beer, mint juleps served in solid silver tumblers, and hot rum toddies became famous nationwide. Actress Sarah Bernhardt enjoyed these particularly. Theodore Roosevelt first visited the Menger in 1892 while hunting for javelinas, as the nasty little wild pigs of the area are called. He returned six years later to recruit his Rough Riders at the hotel bar, and came back in 1905 for a banquet. In 1909 the hotel was again enlarged with an addition to the south side; the main façade was also altered, with Renaissance Revival details in stuccoed brick, pressed metal, and cast iron. A new interior rotunda was constructed to provide light and serve as a circulation hub. The hotel remained a center of San Antonio social affairs and a meeting place for such visiting celebrities as Gutzon Borglum, Mae West, and Babe Ruth.

Although the Menger declined during the Great Depression, in the mid-1940s the building was reconditioned, and its dining rooms restored. By 1951 a new wing was added, and the building completely modernized; it continued to attract the likes of Bob Hope and John Wayne. In 1976 the Menger was added to the National Register of Historic Places as part of the Alamo Plaza Historic District, and again renovated in the 1980s. The hotel now boasts five stories, 316 rooms, and wonderful dining and other services, such as babysitting services, fitness and business centers, a spa, and 11,000 square feet of banquet facilities.

With all of this past greatness and present comfort, it is no wonder that the Menger remains the magnet it has always been. But with such a dramatic past, it should come as no surprise that many of its guests have returned on a more permanent basis. No less than thirty-two phantoms have been spotted in the old hotel. Apparently, Teddy Roosevelt's recruiting session at the bar was a success; it has been reenacted by several of the participants, much to the fear of the hotel employee who saw it in the bar after closing.

Captain Richard King has also returned, apparently preferring the place to his own home—although it would be interesting to learn if he haunts the King Ranch also. At the hotel, he is now and then seen entering his room, the King Suite, by many guests and employees. He does not use the present suite door, preferring to go directly through the wall at the spot where the door was in his day. The unfortunate maid, Sallie White, walks in the hotel corridors, especially at night. Dressed in a long gray skirt with a bandana around her forehead, she is usually carrying towels, although she never delivers them.

But there are other permanent guests, whose names are lost to us. In one room, guests will from time to time step out of the shower of one room, and step into a bedroom. There they will be confronted by a ghostly man in a buckskin jacket and gray trousers, speaking to an unseen presence; the apparition three times asks the question "Are you gonna stay or are you gonna go?" before vanishing. Thankfully, no reply has as yet been heard. In the original lobby, a woman in a beret with tassel, an old-fashioned blue dress, and small metal-framed glasses will be seen knitting. If a staff member should ask "Are you comfortable? May I get you something?" the woman will huffily reply "No," and disappear. She has also been seen reading a newspaper, dropping it down and raising it up. All this activity apparently rouses her appetite, as one banquet waiter has seen her going into the Renaissance Room.

Many more will put in appearances: a Confederate officer may be seen on the patio, enjoying his permanent leave; a plump but deceased maître d' sometimes appears in the Colonial Dining Room. One female guest awoke to see a male ghost grinning at her from the foot of the bed, and then tried to pull the blankets off of her. She and her husband swiftly relocated to a newer portion of the hotel. That by itself may not help: guests in newer rooms facing the Alamo have seen ghosts walking the grounds from their windows. Even modern technology can be affected, as at least one guest has been bedeviled by a TV that kept turning itself on.

These are only a few of the more exciting occurrences; but every few days staff or guests report something, from cold spots, to standard poltergeist activity, to apparitions. But the employees for the most part take their service among the unseen cheerfully, and there is little turnover. For that matter, these occurrences do not seem to prevent a great deal of repeat business. The only apparition this writer has seen there has been expertly prepared venison in the Colonial Room. But then, I wasn't looking. Spend enough time there, and something—or someone—is bound to turn up.

Menger Hotel
204 Alamo Plaza
San Antonio, TX 78205
(210) 223-4361
www.historicmenger.com

At Utah's Historical Society, the Past is Never Truly Dead

U tah, the "Beehive State," is, like Louisiana, a world apart from the rest of the United States. But where Louisiana's uniqueness is owed to its swampy terrain and the French stamp on its culture, institutions, and religion, Utah was made distinctive by its aridity and its Mormonism. The first quality guaranteed a poor quality of life for the state's first Panamint and Ute inhabitants who, with their Nevada brethren, would be characterized as "Digger Indians." Although the area was claimed by Spain and then Mexico, the Great Basin was too difficult to tempt even the hardiest settlers from the south, and too remote for their governments to care about it.

But that very remoteness was its appeal to a column of Mormons, as the members of the Church of Jesus Christ of Latter-Day Saints are called (although in recent years they have come to dislike the term). Founded by Joseph Smith, a young Vermonter who had relocated to New York state, and there been, so he claimed, visited by an angel who called himself Moroni. This spirit gave Smith a set of gold tablets written upon in a language he called "Reformed Egyptian." A set of magic spectacles was also provided, whereby the seer could read them. What Smith said was the translation he wrote down formed the *Book of Mormon*, which he proclaimed to be the equal of the Bible, in that its various books told first of the coming of Israelites to the New World, and their formation of civilization, which eventually corrupted; and then the coming of Christ to redeem these people's descendants after His crucifixion in Palestine.

Smith taught many doctrines at variance with orthodox Christianity: that God has a body, and that He was originally Adam; that He dwells in outer space, near a planet called Kolob; that He is the direct biological father of all human souls; that men have an obligation to produce as many bodies to incarnate these souls as possible; that polygamy, acceptable in the Old Testament, is a good way to increase the supply of bodies; that devout male Mormons may become Gods of their own planets, as Adam did of this one; that living Mormons may baptize their dead ancestors into the Church; that the United States are the actual successors of the Chosen People (an idea held unconsciously by many non-Mormons, to be sure); and much else besides.

In a nineteenth-century America where the various Christian bodies took their own beliefs very seriously, these ideas got Smith and his rapidly growing band of followers into a great deal of trouble. Persecution and hardship followed them as they sought havens successively in Kirtland, Ohio; Independence, Missouri (where Smith and his brother Hyrum were dragged from jail and killed by a mob); and Nauvoo, Illinois. At this last spot, Brigham Young, who had taken over leadership for most of the Mormons (a schism was precipitated when the Smith family refused to accept Young's control; they started a smaller group, based in Independence, where all Mormons believe Christ will rebuild the Temple at His second coming) decided that it was time to leave the hostile east behind.

Young led a pioneer column westwards into the Great Basin. Although it was legally part of Mexico, with which country the United States were then at war, Young was well aware that Mexico had left the land empty. After a grueling journey, the column arrived at the shores of the Great Salt Lake on July 24, 1847. The new arrivals numbered 148—143 men, three women, and two children. When Young first saw the valley, he said, "This is the right place." The day they arrived, the pioneers began tilling the soil and planting crops.

Within a few days, Young drew up plans for Great Salt Lake City; from the center of the city, today's Temple Square, blocks were arranged on a grid pattern in ten-acre squares, separated by streets 132 feet wide: "wide enough for a team of four oxen and a covered wagon to turn around." The newcomers were joined the next year by more immigrants. For a little while, all seemed well. But late frost, drought, and a plague of crickets almost destroyed the harvest. Miraculously, flocks of seagulls descended on the crickets and ate them; enough of the crop was saved to allow the settlers to survive the winter of 1848–49. As a result, the seagull was later designated Utah's state bird. But the occurrence convinced the Mormons both that God was on their side and that Brigham Young's leadership was regarded by Him with favor. The Mormons strenuously recruited Europeans, particularly Germans, Scandinavians, and British. The result was that, despite its religious uniformity, Salt Lake City became quite cosmopolitan over the following decade.

But in the meantime, events in the outside world would affect the infant settlement greatly. When Young and his people arrived, the region was still part of Mexico. But the treaty of Guadalupe Hidalgo signed in 1848 gave it to the United States. Young and his followers decided to form a political entity. They called it the "State of Deseret." In the "Reformed Egyptian" of the *Book of Mormon*, the word means honeybee, which is a symbol of industriousness— this is why Utah's state symbol is the beehive.

The Mormons drafted a constitution for the new state in 1849; its capital was to be Salt Lake City and its borders would encompass the entire Great Basin, including all or part of nine current U.S. states. The city of San Bernardino, California, was founded by Mormons at this time in an attempt to give Deseret an outlet to the sea. Their government up and functioning, the Mormons petitioned congress to recognize them as a state of the Union.

Instead of doing this, on September 9, 1850 Congress created the Utah Territory, comprising modern Utah, Nevada, and Colorado, on the same day that California was admitted to the Union as a state. President Millard Fillmore named Young as Territorial Governor. The creation of Utah Territory was part of the Compromise of 1850, which tried to preserve the balance of power in congress between slave and free states. The first session of the territorial legislature in October of that year adopted all the laws and ordinances that had previously been enacted by the General Assembly of the State of Deseret.

In order to encourage settlement of the barren center of the Territory, Young and the assembly resolved to move the capital into uninhabited land in central Utah. An approximate site for the new capital was chosen 148 miles south of Salt Lake City and dubbed Fillmore in gratitude to President Millard Fillmore for appointing Young governor. On October 4, 1851, the Utah territorial legislature passed a joint resolution that created Millard County from a portion of Iron County, in the area called the "Pahvant Valley." Fillmore would be county seat as well as territorial capital, and the sum of $20,000 was appropriated for this purpose. On October 21, two companies set out from Salt Lake City for the new site. A monumental statehouse was planned; Truman O. Angell, architect of the Salt Lake Temple, envisioned a lavish structure of four wings in the form of a cross with a Moorish dome at the center. Local red sandstone and native timber were used in its construction. Although the first wing was completed in time for the fifth session of the territorial legislature on December 1855, the sixth legislative session soon adjourned to reconvene in Salt Lake City. Never again would Salt Lake City's dominance over Utah be challenged.

However much freedom the Mormons exercised in their territory, their doings were not well regarded back east; polygamy, in particular, aroused constant criticism outside Utah. Meanwhile, attracted by the newly discovered mines of the Comstock Lode, many "gentiles," as non-Mormons are called, began flocking to the western part of the territory. Partly to free them from Mormon rule, and partly to secure the wealth of the Comstock to the federal government, in 1861 the territory of Nevada was created out of the western part of the territory; that same year, a large portion of the eastern area of the territory merged with land formerly part of the Kansas, Nebraska, Utah, and New Mexico territories. Thus was Colorado Territory born.

A blow to Mormon dominance in Utah itself came in 1869, when the railroads arrived simultaneously from California and the east. So displeased by this event were the Mormon leadership that they boycotted the driving of the golden spike at Promontory Summit to complete the transcontinental railroad. Worse still, it was obvious that as long as polygamy was legal in Utah, Washington would never admit it into the Union as a state. Nevada Territory, although far more sparsely populated, was admitted to the Union in 1864; Colorado followed suit in 1876.

It was only twenty years after that, when the president of the Mormon Church received a revelation from God that it would be good to do so, was polygamy discarded by the church, and so the territory. Utah was duly admitted as a state in 1896. But just as some of the Mormons had not accepted Young's headship of the church, some would not abandon polygamy. In certain remote hamlets in Utah and elsewhere in the Great Basin, it survives. But so do other unusual beliefs and practices.

According to the Mormon scriptures (*Doctrine and Covenants*, Abraham 3) this and perhaps all galaxies contain countless planets either already, or soon to be, inhabited by humanoid life. The greatest of these planets is Kolob, because it is "nearest unto the throne of God." The Moon, Earth, and Sun receive their light from Kolob. With such beliefs as part of their scriptures, it will easily be seen why many modern Mormons have no trouble believing in ghosts, UFOs, and all sort of other things. But one belief that goes back to their early days and is still strong in rural Utah is that of the Three Nephites. These are a trio of undying beings, natives of Kolob, to whom God long ago gave immortality. They are described as having bone white feet and long flowing white hair and beards. The Nephites "usually travel singly by most accounts, arriving unseen, unbidden, often seeking a meal or simply a place to stay the night. They come on foot, usually, less often by a rickety cart pulled by an ancient nag. They cure the sick, bring prosperity to the poor. The host who shelters a Nephite never learns his true identity until after he has left. After the stranger vanishes, leaving no earthly trace whatsoever, the Mormon family believes they have been touched by the hand of God. The Nephites remain on earth voluntarily. Although the earliest reports of their encounters with faithful Mormons came from Utah, later stories started coming from all over the world as the Nephites supposedly followed Mormon missionaries who sought converts in every part of the globe." (Michael Normal and Beth Scott, *Haunted America*, 1994).

Stories of these celestial helpers have been told throughout Utah from its first settlement. But benevolent immortals are not the only strange beings said to traverse the Utah wastes. There are also the Gadianton robbers, an evil tribe of Israelites who roam the earth eternally wreaking evil and causing mayhem. Freighters passing through the gorge between Modena, Utah and Pinoche,

Nevada would have rocks thrown down in front of them; a few of the freighters would be crushed. In one Utah town, tools would disappear; women who set their bread out to rise would find it turned upside down. If the women turned their backs, their irons would disappear; the sawmill ran all by itself all night, stopping if anyone came to check it. The Gadianton robbers were at work again. Similar were their depredations at Red Creek in the Uintah basin, where they rode down the canyon on phantom horses.

But while rural Utah was resounding to this supernatural mayhem, Salt Lake City kept right on developing in more material directions. Although construction on the Mormon temple began in 1853, it was not finished until 1892. As feared, the railroads brought in a torrent of gentiles, which torrent further spurred the opening of hundreds of copper, silver, gold, and lead mines in the nearby canyons, including Bingham Canyon. Prosperous mine owners constructed large, gracious homes along South Temple Street.

After polygamy was dropped and Utah became a state, Salt Lake City became, in the early 1900s, rather more mainstream. The state capitol and many other historic buildings were constructed. Ground was broken for the Catholic Madeleine Cathedral on July 4, 1899. Contributed to by every gentile in the city, the massive Romanesque building was completed in a decade. The year 1909 also saw the completion of the splendid Union Pacific Depot.

The following year, the Denver and Rio Grande Depot was built to commemorate the union of the Denver and Rio Grande and Western Pacific railroads. George Gould, the owner of the D&RGW line, spent $75 million in completing the laying of a line to the west coast. He built the depot in an attempt to win contracts and a market share from the Union Pacific. While he did break the UP's railroad monopoly, he was ruined financially and lost his railroad empire a short time later.

Nevertheless, the depot remained and remains something Gould could be proud of. Erected at a cost of $750,000, it combines elements of the Renaissance Revival and Beaux Arts Classicism; it is truly one of the most elegant stations ever built in the United States. But as those old enough to remember will know, elegant stations by themselves could and did not save passenger train travel. Salt Lake City did not need two stations; the depot was sold to the state of Utah for one dollar in 1977. It was lavishly restored, and occupied by the Utah State Historical Society three years later.

The Historical Society has maintained offices, a library, and a museum there since they moved in. But one thing they did not displace was the preternatural. During the 1940s, train crews using the depot believed it to be haunted.

Near the Rio Grande Café, the depot's restaurant, the apparition of a beautiful black-haired woman in a purple dress has often been seen. It is said that she was engaged to a handsome young man, and would come to Salt Lake City by train. Her intended would meet her there; but one day they argued and broke the engagement. The young man threw the engagement ring onto the tracks; his former fiancée ran to get it back, and was mowed down by a train, in similar fashion to the heroine in the fifties song, "Teen Angel." Unlike that fictional character, however, this one does come back.

It is also claimed that a phantom party is occasionally thrown in the cellar. One night, lights went on and off in the depot by themselves. A maintenance worker went down to the basement to check the fuse box, only to find a group of people having a party. Before his eyes, they vanished.

Every night at the same time, a security guard would hear someone walking on an upper balcony. Although he always ran up to check, there was never anyone there. At last, one night he decided to hide and ambush the perpetrator. When he heard the footsteps, he jumped up, but no one was visible. They walked right past him; something brushed him, and then walked on down the stairs.

Many of the staff have had such strange experiences, and don't mind talking about them. *But,* they should be forewarned. In August of 2004, the new State Archives Building south of the depot will be finished; the Archives will move into the building and out of the depot. Extensive remodeling, changing of exhibits, and shift of offices will continue until March 2005. Very often, renovation steps up ghostly activity. The next few years should be exciting ones at the old depot.

Utah State Historical Society
300 South Rio Grande Street
Salt Lake City, UT 84101-1143
(801) 533-3500

In Vermont, a Local Socialite Still Holds Forth in Her Home— Long After Her Death

The first inhabitants of the "Green Mountain State" were the Abnaki. Samuel de Champlain, founder of Quebec, was the first European to discover the Green Mountains. In the summer of 1609, leaving his encampment on the St. Lawrence in Quebec, he joined the Algonquians in an expedition against their enemies, the Iroquois. The journey up the river brought Champlain onto the lake that now carries his name on July 4, 1609. While this trip endeared him to the Abnaki and other Algonquian tribes, and allied them forever to France, it similarly ensured that one day the Iroquois would ally with their English enemies.

Although the first permanent English settlement was established along the Connecticut River in 1724 at Fort Dummer (near modern Brattleboro), it was only a military post maintained by the colonial governments of Massachusetts and New Hampshire as a defensive position against the French and their Indian allies. Not until the French were finally defeated in 1763 would the Green

Mountains be open to settlement. But British hegemony merely opened the door to squabbling between the provinces of New Hampshire and New York as to which had the proper claim to the territory, then called the New Hampshire Grants. Most of the new settlers were from Connecticut or Massachusetts and resisted the authority of New York. Armed bands skirmished on both sides, preserving an atmosphere of instability.

An anomaly in all of this confusion was the little community of Arlington. Chartered in 1761 by primarily Anglican people from Litchfield, Connecticut, and later from Newtown and New Milford, Connecticut, it was a maypole-dancing and Christmas-observing island in a sea of Congregationalists. Not surprisingly, its inhabitants steered a middle ground between New York and New Hampshire, and fielded a fair number of Loyalists during the Revolution.

But most of the New Englanders in Vermont resisted the claims of the "Yorkers." This led to the organization of the Green Mountain Boys under the leadership of Colonel Ethan Allen in 1775. His small army captured Fort Ticonderoga from the British, thus providing the cannon which, mounted on Dorchester Heights, would force them to evacuate that city on March 17, 1776. Nor was this all; Allen and his men would play an important role at the battles of Hubbardton and Bennington in 1777. Nevertheless, if they wished independence from the Crown, the Green Mountain Boys were none too impressed with the rebels either.

On January 17, 1777, Vermonters declared themselves an independent republic in a meeting held at Westminster; although they entered into negotiations with the British, they went nowhere. Vermont minted its own coin and provided postal service until 1791 when it was admitted to the Union, the first state to join the original thirteen.

The Yankees who settled Vermont came equipped with strange tales of "ha'nts" and witches. After the Civil War, droves of

French Canadians arrived, with their own stories of the *loup garou* and *fétiche*. Even today, certain areas of the state, like the abandoned town of Glastonbury with its many disappearances, radiate an eerie atmosphere.

Typical of Vermont towns is Waterbury. In 1763, King George III granted a charter via Governor Benning Wentworth of New Hampshire for land in the Winooski River Valley. The proprietors, mostly from Waterbury, Connecticut, received their charter, naming the new township after their hometown. And in 1783, James Marsh became the first permanent settler.

The stagecoach ran through Waterbury as the state developed, and so, in 1826 the building now known as the Old Stagecoach Inn was erected. Originally it was built in Federal style, while serving as a tavern and coach stop. In 1895, however, it became a private home and was transformed into a Queen Anne Revival house. The large three-story, five-bay building retains its Federal-style one-room-deep profile on the first floor; entry is surrounded by etched glass sidelights, while the extensive porches found on each floor attest to the Queen Anne Revival. For years it was the home of Mrs. Margaret Spencer, a local socialite who also maintained homes in London, Paris, and New York City; she died in what is now Room 2. In 1987 the building was restored and found a new life as a bed and breakfast.

Despite the rough and tumble nature of so many early American taverns, the ghostly echoes of the past do not stem from some nameless Hessian or local stage robber; instead, it is apparently the more respectable shade of Mrs. Spencer who holds forth. Mr. Barwick, the current owner, bought the old inn in 1993. Although he had heard that Mrs. Spencer frequently appeared to guests and employees, he paid little attention—he was a disbeliever in such things. Even so, he was aware that when *Yankee Magazine* did an article on the place, they took a photo of the old owner in Room 2. When this was developed, there was a woman in an old-fashioned dress in the light of the window who had not been there.

But his views have changed. After being there about four years, one of his housekeepers told him that, while working in Room 8, a rocking chair started swiftly rocking back and forth on its own.

About the same time, on a Sunday morning in the summer, three people came down to breakfast. The owner did not recognize them. At first he thought that they had come in off the street, but realized that they had in fact come down the stairs. The only vacancy was Room 3—it was a cancellation that only the owner knew about. He asked where they were staying, and when they had arrived. They replied that they were in Room 3, and had come in around 2:00 or 2:30 in the morning. In reply to the owner's query as to who had let them in, their answer was that they were received by a very friendly older lady, who took them up to their room. She was wearing a long dress and her hair was in a bun. Although the guests didn't notice anything wrong, the owner realized that no one else knew about the vacancy, and there was no one fitting that description on the staff.

In one room on another morning, a housekeeper came down and asked the owner who had slept in Room 2. He answered that no one had. But she insisted that someone had slept in the bed. When they both went up, the bed was indeed rumpled and there were indentations on the pillows. The owner told the housekeeper to smooth it out and forget about it. She went to the linen closet and he went back downstairs. Shortly afterward she came running down, saying that there was someone in the room. When they both returned, the sheets, blankets, and pillows were all folded at the end of the bed. They were staring at a bare mattress cover; the housekeeper would never go up alone again.

The next St. Patrick's Day, some ladies were sitting in the living room having Irish coffee, while a man made the coffee and poured in some Jameson's Whiskey. After serving the ladies he came back to the front room, and asked Mr. Barwick where the whiskey had gone, after noticing that it had disappeared. The owner replied that he did not know and had not seen it. The guest said: "That's gotta be your ghost." They all laughed, but the next morning the owner got up early and came down to make new coffee. He turned on the light, only to find the whisky. It may well be that Mrs. Spencer appropriated it for a little celebration of her own. But whatever the case, the Old Stagecoach Inn is the sort of place people can't help coming back to.

Old Stagecoach Inn
18 North Main Street
Waterbury, VT
(802) 244-5056
www.oldstagecoach.com/index.asp

A Haunted Painting Holds Court
at Virginia's Shirley Plantation

Virginia gets its nickname—"the Old Dominion"—from its status as the first English province in North America, and from its loyalty to the Crown during the English Civil War (1641–49). Technically, it is not a state; together with its two sister colonies Massachusetts and Pennsylvania, and its daughter Kentucky, Virginia is officially called a "commonwealth," although there is no practical difference between the two terms.

Virginians are proud of their origins, dating back to the founding of Jamestown in 1607. Boston may be where the revolution broke out, and Philadelphia where independence was declared. But it is in Virginia that the history of American institutional government begins. The Virginia General Assembly goes back to the establishment of the House of Burgesses at Jamestown in 1619; not only is it the "oldest continuous law-making body in the Americas," it is the second-oldest such assembly in the English-speaking world—only Great Britain's

Parliament is older. Bermuda and Barbados boast assemblies only a few years younger than Virginia's. As with those two countries, and most of the parliaments around the world whose origins lie with Westminster, the Virginia lower house uses a mace—a ceremonial staff first presented to the House of Burgesses in 1700 by the Royal Governor General of Virginia. The current mace was bought in Great Britain and presented to the Virginia House of Delegates in 1974 by the Jamestown Foundation. A symbol of the authority that convenes the legislature, the mace is presented by the sergeant-at-arms in the current house chamber and remains until the house adjourns every day. When the Virginia Senate wanted a seal for itself in 1981, it turned to the College of Arms in London, the Queen's official heraldic body, to design and authorize one. Tradition is very important to Virginians, and a touch of aristocracy pervades the commonwealth.

This is not surprising, given Virginia's settlement patterns. Over her colonial history, Englishmen settled down to raise tobacco in Virginia's river-rich Tidewater country. Further inland, Germans settled much of the higher Piedmont, and Ulster Scots filled the Appalachians. The tobacco-raisers built great plantations worked by slaves, while towns grew up whose merchants bartered the crop for luxury and manufactured goods, and credit in England. Originally, "plantation" meant a settlement in a new country or region—this meaning is preserved today in Rhode Island's official title of Rhode Island and Providence *Plantations*. But in Virginia the word came to mean land that was "planted" and worked by resident labor. Some Virginia planters owned many plantations; not all of these had homes on them.

At first, work on the Virginia plantations was done by indentured servants. These were poor Europeans who bonded themselves over for several years of work to colonial planters; in return they were given passage to Virginia. But by 1705, African slavery was codified into law. The long and complicated relationship between free Europeans and enslaved Africans was under way. It would have an enormous impact, not only on Virginia and the rest of the south, but the rest of the colonies and the future United States. These Africans brought with them the tales and beliefs of their homeland—of magic, ghosts, and witches.

But the Europeans had beliefs of this sort of their own. In Virginia, as in most of the other colonies, witchcraft was a felony. But the courts of the province were not too concerned; those accused of the crime were allowed to counter-sue their accusers for defamation of character. If the accuser was found guilty, he had to pay the supposed witch a large sum of money. There were few such trials in Virginia.

Out in the Appalachians though, then and now, tales of witchcraft were rife. Many stories were told of witches who sold their souls to the devil. The locals might secretly visit such folk for herbal cures and love potions, but always remained on guard against the witch's undoubted malevolence. If a farmer's cow stopped giving milk, he would strike a stone with a birch rod. The bewitcher of the animal would be wounded, and so exposed to the neighborhood. Given the reluctance of the colonial courts to deal with such issues, the matter would usually be settled privately—and lethally.

The same region has given rise to a few vampire stories. Out in Big Stone Gap, in the late nineteenth century, farm animals were found drained of blood. Then the town drunk was discovered in the same condition, as was a traveling salesman. When a strange old recluse was seen by some children happily eating raw meat in his home, a posse was called out. But the suspect had vanished by the time the posse arrived.

In the Tidewater, by contrast, vampires and witches were few. But every plantation home seemed to have a ghost, firmly believed in by both the residents of the ornate and luxurious big house, and by the denizens of the slave cabins. Then as now, such grand old homes were numerous in Virginia, and particularly so in Charles City County.

This county is one of the oldest political units in America, being one of the four "incorporations" into which Virginia settlements were divided in 1619. In the county during the eighteenth century, grand brick homes were on such plantations as Berkeley, Brandon, Shirley, Wilton, and Westover. Their owners, families such as the Harrisons, Carters, Byrds, and Randolphs, were the social and economic leaders of Colonial Virginia. They provided much of the leadership of the revolution, by which they could take complete power from the monarchy and cancel their enormous debts to British merchants as well (living in such grand style was not cheap). After independence, four of the first five presidents, the "Virginia dynasty" as they were called, hailed from the Old Dominion families, as did William Henry Harrison and Benjamin Harrison. But among the greatest and most powerful of these clans were the Carters of Shirley.

Home of the Hill-Carter family for nearly four centuries, Shirley is both the oldest plantation in Virginia and the oldest family-owned business in North America. It was founded six years after the settlers arrived at Jamestown by Sir Thomas West, first Royal governor of Virginia. He called the grant "West and Sherley Hundred," after himself and his wife, Lady Cessalye Sherley. When Sir Thomas died in 1619, much of the grant was transferred to others. Part of it would be sold, thirty-one years later, to Edward Hill I. Colonel Hill was an important man in mid-seventeenth-century Virginia, having been, among other offices, speaker of the house of Burgesses and treasurer of Virginia. His son and grandson, likewise named Edward, maintained similar positions in the province. Their various relations stayed close at hand; Edward II's daughter, Martha Hill Pratt, returned to live there sometime after her marriage.

241

When, in 1723, Edward III's daughter (and only surviving child) Elizabeth married John Carter, eldest son of local magnate Robert "King" Carter, John decided that a grander residence was the only fitting wedding gift he could provide. Building began on the present house, but it was not finished for almost fifty years. No expense was spared, either inside or out. Three brick stories featured dormer windows jutting from the roof on all sides. A couple of two-story porticoes, each with four white pillars, adorned the front of the house. John and Elizabeth's son, Charles Carter (1732–1806), moved his seat to Shirley from Corotomon in 1770. Although he was very Anglophile, Charles supported the various anti-British resolutions and joined various conventions during the revolutionary period.

Little has changed since then. Visitors to the main floor will encounter eighteenth-century hand-carved woodwork, family portraits, silver, furniture, and other decorative pieces that have remained in the family for generations. Part of the house's unique architecture is the famous hanging stairway made of walnut, which climbs the house's entire height without support. On the 720-acre plantation grounds, seven original-out buildings remain today. The plantation remains in the hands of Charles Hill Carter II, the ninth generation to own the property; thus, still family-owned, Shirley Plantation remains a living entity.

For almost 250 years, a wooden pineapple on the Mansard roof between the two giant chimneys has symbolized hospitality to the Carters' guests. Over the centuries, these have included such prominent Virginia clans as the Harrisons, Jeffersons, Byrds, Lees, Washingtons, and Tylers—since the family graciously opened the house to the public, you can take your place in this number. But much has happened in all that time.

When Charles's daughter, Ann Hill Carter, was carrying a silver punchbowl across the dining room, it began to slip out of her hands. Luckily, a gallant army officer standing by came to her rescue. It was Henry "Light Horse Harry" Lee, Revolutionary War veteran and governor of Virginia. The couple was married at Shirley in 1793, and produced a famous son, Robert E. Lee.

During the Civil War, Charles City County was occupied by Union troops. Hill Carter (1796–1870), grandson of Charles, was the owner of Shirley at the time. Shirley was able to survive the war intact because Hill was able to acquire from General George B. McClellan a Federal Safeguard in 1862, which protected the family and property throughout the duration of the war. This was in gratitude for the hospitality shown by the family and their servants to the wounded and dying when Shirley was made into a Union field hospital during the Peninsula Campaign of that year.

Nevertheless, all six of Hill Carter's sons fought in the Confederate Army, only one, however, being killed. When word reached Beverly Randolph Carter at the front that his mother, Mary Braxton Randolph Carter, was dying at Shirley, he resolved to see her one last time. Making his way through the Union lines using secret paths he had known since boyhood, Beverly was able to sneak successfully into the house. Unfortunately, a servant betrayed him and sent word to the Federals that a Confederate spy was in the house. The Union soldiers arrived and searched the house. They were about to leave when one of their officers spied a secret entrance to the attic behind a bookcase. He went in and looked through the attic, while young Carter hid behind the chimney. The officer returned to his men, saying that he had seen no one. After dark Carter made off behind Confederate lines. Years later, a female relative of that officer revealed that he had indeed seen Carter hiding, but that "his conscience overcame his compulsion to duty."

So prominent have the Carters been in Virginia history, that such novelists as Edgar Rice Burroughs (in *A Princess of Mars* and its sequels in the Barsoom series) and H. P. Lovecraft (in his

"Randolph Carter" stories) have created fictional members of the clan to serve as heroes, thus conferring the magic associated with the Carter name on them. With all the history and emotional drama that Shirley has witnessed, it might be supposed that some family and guests have remained after their earthly sojourn has ended. One of these is Elizabeth Hill Carter's aunt, Martha Pratt.

A painting of Aunt Martha is today one of the most prized in the family's collection. But it was not always so. Some years after her death, as part of a redecorating scheme, the painting was taken down from its spot in her old second-story bedroom and placed in the attic. Immediately, the family began to hear the sound of rocking in the attic. On the rocking would go, frightening by its intensity family and guests alike. Those who mustered the courage to enter the picture's hideaway saw nothing, and the rocking would cease; but it would commence again when the door was closed. Admitting defeat, the then-head of the family had Aunt Martha's painting returned to its accustomed place, whereupon the noises ceased.

Even in the most historically minded families, memories fade. In 1974, the Virginia Travel Council, anxious to promote tourism, searched the commonwealth for historical objects to place in an exhibition in Rockefeller Center in New York City. When they heard the story of the rocking portrait, the organizers thought that Aunt Martha would do well as an example of Virginia folklore. But old legends have a way of coming back to haunt us, so to speak. After Aunt Martha's picture was shipped north, and was duly hung in a display case, it began to swing violently; so much so that *NBC Nightly News* filmed it. One morning, workmen found the portrait lying on the floor several feet away from the display case, aiming, so to speak, for the exit. At night, Aunt Martha's painting would be locked up in a closet for safekeeping. But one night the custodians heard knocking and crying from inside the closet, which ended as soon as the door was opened. Although the workers carefully locked up the closet again, the picture was found outside on the floor the next morning. Finally, it was returned to its accustomed place in the second-story bedroom. There it hangs quietly; do have a look—it might just tell you something.

Shirley Plantation
501 Shirley Plantation Road
Charles City, VA 23030-2907
(804) 829-5121
www.shirleyplantation.com

A Prostitute and a Policeman Haunt a Washington Saloon

When one thinks of Washington, what comes to mind are green forests, winding rivers, and the deep inlets of Puget Sound. The cool, misty weather of the region has inspired the brewing of innumerable pots of coffee, and launched attendant coffee houses. This is certainly true of the western part of the state, although the east shades off into the Great Plains, and the extreme southeast is rather arid. Before the coming of the Europeans, such tribes as the Duwanish, Tulalips, Pilchucks, Snohomish, and Snoqualmie inhabited the land. They did no farming, and kept no domestic animal save the dog. They hunted, fished, and gathered in an environment that seemed perfectly suited for those endeavors. Some of the tribes even went whaling. Salmon and shellfish, berries and roots made up much of their diet—often consumed in huge quantities at *potlatches*, communal feasts where the host gave away all of his possessions to his guests, only to get much of it back when one of them threw the next affair. They dwelt in large, well-built wooden houses, clustering into small villages. These would be marked by large, intricately carved totem poles. Within their homes the Indians would tell stories of the animal spirits whom hunters are always careful to propitiate, of witches who lurked, and of fabulous beasts like the giant Thunderbird and the manlike Sasquatch. The latter, at least, is supposed to haunt the area today.

But outside this favored dominion, events were moving swiftly. Although none of these powers had ever seen Puget Sound, the area was claimed by Spain, Russia, and Great Britain. Who would be the first to reach it? The answer came on May 19, 1792, when the British sloop-of-war *Discovery* dropped anchor in Puget Sound between Bainbridge and Blake islands. The following morning, the ship's master, Capt. George Vancouver (1757–1798), sent Lt. Peter Puget and Master Joseph Whidbey to explore the waters to the south. Europe had come at last to Washington.

The Vancouver expedition discovered such spots as Mt. Rainier (named in honor of Admiral Peter Rainier), Whidbey Island, Hood Canal, Puget Sound, Port Gardner Bay at Everett, and Port Susan Bay at Stanwood. June saw Vancouver land near present day Everett to claim the northwest for King George III. This was to forestall the Spanish, Russians, and Americans from taking the mouth of the Northwest Passage, which contemporary educated opinion was sure linked the Atlantic and Pacific Oceans. Vancouver and his men initially thought that either the Columbia River or Puget Sound must be that mouth. Alas, it was not so.

Nevertheless, geographic realities ensured that the different bands of Europeans exploring the interior of the continent in search of furs to trade must eventually reach the Pacific. Eight years after Vancouver's brief visit, another carrier of the Union Jack, David Thompson of the North-West Company (the Hudson's Bay Company's great rival, and also with whom the HBC later merged), reached the headwaters of the Columbia River. It was a brilliant way to enter the new century; the expedition, whose goal (inspired by the arrival of Alexander Mackenzie on the coast in 1793) had been to explore the western slopes of the Canadian Rockies, uncovered a whole new world for trappers and traders.

Five years later, in the name of the United States of America, Lewis and Clark arrived at the Mandan Villages of North Dakota on April 7, 1805. They passed through the Rockies with the aid of their Indian guide, Sacagawea (in token of which, her imagined face now graces our dollar coins). After making the difficult crossing, the Americans reached the Nez Perce country. From thence they followed the Snake to the Columbia River, and followed it downstream, reaching the Pacific on November 15, 1805, having journeyed overland and by canoe more than four thousand miles. After wintering in 1805–06 near present-day Seaside, Oregon, in a stockade they named Fort Clatsop, they began their return journey on March 23, 1806. They finally returned to St. Louis, Missouri, on September 23, 1806, having opened up American claims to the northwest (including present day Washington, Oregon, Idaho, and southern British Columbia, which came to be called the Oregon Country).

But the Americans were not yet prepared to establish a permanent presence in the region. In 1810, David Thompson established Spokane House, at the current city of that name, for the North-West Company. The HBC and the North-West Company merged, and the Oregon Country came under their unchallenged sway. But their activities centered around the valley of the Columbia. In 1825, the HBC founded Fort Vancouver, under the command of Dr. John McLoughlin, who for two decades was the uncrowned king of the area. As we have seen in Oregon City, he apparently presides over a small fraction of his vast domain even today.

The Puget Sound region was for the most part ignored. But American settlers began to pour in over the Oregon Trail. Meanwhile,

Dr. McLoughlin settled retired French-Canadian and Métis employees of the company around Ft. Vancouver, the French Prairie in present-day Oregon, and the Cowlitz Prairie, near modern Toledo, Washington. In 1838, St. Francis Xavier Mission was established in the latter spot, and remains the first permanently established Catholic mission in the state of Washington. The same year, St. James' Catholic Church, destined to be the first cathedral in the northwest, was founded.

But while all this occurred in the Columbia Valley, Lt. Charles Wilkes of the U.S. Navy explored and mapped the Puget Sound area in 1841. Four years later, a treaty between the United States and Great Britain settled the boundary between the two at the Forty-ninth parallel, bringing Fort Vancouver under the Stars and Stripes. In 1847, Congress officially established Oregon Territory; the army sent troops to the area.

After another four years, native New Yorker David Denny led the first group of settlers across the Oregon Trail, intending to settle along Puget Sound. Seeing the possibility for a seaport, the primarily male band founded Seattle. It was a rowdy place, populated mostly by bachelors. One wise civic leader had the bright idea of going to New Bedford, Massachusetts, to recruit wives for the settlers. About fifty-seven answered the call, and returned to the infant town. This was the inspiration for the sixties television show *Here Come the Brides*, a series dear to this author because one of its stars, Henry Beckman, was the father of one of my best friends in high school, now, alas, deceased.

In any case, settlement did not stay confined to Seattle. In 1858, a group of pioneers, drawn to the Snohomish River Valley because of its flat land and deep soil—much better farming country than anything in the Seattle area—set up stakes. The following year, the town of Snohomish was founded at the ferry crossing of the Snohomish River on the military road between Fort Steilacoom and Fort Bellingham. On January 20, 1861, Snohomish became the county seat for Snohomish County, which was carved out of Island County. The city flourished as a port along the steamboat line over the next three decades. Soon hotels, stores, churches, and at least forty-two saloons were built. Learning, literacy, and culture were not neglected: the Atheneum Society provided a venue for such pursuits, and a newspaper, the *Northern Star*, debuted in 1876.

Despite this, it was not culture but timber—green gold—that furnished the lifeblood of the town, and loggers who gave it what passed for its social tone. Augmenting and then replacing the steamships, the Seattle, Lakeshore, and Eastern Railroad (SL&E) commenced rail service between Snohomish and Seattle in 1888, the same year that Snohomish was incorporated. Many shops were opened, and the city boomed. But fires and the Panic of 1893 caused Snohomish's economy to stumble; fearful that its economic doom was on the wall, a fiercely conducted election in 1895 led to Everett's replacing Snohomish as the county seat—a development which has left a lingering resentment even today.

Nevertheless, this was a temporary setback. Logging recovered in 1902, and would reach a peak six years later. The loggers came back to their old haunts, and new bars and bordellos were opened to help relieve them of the stress of their high pay. Although logging finally did begin to wane as the twentieth century wore on, dairy and truck farming businesses supplemented Snohomish's economic base.

One enduring witness to the town's booms and busts is the Oxford Building, housing since 1910 the Oxford Saloon and Eatery, and built in 1889 as Blackman's Dry Goods Store. The old place has seen many tenants come and go. There have been a shoe and boot store, a pool hall, an arcade, and a real estate office; even a lawyer put out his shingle for a time. But entertainment has been the Oxford's primary business. Things could get a bit wild; a policeman was killed during the 1890s trying to break up a knife fight. When prohibition blighted the land, one could gamble and drink upstairs at the Oxford safely; there was also a brothel for less savory pursuits.

The Nagy family restored the Oxford completely in 1992. Of the two floors, the main floor boasts the original oaken back bar, which was brought around Cape Horn to the old Seattle Hotel, and salvaged from that establishment in the 1890s. There is a moose head where long-ago patrons would pitch nickels for beers; there is also Big John, the Knight in Shining Armor. Throughout the place are original as well as restored fixtures of the 1880s. The walls are covered with old photos showing scenes of long-ago Snohomish. There are even stuffed bears over the old walk-in cooler, as well as darts and all the other paraphernalia of pub life.

Given the Oxford's past, one would be surprised if it were *not* haunted. Interestingly enough, its two revenants were apparently on opposite sides of the law. One of the spirits is supposed to be the policeman earlier mentioned, who was killed while upholding the peace during a brawl between two rowdies. In two separate incidents, he was seen in the ladies' bathroom. Both of the women who saw him then picked him out from an old photo of a group of policemen on the wall; a different, decidedly stranger, sort of "police lineup." But that is not the only sort of thing "Henry," as the pub's denizens call him, performs. A waitress while bending down over the oven as she put something in heard her name called. Being rather busy, she didn't turn around, but simply asked, "What is it?" Again, the same voice called her name, in a questioning rather than angry manner. She turned around, but there was no one there—neither in the kitchen, nor outside. This is not an uncommon experience. Things fall off the bar by themselves, and just-straightened pictures will turn crooked. Apparently it is Henry's way of letting folks know that he is still on the beat!

Upstairs, the rooms of the former brothel have been converted into Madame Kathleen's Antiques, named in honor of the former proprietress. But she, too, apparently lingers in her old haunts. Not only has she been seen in period dress in Room 5, but she has appeared down in the pub, and even the main floor where she asked for a T-shirt. One wonders if Henry and Kathleen ever compare notes. Who knows? In between the good food and fun, you might see them consulting on the finer points of the law.

The Oxford Saloon
913 First Street
Snohomish, WA 98290
(360) 568-3845
www.oxfordsaloon.com

Still Saying His Breviary, a Long-Dead Priest Still Walks at His West Virginia Church

Although we have North and South Dakota, and North and South Carolina, only West Virginia gives honor to that direction among American state names. As one might guess from the name, the history of the state is bound up with that of the neighboring Commonwealth of Virginia from which it was carved out in 1863. Although much of West Virginia is so mountainous, wild, and thinly settled (with the exceptions of the northern and eastern panhandles, and the capital at Charleston) as to be real frontier country, nevertheless, thanks to its association with its mother state, its history can be traced back to the seventeenth century.

The first land grants in modern West Virginia were issued in 1669 by King Charles II. All the present state and much of northern Virginia as well (the so-called Northern Neck) was, by 1719, in the hands of Thomas, Lord Fairfax. In 1746, he was officially granted all the land to the North Branch of the Potomac by King

George II. His Lordship had the land surveyed (his team eventually included a young planter named George Washington) and leased to European immigrants on a feudal basis; much was also sold to land speculators.

Nevertheless, much of Lord Fairfax's nominal property was actually in the hands of the French and Indians. The cession of their claims by the French in 1763 seemed to open up the land west of the Alleghenies to settlement. But in keeping with his new treaty obligations to the tribes (once French allies, and now, after their withdrawal, allies of the King), George III issued a proclamation later in 1763 forbidding settlement west of the mountains in an effort to protect Indian lands.

Nevertheless, in 1768 the Iroquois and Cherokee ceded their rights to the territory between the Ohio River and the Allegheny Mountains, resulting in a bonanza for settlers and speculators: one of the most successful of the latter was George Washington, who picked up 45,000 acres of present-day Mason, Putnam, and Kanawha counties. In response, the Shawnee and Mingo of the region (who had not given up their rights) went to war to defend their lands. In 1774, the Royal governor, Lord Dunmore, set out with the militia and defeated the Indians. The way was clear to settle West Virginia en masse.

But history has a strange way of altering things. Tension between the Crown and the dominant set in the colonies erupted into open war in Massachusetts in April of 1775. Lord Dunmore had returned in triumph to Williamsburg from his victory over the tribes in October of 1774; June of 1776 saw him forced to flee to the safety of a Royal Navy warship. The Shawnee, Mingo, Delaware, and other tribes rallied to the Crown, and attacked many of the fledgling settlements of West Virginia. At the same time, however, a number of residents of those villages remained loyal to George III, seeing in him the only alternative to men like Washington, Jefferson, and Peyton Randolph; they had dominated the province before the war, neglecting the western settlers. Now they wished to be supreme. The result was Indian raids on the one hand, and sporadic loyalist uprisings on the other. But rebel victory in 1783 meant both the end of the Indian threat, and the opening of all of West Virginia to settlement.

This proceeded rapidly. In 1790, there were 56,000 people in present-day West Virginia; two decades later, there were 105,000, and in 1857, 377,000. But these folk rapidly became disenchanted with their government in Richmond, for many of the same reasons that loyalism had had such strength among the earlier settlers. Taxes levied by the state were hefty, but public works were few. Also, there was a great deal of difference between the Tidewater Planters, many of whom had dominated Virginia since the seventeenth century, with their great plantations and many slaves, and the hardscrabble settlers beyond the Alleghenies. The Virginia State Constitution, adopted in 1776, restricted voting rights to white males owning at least twenty-five acres of improved or fifty acres of unimproved land. Moreover, representation in the state General Assembly was given at two delegates per county, regardless of population. Since there were many more counties in the Tidewater than in the rest of the state, and many more qualified voters as well, this kept control of Virginia firmly in planters' hands. These worthies strenuously objected paying taxes to Great Britain because no Virginia nabob sat in the House of Commons; they did not, however, object to levying numerous taxes from men who could not sit in Virginia's legislature.

Things did improve for the west slightly after 1816, when the state Senate came to be elected on the basis of population. But despite this, and small incremental improvements, tensions between the two continued, and the west remained very much a backwater. There were many superstitions among the mountaineers, and they treasured their beliefs in witchcraft and ghosts even more strongly than their resentment against the Tidewater. When Virginia seceded from the Union, as with their colleagues in eastern Tennessee, many of the western Virginians refused to follow the lead of their state leadership—in striking parallel to the events of the Revolution. On April 17, 1861, a few days after Lincoln's order to seize Fort Sumter in South Carolina, a convention of Virginians voted to submit a bill for secession to the people. Western delegates marched out of the Secession Convention; many of these organized a pro-Union convention in Wheeling from May 13 to 15. Nevertheless, on May 23, a majority of Virginia voters approved Secession. As in the Revolution, we cannot know where the will of the majority in the west lay.

Between June 11 and June 25, 1861, delegates at the Second Wheeling Convention organized the restored, or reorganized, government of Virginia. On October 24, 1861, residents of thirty-nine counties in western Virginia approved the formation of a new Unionist state; Union troops were stationed at many of the polls to prevent Confederate sympathizers from voting. A constitutional convention met in Wheeling; delegates decided which counties would be part of the new state of West Virginia. Of the fifty counties selected, most of the eastern and southern counties opposed statehood, but were forced to enter West Virginia for political, economic, and military reasons. One of these was Jefferson County, in the eastern panhandle. In 1863, Congress approved the entry of the new state into the Union. The restored government of Virginia moved to Alexandria, Virginia, and then to Richmond after the war ended. Although an election was held to permit Jefferson and Berkeley counties to decide whether they wanted to be part of West Virginia or Virginia, Union troops stationed outside polling places frightened off those who might vote for Virginia. The bitterness of the separation caused feuds in the state that lasted for decades, of which the Hatfield-McCoy was only the most famous. These bloody conflicts left their mark in ghost stories.

Jefferson County's claim to fame was the United States Armory and Arsenal at Harper's Ferry, construction of which began in 1799. This building put Harper's Ferry on the map, attracting many new citizens and turning the small hamlet into a major town. In 1859, John Brown made his famous raid, and the trading of the town back and forth devastated the place. Today, much of it is a National Historic Monument.

Nevertheless, the early growth of Harper's Ferry made it a center of Catholicism in an overwhelmingly Protestant state. But it is not only being such a tiny minority (3 percent of Jefferson County) that sets the local church off from most. It is its strange and ghostly origin, as well as its continued haunting. The first recorded mention of a Catholic in the area dates back to 1765. In that year, Fr. James Frambach, S.J. came to Harper's Ferry, and was welcomed by the news-starved residents of the tiny and remote village because he brought tidings of the outside world. But when the good townspeople learned that he was a Catholic and a Jesuit priest, he was taken to the Potomac; after being warned never to return, Fr. Frambach was thrown in the river and left to swim to Maryland. During the slightly more tolerant 1790s, Fr. John Dubois (later the third Bishop of New York), and Russian convert-priest Prince Demetrius Gallitzin, managed to visit the hamlet without any molestation.

In 1794 Adam Livingston, a farmer and weaver, bought and plowed a great deal of land in Jefferson County, near Midway. Three years later, the Livingstons began experiencing some real problems. A young man had been driving by their farm when his wagon threw a wheel. The Livingstons offered him a bed, but he woke in the middle of the night, and begged the family to fetch him a Catholic priest, because he was dying. They refused, partly because they thought he was delirious, and partly because they wanted nothing to do with any priests; the nearest one, Fr. Dennis Cahill, was in Shepherdstown. But in the morning, the young man had died. The regretful family buried him behind the house. Their regrets would soon mushroom.

One night shortly thereafter, burning logs jumped from the fireplace. The next morning, an invisible rope barred carriages from passing by the house until it was "cut" with a knife. After that, the fun really began. The sound of shears clipping was heard inside the house; but the disembodied noises did real damage as linen, clothing, boots, and saddles were cut and slashed. Heavy objects floated around the rooms of the house, while at night fires erupted and invisible horse-drawn wagons were heard. Folk came from miles around to experience the weird goings on, and eventually began calling the area "Cliptown" or "Wizard's Clip."

Hoping to rid themselves of their unwelcome guest, the Livingstons invited ministers of several denominations to try their hand at purifying the place. All were repelled with unpleasant results. At last, they sent for Fr. Cahill, who blessed the house and the young man's grave, and offered Mass for the repose of his soul. The unpleasantness stopped, but mysterious occurrences kept occurring. For a number of years after Fr. Cahill's first visit, a disembodied "voice" instructed the Livingstons in the Catholic faith, prayed with them, gave them spiritual advice and admonitions, and made prophecies. Not too surprisingly, the Livingstons converted. Wanting to know the truth of the matter, Fr. Demetrius Gallitzin was dispatched by Bishop John Carroll to investigate. He concluded that the events were authentic.

Adam Livingston was so grateful that in 1802, he deeded thirty-four acres near the Opequon Creek to Fr. Cahill and four other trustees of the Catholic Church; the "voice" assured him that "before the end of time, this will be a great place of prayer and fasting and praise." But after all of the trustees had died, one of their heirs seized the land for himself. In 1922, the diocese brought suit to regain the property. The court ruled in favor of the Church, and declared that a trust cannot be violated just because the trustees have died. Bishop O'Connell offered a Mass of thanksgiving for the recovery of the land. It is now the location of the Priestfield retreat center, one of four pastoral centers in the Diocese of Wheeling-Charleston. But perhaps recent changes in Church liturgy and teaching have displeased the young man. In recent years the apparition of a man in a black cape has been seen passing into the chapel on autumn nights, and tourists have reported clothing, purses, camera straps, and other items mysteriously cut to pieces.

With these sorts of origins, it should not be too surprising that the shadow of the strange lies over the oldest church in the county, St. Peter's, Harper's Ferry. In 1828, it was decided to make missions of Harper's Ferry, Shepherdstown, and Martinsburg into a separate parish, with Harper's Ferry as the main church under the name of St. Peter's. A flood destroyed the first building, and in 1830, the cornerstone of the present church was laid; it was completed three years later. The Civil War saw the church menaced frequently when either side occupied the town. But Masses were said throughout the war; Union and Confederate alike respected the sanctity of its grounds, thanks in no small part to the alternating tact and bluster of the then-pastor, Fr. Michael Costello. Nevertheless, a babe in arms was killed on the steps of the church by a fragment from a mortar burst. During the battle for Harper's Ferry, the Church and rectory were used as a hospital. In 1896, the building was expanded to its current dimensions. Today, St. Peter's Church in Harper's Ferry is no longer a parish church; still, it is kept open by the Diocese of Wheeling-Charleston as an historic church in association with the National Historic Park. The pastor at St. James in Charles Town has responsibility for this church, and it is being renovated.

But despite lack of a corporeal resident pastor, there does seem to be one priest in perpetual attendance. His ghost walks the path along the north exterior wall of the church, reading his breviary; he then turns abruptly and steps into the wall, at the spot where the original 1833 church's front facade probably stood. Is this Fr. Costello? If so, one wonders what he makes of the cries of the baby killed by the mortar on the stone steps leading into the east entrance of the church. Some people have heard the screams of wounded and dying soldiers, presumably from the times during the war when the church served as a hospital. Priest, infant, and soldiers; it is a strange congregation for a church, to be sure. But even if you don't see or hear them when you visit, you might say a prayer for them. After all, you and I may want such help ourselves one day.

St. Peter's Catholic Church
Harper's Ferry National Historic Park
Harpers Ferry, WV 25425
(304) 535-6298

Wisconsin's Fairlawn Mansion
Is Still Served By a Murdered Maid

The "Badger State" enters world history in 1634, when the French explorer Jean Nicolet came ashore at Green Bay. The tribes resident in Wisconsin at the time were the Ho-Chunk (Winnebago), Potawatomi, Ojibwa (Chippewa), and Menominee, who allied with the French. Hunters, fishermen, and farmers, these tribes had a very high standard of living before the Europeans came. As partners with the French in the fur trade, they became very well-to-do, indeed. When French power in the region ended after 1763, they took part in Pontiac's Rebellion against the new British rulers, but then entered into a firm alliance with George III, which only ended after the War of 1812. The Americans pioneered their policy of shifting eastern tribes westward (which culminated in the creation of Indian Territory by bringing such tribes as the Oneida, Stockbridge Mohicans, Munsee (a branch of the Delaware), and Brothertons from New York during the 1820s.

Although the French-Canadians were the earliest European group to have settled in Wisconsin, pioneering such towns as Green Bay and Prairie du Chien, by 1850 a good 36.2 percent (106,000) of the total population were immigrants from the British Isles. But after 1850, the tide of migration became much more multi-national. More French-Canadians arrived, but Germans, Scandinavians, Swiss, Dutch, and Poles poured in, establishing ethnic enclaves. The folkways of all these groups as well as the Indians put a definite mark on the strange tales told in Wisconsin. But of these, the largest group of all were the Germans. Their mark was especially obvious on Milwaukee.

Away up in the northern part of the state was and is Douglas County, on the shores of Lake Superior. It was first inhabited by the Mound Builders, that mysterious race of people who left their tracks all over the Midwest, and who seem to have been quite advanced. Mining copper in the Minong Range and at Manitou Falls on the Black River, they pounded the metal into weapons, implements, and ornaments that were buried in mounds with their dead. But like the Romans they were overwhelmed by less advanced peoples a few centuries before the arrival of Columbus.

In 1847, the Chippewa signed away all their rights to the region; five years later, the government survey of townships in the country was completed, and the city of Superior was founded. On February 8, 1854, Douglas County was separated from the county of La Pointe and Superior selected as the county seat, although it would not be incorporated as a city until 1887. On December 17, 1881, the Northern Pacific Railroad formally opened to Superior; the city's expansion would now begin in earnest. With the railroad, local mining and lumbering interests would transform Superior. Fortunes were made, and, in true Victorian style, displayed in great houses. Typical of this development was Martin Pattison, builder of Fairlawn Mansion, one of Superior's finest homes.

Born in 1841, Pattison was a real go-getter; by his twenty-fifth birthday he was a full partner in a lumber company. Five years later, he was elected to the state legislature, and at thirty-two he moved to northern Michigan where he continued to operate a second lumbering company. In 1879, Pattison came to Superior and logged along the Black River. Realizing that ore could bring more than wood, he sold his lumber company and searched for iron on the Vermilion Range, ninety miles north of Superior. He opened the Chandler and Pioneer group of mines, becoming the greatest owner of iron lands in Minnesota.

With his wife Grace, Pattison began his dream house in 1889; spending $159,000 (in today's money, at least ten times that amount), he completed it two years later. The Pattisons were very happy there. Pattison remained interested in public service. Serving as sheriff (one term) and mayor of Superior (three terms), he donated large sums to build several churches and the Masonic Temple. The Pattisons sponsored many Scandinavian immigrants to Superior, paying their passage to America in return for a stated time of service, in a latter-day version of indentured servitude. Unlike many of the colonial-era masters, Pattison was a very kind man. His servants were treated more like family—of course, this bred deep loyalty on their part. In 1917, When Pattison learned of a plan to build a power dam on the Black River, which would have destroyed the waterfalls there, he secretly purchased 660 acres from a large number of owners along the river and near the falls. The following year, he gave the land to the people of Wisconsin for a state park—Pattison Park. He said at the time, "In being able to grant this site to the public, I have accomplished one of my chief ambitions. For years I have spent so much time amid the surroundings of the falls and have received so much real enjoyment there that it gradually became a part of my life."

But death comes to us all, even to the wealthy and joyful. When Pattison died in 1918, his wife donated Fairlawn to the

Superior Children's Home and Refuge Association as an orphanage, and the interiors were radically altered. Approximately two thousand poor children called Fairlawn home during the years 1920 to 1962. In that final year, the orphanage closed. Grace's will had required that Fairlawn be razed if that should ever happen. Civic leaders and members of the Pattison family were able to save Fairlawn through a loophole in the will, and in 1963 the city of Superior purchased Fairlawn for $12,500. Since then it has been operated as a city-owned museum.

The city of Superior, Douglas County, the Douglas County Historical Society, and the Jeffris Foundation, poured millions of dollars into the mansion, in order to return Fairlawn's exterior and first-floor interior to their original grandeur. The ceiling of Mr. Pattison's office is the only interior feature to remain intact. The painting on the ceiling's *trompe l'oeil* panels appears as raised plaster surrounding a painted open oculus with clouds, sky and vines. There are forty-two rooms in the mansion, which is built in Queen Anne Revival architecture exemplified in the prominent porch, steeply gabled roof, and the contrasting colors and textures on the exterior trim. But most prominent of Fairlawn's features is a four-story turret. Visible on the Harborview Parkway, it has become a symbol of Superior.

Fairlawn is a very popular museum, and its docents wear period dress. But one of them is as authentic as Mr. Pattison's office ceiling, because she has never worn anything else. Not on the roster of official guides, but sometimes just as helpful to visitors, she is often mistaken for a living person. The revenant often helps visitors find displays they are interested in, only to disappear. A cold, damp chill accompanies these appearances.

But just who is she? Noted ghost author Dennis William Hauck believes, on the basis of his research, that the apparition is a servant girl murdered by her husband, shortly after her term of service ended. Apparently the loyalty the family engendered in her has not ended at death. But whoever she is, she does not walk alone; the period of the orphanage has also left its mark at Fairlawn: two child ghosts are often seen and heard playing near the old swimming pool in the basement. There are no records of any children having died in the house; but perhaps two adoptees ended up preferring the orphanage to the lives they encountered afterwards. Whatever the case may be, the ghosts of Fairlawn appear neither menacing nor unhappy.

Fairlawn Mansion
906 East 2nd Street
Superior, WI 54880
(715) 394-5712

Buffalo Bill May Be
the Only Person Not Haunting
this Wyoming Hotel

W yoming is renowned for its natural wonders; Yellowstone, Grand Teton, and so forth are truly spectacular places. Even today, much of it is wild, and it takes little imagination to see in the mind how it must have appeared to the Arapaho, Arikara, Bannock, Blackfeet, Cheyenne, Crow, Gros Ventre, Kiowa, Nez Perce, Sheep Eater, Sioux, Shoshone, and Ute. Of these, only the Shoshone and Arapaho remain, on the Wind River Reservation. Before the Europeans came, they told strange tales of the wondrous beings that had constructed the bizarre geography of places like Yellowstone.

The geysers and other odd phenomena intrigued John Colter as well, when he arrived in Wyoming in 1807; his reports earned the area the name "Colter's Hell." (It is now Yellowstone National Park.) In his wake followed the mountain men: Kit Carson, Jim Bridger, Davey Jackson, and Jedediah Smith, to name a few. The Oregon Trail was forged through Wyoming, and soldiers followed the wagons. The frontier was considered closed in 1890.

One of the most famous people in nineteenth-century Wyoming was William F. "Buffalo Bill" Cody. Not only did he found Cody, Wyoming (which now boasts a museum in his honor), but he also took his "Wild West Show" to the east and Europe. He produced for his audiences, on stage, the romantic west they wanted to believe in. But although he was really a showman, by virtue of his acquaintance with Kit Carson and similar figures he was a true bridge between eras.

In some ways, Wyoming would be considered forward-looking; women were given the right to vote there in 1869. That year, when Wyoming Territory was organized, the citizens began talking of statehood. But it would not eventuate until 1890, the year the frontier closed. As with so many other western states, one of the biggest catalysts for development was cattle.

Sheridan was founded May 10, 1882, by Union veteran John D. Loucks, who named it after Phil Sheridan, under whom he had served during the Civil War. Naming the streets mostly after himself and other pioneers, Loucks was able to obtain title from the government to the site; by 1890 there were 281 people. Some of these folk were foreign aristocrats like the polo-playing Moncrieffes. These sorts of folk managed to carve out a life for themselves reminiscent of what they left behind.

The year 1892 saw the railroad come to Sheridan; coal, wheat, and cattle went out, more and more people came in to visit or to settle. This resulted in a need for accommodation. The need for accommodation was answered by the Burlington and Missouri Railroad that joined together with the Sheridan Land Company when they built the lavish Sheridan Inn during the winter of 1892–1893. It was patterned after a hunting lodge that the inn's architect, Thomas Kimball, had seen in Scotland.

For its day, the Sheridan was both up-to-date and lavish. At a cost of $25,000 to construct, the inn featured hot and cold running water, two bathrooms, and steam heat. When the hotel opened on May 21,

1893, it had the first electric lights; a telephone was soon installed. The lobby, main dining room, and bar were all given exposed hand-hewn beams made from Georgian pine, and the oak and mahogany "Buffalo Bill Bar" was a gift from Queen Victoria to Buffalo Bill. It came across the Atlantic by ship, and then via rail from New York City to the "Custer Station" in Montana. From there, an ox-drawn freighter brought it to Sheridan. After the Sheridan was built, Buffalo Bill leased the building interior and auditioned his Wild West Show performers from the front porch. The first managers were a couple hired by Buffalo Bill: named George and Lucy Canfield they maintained their positions for many years. Buffalo Bill owned the business side of the inn from 1894 to 1901 and gladly kept the Canfields on.

The list of the celebrities who have stayed at the Sheridan is astonishing: Ernest Hemingway, Herbert Hoover, Thomas Dewey, Wendell Wilkie, Will Rogers, Dwight Marrow, Mary Roberts Rinehart, Charlie Russell, Robert Taylor, Bob Hope, and many more. A fairly lethal drink, the "Wyoming Slug" (a mix of whiskey and champagne), was invented at the bar.

The inn was rescued from wrecking in 1967, two years after what the community feared would be its final night. It is now owned by the non-profit Sheridan Heritage Center, Inc. Although there are no overnight accommodations currently available, it is envisioned that eventually there will be twenty-some-odd rooms.

As mentioned, Buffalo Bill did a lot at the Sheridan. He lived there when he wasn't on the road, and held many dances in the dining room. It was at the inn that he planned the Irma Hotel in Cody (which he named after his youngest daughter, Irma). When that hotel was built, the Codys stayed at the Irma but continued to visit the Inn. His son-in-law, Horton Boals, husband of his daughter Arta, committed suicide in his room on the third floor of the inn. A copy of his suicide note is at the Inn.

A rather nicer memory of the inn is that of Catherine B. Arnold, called "Miss Kate" by long-time visitors and friends. Miss Kate was twenty-two in 1901, the year she came to the inn to work as a seamstress. She stayed on for sixty-four years, working as desk clerk, housekeeper, hostess, and babysitter. She raised the flowers used in the hotel on her own land. Miss Kate, in other words, was absolutely devoted to the hotel and its guests, body and soul. She only moved out in 1965 because of the threatened demolition. Thankfully, she lived to see the Sheridan rescued. But when she died in 1968, she asked that she be cremated and entombed in a wall in the room she had occupied on the third floor. This was done; her room has since been renovated by the Preceptor Tau Chapter of Beta Sigma Phi Sorority.

Apparently, however, she has left more than a mere material presence behind. Very frequently, lights turn on and off and doors open and close by themselves. Miss Kate may be felt in her former room (her rocking chair is often seen rocking by itself), near the front downstairs windows, or in the ballroom. Sometime there is a moving cold spot, sometimes only disembodied footsteps are heard. Passersby have seen lights on at night, when no one was there. But Miss Kate is apparently not the only permanent guest. A little girl is sometimes seen, as is Buffalo Bill's son-in-law. The Sheridan is definitely worth dropping by for a meal, and when the rooms re-open it ought to be irresistible. But apparently it is not only the living who find it so!

Sheridan Heritage Center, Inc.
856 Broadway Street
Sheridan, WY 82801
(307) 674-5440

Afterword

Now, at last, we have completed our journey through these United, and haunted, States. It will, perhaps, be obvious by now that ghosts are an integral part of our history and culture as Americans. People have come here from all over the globe, spectral beliefs in hand—or, more properly, in head. They and their descendants have maintained and added to those notions. The Indians, of course, had a whole set of their own such ideas. Beyond a doubt, ghosts are as American as apple pie.

But just what are they? I am afraid that our survey helps us very little here. Some appear to be mere repetitive images, rather like movies on ether, without any intelligence, and oblivious to what goes on about them. Many modern researchers in these areas would claim that these are actually mere natural phenomena, implanted in ways as yet undiscovered upon certain places by the unleashing of great emotion. This is actually not a new theory: it was suggested by St. Thomas Aquinas in his *Summa Theologica*.

But what of the others, who appear to be haunting with a purpose, and who interact with their viewers? Many professional ghost hunters have a whole set of quasi-religious answers, familiar to anyone who has seen the *Poltergeist* films. For these folks, the intelligent type of ghosts are human souls who are confused or frightened, and often do not know that they are dead. They require "rescue" ceremonies to coax them toward the light.

Myself, as a Catholic, I subscribe to the view mentioned in the introduction—that they are, depending on the particular case, damned souls, demons masquerading as the dead, or souls returning from Purgatory to ask for aid or to right wrongs. One recalls Hamlet's father's ghost, doomed by day to languish in Purgatory fires, and by night to walk. Certainly, anyone who has visited Rome's Purgatory museum at the church of Sacro Cuore del Suffragio, with its macabre collection of various artifacts bearing burn marks from being touched by "returnees" (who ask for a certain number of prayers or Masses to spring them from Purgatory) cannot fail to be impressed by the idea. It does give one's praying for the dead a whole new urgency.

There is also the possibility that some of these activities (particularly of the poltergeist nature) are entirely non-human (or demonic) in nature. Those who hold this view posit the existence of another race of beings on this Earth of a different physical nature to ours. Neither is this a new idea; our ancestors told such tales of the fairies and elves. Even such medieval theologians as Lodovico Sinistrari, O.F.M., in his *Daemoniality* held these views. Certainly, it would be an explanation of such diverse phenomena as the UFOs, alien abductions, and the so-called mothmen, if indeed those oddities exist.

But while our survey has not and could not answer the questions, one thing is sure: the vast majority of hauntings are not caused by happy events. Murder and mayhem, hate and fear, betrayal and neglect—these are the ingredients of which ghosts are made. We may not be given to know, this side of the grave, the who or the how of hauntings, but we can suppose the why.

Of course, we all must cross over into the afterlife. The dead who walk are a source of endless interest and speculation to the living; books of this nature have been written since the advent of printing, ghost stories have been told as far back as we can trace, and without a doubt they shall continue to be so. Let us live our lives in such a way as to avoid being ourselves the subjects of such tales, when we, too, come to "shuffle off this mortal coil."

Charles A. Coulombe
Arcadia, California
Walpurgis Night, 2004